Pianos, Toys, Music and Noise

Pianos, Toys, Music and Noise

Conversations with Steve Beresford

Andy Hamilton

BLOOMSBURY ACADEMIC
NEW YORK • LONDON • OXFORD • NEW DELHI • SYDNEY

BLOOMSBURY ACADEMIC
Bloomsbury Publishing Inc
1385 Broadway, New York, NY 10018, USA
50 Bedford Square, London, WC1B 3DP, UK
29 Earlsfort Terrace, Dublin 2, Ireland

BLOOMSBURY, BLOOMSBURY ACADEMIC and the Diana logo are trademarks
of Bloomsbury Publishing Plc

First published in the United States of America 2021
This paperback edition published in 2022

Copyright © Andy Hamilton, 2021

Cover design: Louise Dugdale
Cover image © Blanca Regina

All rights reserved. No part of this publication may be reproduced or transmitted in any form or by any means, electronic or mechanical, including photocopying, recording, or any information storage or retrieval system, without prior permission in writing from the publishers.

Bloomsbury Publishing Inc does not have any control over, or responsibility for, any third-party websites referred to or in this book. All internet addresses given in this book were correct at the time of going to press. The author and publisher regret any inconvenience caused if addresses have changed or sites have ceased to exist, but can accept no responsibility for any such changes.

Whilst every effort has been made to locate copyright holders the publishers would be grateful to hear from any person(s) not here acknowledged.

A catalog record for this book is available from the Library of Congress

ISBN: HB: 978-1-5013-6644-4
PB: 978-1-5013-6956-8
ePDF: 978-1-5013-6646-8
eBook: 978-1-5013-6645-1

Typeset by Deanta Global Publishing Services, Chennai, India

To find out more about our authors and books visit www.bloomsbury.com and sign up for our newsletters.

To Derek Bailey (1930–2005), musician

Contents

List of Steve Beresford's Top Tips for Improvisers	ix
List of Figures	x
Foreword by Stewart Lee	xi
List of Contributors	xiii

Introduction		1
Short Biography of Steve Beresford		5
1	Early Life, 1950–74, and Musical Education *(Martin Mayes)*	7
2	The Portsmouth Sinfonia *(Gavin Bryars)*	17
3	Second-Generation Free Improviser *(Brian Marley, Mike Cooper)*	27
4	Derek Bailey	41
5	Company Week 1977 + The Dutch School + Alterations + White String's *(Eugene Chadbourne, David Toop, Terry Day, David Brown)*	59
6	Saxophonists: Evan Parker, Tony Coe and Lol Coxhill *(Evan Parker, Mark Sanders)*	77
7	Piano, Toy Piano, Toys *(Chris Burn, Alex Ward, Adam Fairhall)*	87
8	Jazz, Free Jazz, and Free Improvisation *(Rachel Musson)*	105
9	Teaching Improvisation	141
10	The 1980s and 1990s *(Kazuko Hohki, Jean Rochard, John Butcher, Paul Hession, Hannah Marshall)*	147

11	Film Music + Christian Marclay + Video Artists + Visual Art *(Helen Petts)*	165
12	Graphic Notation + John Cage + Classical Music *(Philip Thomas, Tania Caroline Chen, Mandhira de Saram)*	179
13	The Improv Scene + The Audience	197
14	Post-2000 *(Alan Tomlinson, Elaine Mitchener, Blanca Regina, Leila Adu-Gilmore, Cara Stacey)*	209
15	Comedy and Entertainment	219
16	Popular Music, Popular Culture *(Tessa Pollitt, Adrian Sherwood)*	235
17	Electronics, Sound, and Recording *(Pat Thomas)*	251

Steve Beresford Discography	261
Bibliography and Discography	267
Index	270

Steve Beresford's Top Tips for Improvisers

1	Never pay to get into one of your own gigs. (Chapter 1)	15
2	Always bring spare batteries. (Chapter 7)	96
3	"Don't worry about being wrong, just worry about being uninteresting" (Whitmer). (Chapter 8)	112
4	Don't rehearse your improvisations at home. (Chapter 8)	114
5	Extend your listening past the usual tropes. (Chapter 9)	143
6	If you're playing something the audience don't like, you don't have to stop doing it. (Chapter 15)	230
7	Don't expect to make a living from improv. (Chapter 17)	259

Figures

1	Steve Beresford, euphonium and cat	125
2	Steve Beresford, Tristan Honsinger, Derek Bailey	126
3	Steve Beresford and Han Bennink looking snazzy	127
4	Steve Beresford switched on	128
5	Company (Derek Bailey, Maarten van Regteren Altena, Lol Coxhill, Steve Beresford, Anthony Braxton, Tristan Honsinger, Han Bennink, Evan Parker, Wadada Leo Smith, Steve Lacy)	128
6	The Steve Beresford twinkle-toes piano method	129
7	Steve Beresford and Nigel Coombes	130
8	John Zorn, Steve Beresford, David Toop, Tonie Marshall	131
9	Steve Beresford conducts the LIO	132
10	The Melody Four (Lol Coxhill, Steve Beresford, Tony Coe)	133
11	Alterations (Terry Day, Steve Beresford, Peter Cusack, David Toop)	134
12	Steve Beresford on electronics	135
13	Megaphone diplomacy	135
14	Talking to David Toop	136
15	With Satoko Fukuda	136
16	Table-top	137
17	With Mandhira de Saram (violin)	137
18	With Tania Caroline Chen, recording session	138
19	Playing melodica with General Strike	138
20	Looking at Derek Bailey records	139
21	Table-top with ukulele	139
22	Stewart Lee, performing Cage's "Indeterminacy"	140

Foreword: Steve Beresford – If I Don't Write It, Andy Hamilton Will

Like Steve Beresford, I was born in Wellington in Shropshire. Beresford eventually left the small market town to become a leading light of the British free improvisation scene, whereas I was immediately dispatched to an orphanage in Lichfield, where I lay alone in a charity crib, crying. Those who struggle to appreciate the merits of the musical world Beresford has made his own might wonder which destination was the most disadvantageous to long-term mental health.

Andy Hamilton knows Steve Beresford, in the context of this book, as a subject of study. I know Beresford as a wit and an epicure; as a fount of musical knowledge and a great conversationalist who is disproportionately popular with the capital's cleverest women; as a man who will never turn down a Kir Royale cocktail if one is available; and as someone who will not let the far-flung nature of the night's gig venue deter him from seeking out the finest fusion food restaurant for dinner after the show.

Whilst younger music fans wilt and wither, Beresford, at seventy, is still to be seen most nights, abroad in the city, quietly digesting a diverse array of cultural influences, all of which inform his musical practice, irrespective of whether the guardians of taste have deemed them high or low culture.

It's a trait Beresford shares with Derek Bailey, who found space in his mind-map for both the Scottish music hall comedian Chic Murray and the Austrian composer Anton Webern. Indeed, it was Beresford who steered me towards both the Ethiopian jazz saxophonist Getatchew Mekuria, and the subversive American horror movie *Get Out*. And it was Beresford who made me, a lowly stand-up comedian, into a conduit for the high art of John Cage.

I think I first saw Beresford playing in the flesh as part of Evan Parker's Foxes Fox group at the old Vortex in Stoke Newington towards the end of the last century. But I almost certainly experienced him before in endlessly recombined line-ups of London improvisers at venues that I attended in a spirit of bewildered curiosity in the early 1990s, without knowing who or what I was watching.

I owned The Flying Lizards singles as a teenager, thinking they were funny novelty records, and would have skanked alone to the punky reggae of The Slits as I grew older, without necessarily knowing Beresford was in the mix of so many of the tracks I loved.

Beresford was post-war music's version of Leonard Zelig, the chameleon-like Woody Allen character who moves through the history of the twentieth century, present at every major event, but not necessarily noticed by anyone outside a circle of adepts. Andy Hamilton's *Pianos, Toys, Music and Noise* aims to redress this oversight.

From the opening salvo it is clear that Hamilton has attempted to write a book about musical improvisation, and a musical improviser, in the same spirit of interrogative playfulness that his chosen subject Steve Beresford brings to the scene in which he has seen fit to ensconce himself.

In an effort to be true to the spirit of chance musical meetings conducted in real time, Hamilton edits the pair's conversations as lightly as possible. Discursive tributaries are followed wherever they may flow, leading us to Beresford's time in both the proto-pub rock band Roogalator and the orchestral anarchists, the Portsmouth Sinfonia, and to his knowledge of Britain's best commercial whistle manufacturers and Britain's finest Asian restaurants.

Beresford and Hamilton listen to each other, engage, look for some common ground and find a way forward. Hamilton's questioning of Beresford, and the wide-ranging answers given, mean that the book expands outwards from its initial subject, like ripples from a tossed pebble, until it becomes an accidental, and vital, history of free improvisation in Britain, albeit one hinged at an oblique angle to the multi-platform presence of Steve Beresford.

As a dedicated comedy fan, Beresford would doubtless know that Eric Sykes' 2005 autobiography *If I Don't Write It, Nobody Else Will* takes its title from a warning a fellow comedian gave him, that maybe he should take his legacy into his own hands. But auto-memorialisation isn't the sort of thing a self-effacing gentleman-artist like Beresford could do. In the end Steve Beresford wouldn't write this, so Andy Hamilton had to.

Stewart Lee, writer/clown, Stoke Newington,
October 2019

Contributors

Leila Adu-Gilmore
David Brown
Gavin Bryars
Chris Burn
John Butcher
Eugene Chadbourne
Tania Caroline Chen
Mike Cooper
Terry Day
Mandhira de Saram
Adam Fairhall
Paul Hession
Kazuko Hohki
Brian Marley
Martin Mayes
Hannah Marshall

Elaine Mitchener
Rachel Musson
Evan Parker
Helen Petts
Tessa Pollitt
Blanca Regina
Jean Rochard
Mark Sanders
Adrian Sherwood
Cara Stacey
Pat Thomas
Philip Thomas
Alan Tomlinson
David Toop
Alex Ward

Introduction

For nearly fifty years, Steve Beresford has maintained a career in improvised music – a career totally against the odds, because financially it is almost impossible. Since the 1970s, this second-generation free improviser has opened up the genre from its more austere beginnings and tendencies. He is an enigmatic Dadaist – a modest entertainer, free of ego both in performance and in life. Steve has been involved in many areas of music – as well as improvisation, these include audiovisual collaborations, composing for film and TV, promoting gigs and working with comedians such as Ivor Cutler, Vic Reeves and Stewart Lee. He is one of music's great survivors. He has always supported younger musicians and attends an amazing number of gigs every year. Indeed, Steve is an icon for younger players. These polymathic activities make him an ideal subject for a biography in conversation – one that offers a kind of prism of the UK improv scene since the 1970s.

Steve is an eager and opinionated conversationalist – he's even been called a raconteur – and is modest but not shy about his talents. The book covers a broad range of topics – biographical, music-historical and philosophical – and he provides valuable insights on each. His knowledge is eclectic but deep, and the conversations show how the genre of free improvised music is embedded in a broader cultural context. As Steve's collaborator Mandhira de Saram perceptively comments, "I don't think he sets out to say anything profound – in fact, he might dare you to find such truths in music. But I [wonder] if perhaps he does unwittingly present something which at least closely resembles such a truth." I hope that these conversations vindicate what Mandhira says, even if we struggle to articulate that truth.

Musician autobiographies have involved collaborations ranging from "as told to" to shared writing credits and ghostwriting. The case of Quincy Troupe's *Miles: The Autobiography* shows how problematic traditional forms can be – apparently, without comment, Troupe added material not found in his interviews. I've favoured a development of the interview form, a staple of music journalism, into a whole book. When my collaboration with Lee Konitz appeared in 2007, one of the few other jazz examples was Meehan's *Time Will Tell: Conversations with Paul Bley* – though there were collaborative titles with Stravinsky, Xenakis, Boulez and Messiaen in classical music. Konitz had, quite correctly, vetoed our original "as told to" format as inauthentic – once the interviewer's questions are removed, it's hard to see what motivates the subject's remarks. When the conversation is obscured in this way, honesty and candour are undermined. With an interview format, the contributions of the writer/editor are more explicit.

This book adopts a similar approach to the Lee Konitz biography. Beresford's life is discussed chronologically, broken up by thematic chapters on free improvisation, the instrument(s), film music, musicians and other topics. The question of authenticity recurs – inevitably, the author's interests and concerns influence the discussion and editing, but more explicitly than in traditional formats. The format proves fruitful in engaging Steve in aesthetic and philosophical debates, including the relation between improvisation and composition; its connection with debate over the aesthetics of imperfection versus perfection; and the relation between art and entertainment. I've benefited a lot from Steve's insights, as a working musician, into these issues. A perennial question is how genuinely spontaneous improvisation can be – which implies the question "What exactly *is* improvisation?" In fact, as we discuss, it's not clear that many listeners really understand what improvisation is. For most people, composition is the norm – whether in pop or classical music, the model is that someone composes something and someone else performs it. Misunderstandings arise, I believe, from the fact that "composition" has two senses – the general meaning of "creating an aesthetically effective design," and a particular musical meaning of a "desk-worker who produces scores." When these are distinguished, it's clear that all musical improvisation is, in a broad sense, a method of composition.

The conversations, as they appear here, are constructions, not literal transcriptions, suggesting parallels with post-production techniques in recording. It is difficult to transfer the feel of speech to the written page, and I have rearranged phrases within sentences, changing individual words to improve the flow. Over the years of conversation, Steve and I have addressed several key topics more than once. A degree of repetition is therefore inevitable, and not all repetitions can be removed without also removing valuable context. I hope that the remaining ones are not too distracting. The linear narrative is broken up by "interventions" or short pieces by collaborators and commentators. As with the Konitz book, these were an afterthought which burgeoned, and most were conducted as the book was nearing completion. The musicians showed a lot of warmth towards Steve, which he and I have greatly appreciated.

Steve has accommodated my endless questions with grace and humour. He's been a close collaborator, reading successive drafts of the manuscript and making corrections and additions. Having these conversations with Steve has been an education for me, in many ways. His musical tastes are some of the broadest I know, and I've learned much about the history of improvised music. I've also learned a lot about popular music, including that of obscure artists like The Shaggs and Ace Cannon, and byways such as Spouge – Barbadian pop music of the 1960s that fused ska with calypso – not to mention bigger names about whose music it's too embarrassing for me to confess my previous ignorance. Steve constantly reminds me of the great sounds out there that focused interests have kept from my ears. He's also educated me in non-musical matters, especially the range of Asian restaurants found in London – the locations of many of our conversations.

The project began nearly a decade ago, and I inherited it from Brian Marley, in circumstances that neither of us can precisely recall. He has been a stalwart collaborator throughout – advising on matters large and small, commenting on several drafts and editing the photo section. Tony Herrington of *The Wire* magazine, in which I have written about Steve and colleagues such as Derek Bailey, Evan Parker and Rhodri Davies, has provided much-needed support and encouragement – as has editor Derek Walmsley, and fellow writer Philip Clark. *The Wire* has been the most important home for my writing on jazz, improvised music and contemporary composition since the late 1980s, when its editor Richard Cook was my journalistic mentor. My career as a music writer would not have been possible without it.

Many thanks are due to the colleagues and fans of Steve who have enlivened the conversations with their reminiscences or interviews. Rhodri Davies gave crucial early advice and read versions at two different stages. Many thanks also to Daniel Garel for compiling the discography; to Gareth Thomas for help with biographical information; and to anonymous referees for Bloomsbury. Thanks to Martin Davidson of Emanem for his assistance, and to photographers Caroline Forbes, Helen Petts, Sean Kelly, Roberto Masotti and Fabio Lugaro for their invaluable cooperation under pressure of time. My gratitude to Sam Horlor for help in compiling the index, and for his invaluable assistance over recent years in my Aesthetics of Imperfection research project, of which this volume forms a part. Many thanks to Blanca Regina for her excellent cover image and design, and to Leah Babb-Rosenfeld at Bloomsbury for her patient editorship. Finally, thanks to readers and commentators Chris Abrahams, Douglas Benford, Paul Bream, David Brown, Chris Burn, Peter Cheyne, Trevor Barre, John Butcher, Mike Cooper, Angharad Davies, Adam Fairhall, Tim Fletcher, Paul Hession, John Kieffer, David Lloyd, Rachel Musson, Brian Olewnick, Lara Pearson, Gerard Tierney, David Toop and Lloyd Swanton.

Andy Hamilton
Durham, July 2020

Short Biography of Steve Beresford

Steve Beresford was born in Wellington, Shropshire, in 1950. Principally a pianist, he also plays bass guitar, trumpet, euphonium, small instruments and electronics. After moving to London in 1974, he worked with improvisers including Derek Bailey, and played with the Portsmouth Sinfonia – on trumpet – along with Brian Eno and Gavin Bryars. He has become internationally known as a free improviser on piano and electronics, working with The Slits, Han Bennink, Ivor Cutler, Prince Far-I, Alan Hacker, David Toop, Najma Akhtar, Evan Parker, Adrian Sherwood, The Flying Lizards, Otomo Yoshihide, John Zorn, Jason Yarde, Roger Turner, Mark Sanders, Hannah Marshall, Sharon Gal, George Lewis, John Butcher, Okkyung Lee, Tania Chen, Kazuko Hokhi, Lore Lixenberg, The Shaking Ray Levis and many others. His regular groups have included Alterations; The Melody Four with Lol Coxhill and Tony Coe; and a long-running duo with drummer Han Bennink. He also has a long association with Swiss artist/musician Christian Marclay, and with stand-up comedian Stewart Lee.

Beresford's work is marked by irreverence, humour, virtuosity, anti-virtuosity and playfulness. As well as free improvisation, he has also been involved in dub reggae and post-punk, and has produced pop and commercial music for TV documentaries, feature films and commercials. He has appeared on a record by comedian Vic Reeves. In 1975, Beresford was a key figure in the formation of the London Musicians' Collective, a charitable organisation that promoted free improvisation and experimental music. With the London Improvisers Orchestra, Beresford has been conductor and pianist, with a line-up including Evan Parker, Caroline Kraabel and BJ Cole. He has been arranger and producer for the Dedication Orchestra, and Butch Morris's London Skyscraper. In 2014, he toured *Indeterminacy*, in which comedian Stewart Lee reads one-minute texts by John Cage whilst Beresford and fellow pianist Tania Chen performed. Recent collaborators include Elaine Mitchener, Blanca Regina, John Butcher, Satoko Fukuda and Shabaka Hutchings. Steve was awarded a Paul Hamlyn Award for Artists in 2012.

1

Early Life, 1950–74, and Musical Education

Steve Beresford was born in Wellington, Shropshire, in 1950, and started playing piano at the age of seven, studying the classical repertoire. From age fifteen, he played trumpet in the Shropshire Schools' Symphony Orchestra. He played Hammond organ in a soul band in Wellington, called Hooker Green – named after a paint colour – and remained a band-member during his first year of studying music at York University. After graduating, he stayed in York to work in theatre groups and working men's clubs, also playing improvised music in Bread and Cheese, with Dave Herzfeld (drums) and Neil Lamb (guitar). He worked in a group with drummer Dave Solomon, whose repertoire included Otis Redding, Sam and Dave and Motown hits, before joining US guitarist/singer Danny Adler's pub rock band Roogalator. He moved to London in 1974. This chapter covers musical developments up to that date, before Beresford began his close involvement with leading free improvisers.

Your fellow improviser Rhodri Davies says that you used to be polemical and acerbic. Have you mellowed?
I wasn't conscious of being polemical and acerbic, but I think I was, from what people tell me.
Did you begin in jazz?
No. But my father [Les] was a singer in a semi-pro dance band. He also played a bit of guitar. When he used to sing with a big band, the Musicians' Union rule was you didn't get paid if you were a singer – singers didn't count as musicians. So my dad had to play probably rather quiet rhythm guitar to get paid. He loved singing standards.

His collection of 78s was mainly Swing, quite a lot of Glenn Miller, Tommy Dorsey, a bit of Louis Armstrong, Duke Ellington – he loved Johnny Hodges, Benny Goodman, Archie Shaw, that kind of period. During the war, when my mum and dad were courting, there were three gigs a day at the local dance halls – there was one at the top of the high street in Wellington, and a ballroom at the major employer called Sankeys. My dad performed many times at the dance hall at the top of the high street.

[Beresford adds: *Hang on, there's a typo there – it's Artie Shaw, not Archie. Maybe there's an Artie Shepp further on. A few years ago, a Barbican press release for McCoy Tyner described him as the piano player in Robbie Coltrane's famous quartet.*]

You could go to a lunchtime concert, an early evening concert and a late evening concert, and they went dancing all the time – they loved dancing. My mum's family was musical. Her dad had played cornet in a very early English dance band that toured America – extraordinarily, I think, in the 1920s. His name was Fred Hands, and he played cornet with his brother, Jim, who later became a piano player with the Debroy Somers Society Orchestra – a big, posh dance band in the 1930s. Jim played piano and also accordion, apparently for Gaumont British films.

A big story in my family that I still haven't been able to prove, though I've looked at all the books, is that Jim Hands – my great-uncle – played piano for Louis Armstrong in 1931 or 1932, when Louis was here. That's fantastic if true – I'm thrilled just by the rumour! The first time Louis came he was escaping the Mob, I think – they thought "This guy's making money, we want a piece of him." I think he finally had to come to some arrangement.

My maternal grandad remarried – his first wife died – and then gave up jazz and was slightly embarrassed that he'd ever played it, I think. He played classical violin.

So, my mother [June] had a musical background. She didn't play an instrument, but she liked singing and dancing. My paternal grandad played a bit of harmonium, so both sides of the family had a musical background. I have a sister, Anne, who produces dance and music films, plays piano and has always danced, and a younger brother Pete, who plays piano and other instruments, is versatile and runs bands.

My parents loved jazz, so I grew up listening to it. The first record I bought was "Good Golly Miss Molly" by Little Richard, on a 78 – I was seven when that came out. I still think that's a fantastic record; I'm very proud that that was the first record I bought.

I soon started listening to Charlie Parker. There was a stall in the market that sold EPs – this was Wellington in Shropshire, a market town twelve miles from Shrewsbury. At that time, this guy specialised in EPs, and I got Monk and

Coltrane – "Trinkle Tinkle," "Ruby, My Dear" – and Miles Davis and Coltrane. It was a little too much for my parents, but they didn't hate it.

The first book I read about jazz in was Brian Rust's Penguin – *Jazz Records 1897–1942* (1961). Rust thought that Coleman Hawkins could have been a good player, if he'd played the clarinet – and that a band with a guitar and not a banjo was unacceptable. He thought instrumentation should stay as it was in 1923 – a ridiculous purism about jazz. Then I read Sidney Bechet's autobiography *Treat It Gentle*.[1] It wasn't that there were millions of books on jazz coming out.

Did you have piano lessons?
Yes, I started when I was seven, initially with a lady called Mrs Edwards – but then it transpired that she wasn't really teaching me to read music, I was just copying her fingers. Then I had Mrs Evans, who was a much better piano teacher, but we never saw eye to eye aesthetically. I wasn't playing by ear, I was playing by sight, I was looking at the fingers – I don't think I played by ear. But I learned to read music with Mrs Evans.

I did the Associated Board piano exams. When I went to university I had a few lessons with a guy whose name I forget – but he tried to look exactly like Stockhausen, with the same floppy haircut and safari suits. He was very much in the mould of the extremely severe classical piano teacher, and I don't think he thought much of me.

At about the age of fifteen I joined a soul band called Hooker Green – by this time I was playing trumpet as well. I was listening to Thelonious Monk and Cecil Taylor, but I had no idea how this music was constructed. I'd never heard anyone play piano like Cecil – I thought he just banged piano with his fists, but it didn't sound the same when I did it. I didn't know about chord sequences – I was living in Shropshire and nobody round there could tell me how to voice chords or anything.

The thing about jazz piano from that era, the bebop era, is that chord-shapes are very hard to hear – what the hell are they playing in the left hand? I went through my whole university career asking various jazz pianists what the hell you do with your left hand, and nobody would tell me. But when I listened to "Green Onions" by Booker T and the MGs – which I still think is a fantastic record – I could work out what the organist, Booker T Jones on Hammond B3, was doing. "Green Onions" was a sufficiently simple piece of music, so I began to figure out how you could improvise over a chord sequence.

This would be about 1965, and we were playing Stax and Motown tunes, around Shropshire and Wolverhampton. This was before uni, and during the first year, when I went back home. We were a relatively successful local band, but probably we were terrible. They finally got me a small Hammond organ to play, and I did more on that. That's definitely what got me into improvising. I wanted to sound like Cecil Taylor but obviously I couldn't start off that way.

I love soul music, I think it's great. I think I was a bit snobbish about it in those days, though. I would say "Of course, Coltrane is miles better than Junior Walker." These days I love Junior Walker as much as Coltrane, and I think the song-writing is incredibly impressive in that period of Stax, Motown and Atlantic. I love that period of soul music – Aretha Franklin's "I Never Loved A Man," and the slightly later stuff like Sly and the Family Stone, and Curtis Mayfield's *Curtis/Live!* – that's an amazing record. At university everyone laughed at my soul records, because they were hippies.

Hippies didn't like soul music?
They didn't like it at all, because it was on singles [rather than albums], and showed you weren't intellectual enough. Also there wasn't much of an interest in African-American music – except for Arthur Lee, Richie Havens, and Jimi Hendrix. Anything that was dancey, they didn't like.

What did your parents think about your music?
Especially coming from that period, and that they probably didn't find free improvisation that congenial, they were very supportive.

I think they saw the soul band once. I don't think they ever went to one of my free improv gigs, because I never played free improv in Wellington. And they never came to London – I mean, they weren't very mobile towards the end.

They sort of liked the Portsmouth Sinfonia.

I think they were very happy that I was doing what I enjoyed.

I'd wanted a gap year, but the feeling then was that it wasn't a good idea. I don't think the soul band would ever have taken off, particularly.

Did you know [former Labour Party leader] Jeremy Corbyn, who was born in nearby Telford, a year before you?

What's super-embarrassing is that decades ago I had a drink with *a* Corbyn in the pub near my parents' house – and I can't recall if it was him, or his slightly creepy right-wing brother Piers, the climate-change denier.[2]

You studied at York University.
I studied music there, starting in 1968. Wilfrid Mellers was professor. He used to wear boot-lace ties, like cowboy ties, and he would sit cross-legged on the table and talk about Bach – he was fantastic talking about Bach. He would pummel out a prelude, get all the notes wrong, but he'd play it with fantastic enthusiasm.

It was a very good music department, wasn't it?
Well, it wasn't great for me. The first lecture was by David Blake, who I later discovered to be an ex-student of Eisler's. He was, I'm guessing, a pretty unreconstructed Stalinist. His first lecture was about Webern, who I'd never heard of – though by this time I'd got as far as SME [Spontaneous Music Ensemble], and I'd heard Sun Ra, Ornette, Coltrane, maybe a little bit of Cecil.

I had the same response to Webern as my friend Shirley Thompson, a composer I later shared an office with at University of Westminster in Harrow. We both went, "Oh my God, this is great, I love it!" – instantly! It's completely opposite to what everyone says about Webern: "Oh, it's completely constructed and totally artificial, it's too intellectual," and so on.

So I went up to David Blake afterwards and said, "That was great! Did Webern write any solo piano pieces that I can look at?" And he said, "You'll never be able to play that stuff." This was the first thing I heard from a lecturer, and he was telling me I was a failure.

How did he know?
He didn't know, he knew nothing about me. The music is hard, of course, but there's a children's piece, actually, and the slow movement of the *Variations* isn't so difficult. But even if it's true, why would you say it? It makes no sense. You're telling a student who's just arrived from Shropshire...

You took that to heart.
I remember it to this day, and as a lecturer at a university, I really hope I've never said anything that horrible to any of my students. But all the lecturers there were sort of frustrated composers – composers who couldn't make a living out of it, which is fair enough, it's very hard to make a living out of composing. It's almost impossible.

My impression was that the lecturers thought I was a total idiot – except Bernard Rands, who was really supportive.

David Blake wrote an opera about Toussaint L'Ouverture [*Toussaint*, 1974–77], I think that was his best-known thing. Also in the department were Peter Aston, Robert Sherlaw Johnson and Richard Orton.[3] I think I got in on the strength of an interview with Wilfrid – I knew who Ornette Coleman was, and I think probably nobody else did in that year. The students at York, like most music students, were incredibly conservative. Wilfrid Mellers, to his credit, brought in Feldman, Cage and Bert Turetzky – we didn't get to speak to these people, but they gave lectures. That was amazing.

It's sometimes surprising how little musicians know about the history of their music.

A decade ago, Mark Sanders was working with some very good, contemporary, London-based jazz saxophone players, and none of them had ever listened to an Evan Parker solo record, which strikes me as astounding. They weren't that young – thirty-five-ish. They'd never wondered, "I wonder what Evan Parker's solo sounds like?" And the guy lives down the road!

It is surprising, but I have to say that the people I was around when I was coming up – particularly Evan, Derek Bailey and John Stevens – were incredibly well-informed.

You've always been attracted to mavericks – you've always been kicking against the establishment.

Yes – but I was really crap at playing conventional music. I'd been told I had to learn an orchestral instrument, but I never got any good on trumpet.

But you got to Grade VIII on piano, so you couldn't have been crap on that!

I did a performance in my last year at university, Schoenberg op. 33a – I love that piece – a Bach Prelude and Fugue, and Satie's "Sports et Divertissements."

I didn't meet any nice classical musicians then. Now I know lots of nice classical players! Ilan Volkov, Aisha Orazbayeva, Satoko Fukuda, Mandhira de Saram... they're delightful – they would never be horrible and snobbish.

When did you first get to know the work of John Cage?

Probably like a lot of people I read his books before I heard the music – there was nothing on any easily-available label. When I went to university it was getting a little easier – Nonesuch released the Concerto for Prepared Piano and Chamber Orchestra. Years later I heard John Tilbury play it at the Proms, and I realised I knew that piece off by heart, though I hadn't heard it for years. We had small record collections as teenagers, because we didn't have any money, and we played those records obsessively – so I knew the Cage piece.

Did you listen to radio much?

Yes – I first heard SME on Charles Fox's jazz programme on what was then the BBC Third Programme, though they certainly weren't playing jazz. Charles Fox was amazing, a very nice man.

I left university in 1971, and stayed in York for three years – I moved to London in 1974. First of all, I taught music at Archbishop Holgate Grammar School, where the headmaster was Fred Frith's dad, who's a really nice man. But I was the world's worst teacher, and the kids just came in and broke all the instruments. It was embarrassing. I had no control – I was terrible.

I must have signed on – then I got this job, playing in working men's clubs. I think I made eleven pounds fifty shillings a week, and that was plenty. I think our band did two nights at this working men's club – it was Jan Steele's band, he was a saxophone player, and the drummer was a guy called Arthur, who I think moved to Australia. We had a lot of free time. Rent was nothing.

I think they had Gallien Kruegers in those days, those tiny little PAs. We'd back singers, always male – I don't think we ever backed a female singer. They would always show up with a microphone stand, a stool with a little switch to turn the reverb on, and lots of frilly shirts. You'd have to turn the reverb off between tunes, so you could tell jokes – you can't be a comedian with reverb on your voice. But when you sing, you should sound glamorous, so you need reverb. Surely you know the semiotics of popular music?

You just click it in, as part of the reverb unit – actually, it was probably built into the amp. They would always tell us, "Right, *colla voce*, and *segue* into a *paso doble*." We didn't know what any of these words meant. Now I do. But when people told us "*colla voce*," "*segue*" and "*paso doble*," we just said, "Oh, OK, fine." "*Colla voce*" means you follow the voice, so you're out of tempo – you're waiting for the voice and then you're playing behind. "*Segue*" is following immediately with another tune. So I did three years of that.

What were you playing?
God knows. "Beautiful Sunday" by a singer called Daniel Boone was one hit we played – he was a sort of manly singer. This was 1972, not pre-rock-and-roll.

You were backing crooners.
They were showbiz singers. They'd probably do an Elvis tune or two, and they'd always do "Beautiful Sunday" because it was always on Sunday. We played "Tie A Yellow Ribbon" a lot. Years later there was a tune called "Silly Games" by Janet Kay, the ultimate in British Lover's Rock – it was quite sophisticated reggae, out of the Tottenham area, a really great bass-line, brilliant drum track. Janet Kay had an incredibly high range – years later [with The Slits] I worked with the writer and producer of that tune, Dennis Bovell, and he said, "I stole the entire chord sequence from 'Tie A Yellow Ribbon'", which was hilarious.

Did you think, "God, at last I'm a musician"?
It paid the rent. I think it was a challenge, because that wasn't really our kind of music. At the same time I had a free improv group called Bread and Cheese, with a guitarist called Neil Lamb and a drummer called Dave Herzfeld, both from the States. Dave was from New York, I think, and Neil was from New England or somewhere. That was the first free improv I did. We always played at the university – by that time I'd left but was still around, so I worked with people that were still there.

Your first appearance on record was on a disc by Trevor Wishart, the electro-acoustic composer.[4]
It was Trevor Wishart's *Journey into Space* – maybe two of us played squeaky toy trumpets, but there's millions of people on it. I think it was me and Neil Lamb – this was the year after I graduated, and before the Portsmouth Sinfonia. Trevor was doing a postgraduate degree at York University. After that I didn't have much contact with him.[5]

One influence while you were at university was The Bonzo Dog Doo-Dah Band.
At uni we had a band called The Inedible Cheese Sandwich, which was slightly influenced by them – it was to do with parodying groups that were taken very seriously, like The Velvet Underground.

Who were the Bonzos parodying?
They started out as a sort of Dixieland band, like Bob Kerr's Whoopee Band – they had banjos and cornets. They dressed like Edwardian gentlemen, with beards and tweed jackets. They mixed up 1920s jazz with Edwardian clothes – and being quite posh, and also interested in Dada, or Satie. They had a theremin piece, and a parody of Micky Spillane, with a John Coltrane pastiche in the middle. They were very adept. They had a robot with a three-necked guitar, who played the blues.

Were they not just pure entertainers?
I think so. It was a good combination. Neil Innes was more of a conventional musician, who had a kind of pop sensibility – he wrote their hit "I'm The Urban Spaceman." Others were more from the art world.

Until I saw a BBC documentary recently, I didn't realise how amazingly good they were – and what a sad story it was.

You played Hammond organ in a soul group with Dave Solomon, performing Otis Redding, Sam and Dave and Motown hits – you said Dave Solomon was listening to James Brown on the one hand and Han Bennink on the other. Then you joined Danny Adler's pub rock band Roogalator.
When most of us moved to London around 1974, the rhythm section – Dave Solomon on drums, Nick Plytas on keyboards and me on bass – also played for Roogalator.

In the period after you graduated, between 1971 and 1974, when you were still in York, you also had a duo with drummer Dave Solomon called Sorry – because every time Dave did something wrong, he'd say "Sorry!"
I was also getting to know my generation of free improvisers, the people who were on Teatime – John Russell, Garry Todd, Nigel Coombes, as well as Dave Solomon.

How did you get to know them?
I was going down to London regularly, to the Little Theatre Club, that was the main place to hear free improvisation.[6] I guess I met them at gigs – I was sitting in on gigs, I think. I wasn't taking notes at the time [for my autobiography], but I'm sure I sat in.

Nigel is shy – so is Dave Solomon. Dave went to a gig where he was down to play, and he was so shy he paid to get in.

That's completely bizarre.
Was there a point when you realised you were committed to improvisation? Was the fact that the music was improvised always a big thing about it?
It must have been at some point in the three years after I left university, while I was staying in York. By the end of my undergraduate years, I was doing some improvising, because I was in this Love Rock musical. We played in a student theatre festival in Poland.

I was committed to free improvisation, but not to the exclusion of everything else.

TOP TIP No. 1: Never pay to get into one of your own gigs.

French horn-player and alphornist MARTIN MAYES was born in Edinburgh, and was a near-contemporary of Beresford at York University. He has worked with Evan Parker, Cecil Taylor, David Jackson and the Italian Instabile Orchestra, and lives in Turin. He has performed in a myriad of different places, from historic buildings and trade fairs to the sea and underground caves.

Martin Mayes writes:

> *I first met Steve in 1971 when I was in my first year at York University – he had graduated but remained very present around the Music Department, as well as performing in the York area. The Music Department, created by Wilfrid Mellers, was an amazing backwards prism which took all the musical and cultural threads of the previous hundred years, creating an intense white light which illuminated what they might mean. This light was then projected through a forwards prism which suggested many possible musical and artistic paths.*
>
> *Steve was a major presence and his restless energy, coupled with an ability to be provocative and controversial, helped me transform my intellectual curiosity in twentieth-century ideas into a sounds-on, tactile exploration, manipulation and enrichment of audible vibrations. I had been chasing intangibles – Steve revealed the tangible within the intangible through tumbling head over heels in the process known in music as improvisation, encouraging and participating in student groups*

and inviting unheard-of names such as Derek Bailey, Evan Parker, Fred Van Hove and Peter Brötzmann to come to perform.

In his performances he demonstrated how a visual gesture could be as musically important as a sound played. His interest in and knowledge of areas of music that I had never heard of gave him a contact with the real world – both musical and non-musical – that proved a revelation.

Notes

1. Bechet (2002).
2. There are four Corbyn brothers in total, in fact.
3. Martin Mayes adds: also Neil Sorrell (world music) and John Paynter (music in schools).
4. Born in Leeds in 1946, Trevor Wishart is a composer and author, influential in the area of electroacoustic music. Following a postgraduate degree at the University of York, his early work included improvisation using found objects and tape manipulation. His interest later shifted towards technology and electro-acoustic composition, with a particular focus on the human voice, heard for instance in *Red Birds (A Political Prisoner's Dream)*. Wishart has written several books – for instance, *On Sonic Art, Audible Design* and *Sound Composition*.
5. "Journey into Space" was made in the University of York Electronic Music Studio between January 1970 and December 1972; it was originally released as two LPs privately pressed in 1973. (1970/72, *Journey into Space*, York University (no label) [Double album]. Trevor Wishart; 1970/72, *Journey into Space*, Paradigm Discs PD18. Trevor Wishart. CD re-issue of York University LPs.)
6. The London venue is widely regarded as the birthplace of free improvisation, through its open nights run by drummer John Stevens.

2

The Portsmouth Sinfonia

Steve Beresford's first appearances on disc were on a recording by electroacoustic composer Trevor Wishart, followed by a York "pop music" album. He then appeared on an album by the Portsmouth Sinfonia, on which he played trumpet. The Sinfonia was founded by composer Gavin Bryars and his students at Portsmouth College of Art in 1970. Bryars entered the talent competition Opportunity Rocks with a scratch band called the Portsmouth Sinfonia, which drew on players who either were without musical training or played an instrument they were unfamiliar with. Brian Eno, who later in 1970 became one of the Sinfonia's clarinetists, remarked that "The philosophy of the orchestra was that anybody could join; there was no basis of skill required."

Heralded the "world's worst orchestra," the Sinfonia became a cultural phenomenon, with a record deal, a film and a hit single. It last performed publicly in 1979. Its philosophy paralleled that of other ensembles of unskilled players or strange instruments – Sun Ra's Strange Strings (1966) and Cornelius Cardew's Scratch Orchestra (early 1970s). Later Sinfonia members included composers Simon Fisher Turner and Michael Nyman, who located the ensemble in the avantgarde tradition:

> We were all serious artists or experimental musicians. . . . Because of the skill structure of the Sinfonia, you couldn't fail to come up with outlandish results. But we weren't deliberately incompetent. And the combination of everybody's individual errors built a musical structure that was incomparable.[1]

For Martin Lewis, the Sinfonia's manager from 1973, the Sinfonia predated punk: "Four years later, you had punk: the same notion of people picking up instruments they couldn't play but wanted to play."[2]

Composer and bassist GAVIN BRYARS, born in 1943 in Yorkshire, began his career as a jazz bassist with Derek Bailey and Tony Oxley in the early 1960s. Bryars has seen extensive success as a composer from the release of his first major works, *The Sinking of the Titanic* and *Jesus' Blood Never Failed Me Yet*. He has composed for the stage, his first opera, *Medea*, performed in 1984 by the Opera de Lyon and the Opera de Paris. Bryars has also composed string and chamber music for his own ensemble, founded in 1981, as well as being involved in numerous collaborations, including with visual artists.

Gavin Bryars writes:

> *Steve is almost entirely an improvising musician but of a very rare kind. The vast majority are deeply serious about their work, have a clear sense of direction allied to an often-fierce intensity in performance, strive for high technical standards and move within clearly circumscribed territory. To his eternal credit, Steve is seldom any of these things, and never all of them at the same time. He can be whimsical, wilfully comic, and proudly maladroit, and at the same time seek out performing situations that are far from obvious. I first encountered him within the community of improvisers that included old friends of mine such as Evan Parker and Derek Bailey, but even there he was performing in a self-effacing, slightly anarchic manner that was very refreshing. He joined me in the Portsmouth Sinfonia in the early 70s where he was an entirely respectful member and grasped immediately an ethos that was close to his own musical practice. Membership of the Melody Four, for example, also exercised his rare gift for self-deprecation. That does not imply that he is not a serious musician, but rather that he is capable of seeking out a much broader range of companionships than most other improvisers, and he is deeply aware of the wider area of experimental music – his work with Tania Chen and comedian Stewart Lee on the Cage lecture Indeterminacy is a masterpiece. Steve is one of the great originals.*

How did you come to join the Sinfonia?
I think Nigel Coombes was already in it.

I heard that when Gavin Bryars formed the group at Portsmouth College of Art, to enter a talent contest, they each went out and bought an instrument and a *Tune A Day* book.

Their first recording was the "William Tell Overture" – a flexi-disc with a huge amount of applause badly stuck onto the end of the performance, obviously not an audience in that room. It was virtually unrecognisable as the "William Tell Overture," which we knew as the theme to *The Lone Ranger*, which we all watched avidly in our youth. Gavin liked "Sinfonia" as a pretentious name for an orchestra – clearly one of his targets was the pomposity and conservatism of conventional classical music.

In those days, art colleges were very encouraging to experimental music – much more than music departments in universities and music colleges, which were conservative. Gavin Bryars' early pieces are wonderful, they're really inspired. But can you imagine any conservatoire taking him seriously as a composer? In an art college, you can sneak these things in. There's a fantastic piece by Gavin called "Marvellous Aphorisms AreScattered Richly Throughout These Pages" – a man stands in a raincoat with little squeaky toys and other sound sources concealed in his clothing, and tries to play them without moving.

What was the point of the Sinfonia?
The point was to have fun.

You can have fun, and make an artistic point. It sounds like Dada.
It had a Dada thing. Beethoven's Fifth – for God's sake, how many times do we want to hear this piece of music really? It's funny because with any great piece of orchestral music, Nigel Coombes will have half a dozen versions of it – I'll just find the Naxos recording and buy that, because it's the cheapest, and usually okay.

I think all funny jokes have serious points because they point out something about life or society or something.

Unless it's slapstick.
Maybe not slapstick.

Anyway, the idea was to do Mendelssohn's "Fingal's Cave," a Rachmaninov Piano Concerto, the "Hallelujah Chorus." All this stuff bored me stiff. . . . Everything was hackneyed.

There were spin-off groups that did other things, for instance, we had a trio of Nigel, me and James Lampard called the Wandsworth Trio – I was living in Wandsworth at the time. We did stuff we really liked like Erik Satie and Kurt Weill, and we also wrote things.

These were things you were trying to play as well as you could?
We were trying to play them as well as possible but accepting the fact that they won't come out right. There was a group called The Majorca Orchestra. I can't remember what they played – maybe the pieces Ives wrote for small orchestra and marches, which are really great. There was a band called the Ezra Read Orchestra, who only played music by Ezra Read – a very hackneyed Edwardian composer who wrote "characteristic intermezzi." There'd be one called "Fire Fire" and the sheet music would have firemen running to a fire – and lots of battle pieces; the Edwardians loved them. There was a group called The Garden

Furniture Ensemble who played original music by John White.[3] So there were lots of these little orchestras.

Was it frustrating to you that the Sinfonia made mistakes, or did you enjoy making them?
I don't think anybody minded you making mistakes. It wasn't like the Shropshire Schools' Symphony Orchestra, where people wanted to kill you when you made them.

There's lots of ways of approaching Western tradition and I think Cage's was one way and Portsmouth Sinfonia's was another. They're related, because Gavin Bryars studied with Cage – though I don't think Cage would have been very interested in an incompetent orchestra.

Were you laughing when this was going on?
Sometimes. The whole point really was that there were no set funny bits except perhaps the introductions at the Albert Hall which had been pre-written.

What size of audience were you getting?
Huge. It was packed.

So, somebody must've made a bit of money?
Yeah, I think we got paid for it. It wasn't too bad.

And the audience were laughing?
Oh God, yeah. Aside from a few red-faced majors who stormed out saying "How dare you?" Because, of course, the whole thing was always presented seriously. "The Portsmouth Sinfonia will perform *Thus Spake Zarathustra*." If you looked at the programme, it's far too long – Beethoven's Fifth, Tchaikovsky, Richard Strauss . . .

And some people came who were deluded?
There were one or two deluded people.

None of the three LPs has been reissued, which is a pity. The first two were on Transatlantic – the studio album and the Albert Hall one – and the other was on Phillips. Transatlantic just fell apart. It was a pretty successful label, mainly covering English folkies of that era, John Renbourn and people like that, and it did some really great records. I think it put out one of the first Albert Ayler albums. The Phillips disc was called *Twenty Classic Rock Classics* [1979], a parody of that tradition of shameless symphony orchestras doing those awful versions of "Nights In White Satin" – which is a song I detest anyway, so for me that was revenge. *Classical Muddly*, released by Springtime!/Island Records in 1981, was a cut-up of existing tracks.

You'd think there was some money to be made from reissuing.
I did a gig with Zorn, and this young guy who was Woody Herman's drummer, in New York. As soon as he discovered I played with the Portsmouth Sinfonia, he said, "Oh, that's my favourite record." And one of my students came in one day and his start-up jingle was *Thus Spake Zarathustra*, and I told him, "Do you hear that really bad trumpet player? That's me." You're probably right, but record companies don't work like that, do they?

The Sinfonia were sincerely trying to do their best. Were there participants who didn't realise how bad they were?
That's the grey area. I think that's what makes it interesting – irony and vagueness. On the Bonzo Dog Doo-Dah Band's "Jazz, Delicious Hot, Disgusting Cold," which is an absolutely brilliant pastiche of awful English trad, everybody played badly deliberately. We weren't doing that. We were definitely playing whatever instruments we had as well as possible. Michael Nyman, who sat next to me, had this weird, conical sort of circular euphonium – I don't think he knew what it was called, and I think that's great, to play an instrument you don't really know what it's called. Gavin Bryars played cello because, of course, he was a good bass player but I don't think he was a very good cello player. Alan Tomlinson played trombone and he was really good on it – he's listed on *Hallelujah*. [*"Hallelujah!" – The Portsmouth Sinfonia at the Royal Albert Hall* (1974), their second album]

Nigel Coombes was in the band, my brother was in the band on violin, Brian Eno played clarinet – which he definitely couldn't play. The idea was that somebody would do a simplified version – they weren't full versions of Beethoven's Fifth.

One of the great advantages was to have the least assertive person I've ever met as the conductor. That was John Farley. He was built up like the cover star of the second album, *Live at the Albert Hall* – and you couldn't tell if he was conducting or scratching his head, so half the band would come in and half wouldn't. He absolutely couldn't communicate anything.

You'd have to be a real idiot not to get the joke! But there were people who probably nurtured a secret desire to be in a symphony orchestra and knew they weren't good enough, so they could be in the Portsmouth Sinfonia.

I'd had a horrible experience in the Shropshire Schools' Symphony Orchestra. You can imagine what that was like; horrible snobby little twits with their shiny trumpets, and composers who treated us like we were idiots. Awful, awful, awful. Real old school provincial classical music scene.[4]

Famous composers?
Yes. I said to one of them, "Oh yeah, some of it sounds like Bartók" – I was sixteen for God's sake – and he said, "Well, yes, you would say that, you don't know anything about contemporary music." How would you know how to talk about my music, you spotty little twit – that kind of attitude. So that was horrible, anyway. And I was a terrible trumpet player, I should never have been in it in the first place – so it was great to be in the Portsmouth Sinfonia.

Portsmouth Sinfonia performances had something in common with Florence Foster Jenkins – a rich woman who aspired to be a singer. I think her story is about privilege – she went around her whole life without anybody telling her she was a terrible singer. Of course, people knew she was, that's why they went . . .[5]

Nobody told her?
Well, they laughed, but . . . I don't know.

The film about her, with Meryl Streep, got quite poor reviews, but I thought it was great – it's funny, and quite moving. It left you with a question mark over how the people around her related to her obvious lack of talent as a singer. I don't think anybody was ignorant – people perhaps loved her, she was a very nice lady. And she was rich, and one is encouraged to like rich people, by this culture.

I'm not sure anybody was being hypocritical about her.

You had to tell her that she was great when she came offstage – you couldn't tell her she was singing out of tune all night.

Everyone thought she had a talent of some kind?
We could call it that [laughs].

Isn't it close to naïve artists like L. S. Lowry and Douanier Rousseau?
I think there might be something of the naïve artist about Florence Foster Jenkins.

You're not just laughing at her.
My favourite story about her was one that I heard from Annie Ross on Desert Island Discs – who I love, she's one of my favourite singers, really good technically and very hip, and with a really good sense of humour. She chose a Florence Foster Jenkins record to take to the desert island. Understandably, [presenter] Roy Plomley asked why.[6] Annie replied, "Because she believed." I think that's a fantastic answer. She believed in her own talent.

She would change costumes. The famous picture of her is in a dress with angel wings.

The film *Florence Foster Jenkins*, with Meryl Streep and Hugh Grant, suggested that she didn't know how awful she was.
She was quite well off, that's how she could afford to hire Carnegie Hall – and rich people float around in a sort of bubble.

I don't like the repertoire she sang – popular operatic arias, that stuff.

I was sitting with [the pianist] Ian Pace in a pub, after a gig he'd played, and he was having a very rarefied conversation about opera with an ex-student – I realised I knew not the first thing about opera.

Florence is like the world's worst poet . . .

William McGonagall?
Yes, he would go out and give recitations.

He walked to see Queen Victoria.
He walked right across Scotland in the rain to see Queen Victoria, believing that her letter, which just said "Thank you for your volume of poetry," was an invitation to go and see her. People can be very self-deceiving.

Self-deception is a really interesting area. It's sort of the basis of *Songs in the Key of Z*, Irwin Chusid's book about what he calls "outsider music." I think that's one of Chusid's definitions of outsider music: people trying to do conventional music but failing to be conventional, and thereby becoming interesting.

The Shaggs are a rather different example. The Shaggs with two "g's" – it's not rude in American – wanted to be like The Carpenters. They covered "Yesterday Once More" on their second album. But they hadn't worked out basic things about music – like you have bar lines and beats. The drummer is somewhere else most of the time – she occasionally coincides with the first beat of the bar. I think they thought they were on their way to being The Carpenters and there were just a few little glitches to be sorted out – but, of course, what was interesting were those glitches, which were actually quite big. They were doing songs that feel like they should be in 4/4, but aren't.[7]

Harrison Birtwistle is another example. Percussionist Paul Clarvis, who performed Birtwistle's "Panic" at the Proms, said that "[He] doesn't hear things rhythmically – I played him some Count Basie and he said, 'It's a bar of 13 and a bar of 7, isn't it?' and it's very strange what he heard . . . ."[8]
He probably played him "Splanky" or some really straightforward Neal Hefti arrangement of a 12-bar blues. It's a fantastic record, but there's nothing confusing about it.

Except Birtwistle was confused.
He *was* confused! [laughs]

Victor Borge was a great virtuoso – the funniest. He could play piano really well, and he worked that stuff out to the last note.[9]

The Portsmouth Sinfonia weren't playing the music because they hated it – that would be silly. People talk about Coltrane "murdering" popular songs like "My Favourite Things," but he loved them. He probably didn't like Julie Andrews' version very much – but he also did "Chim Chim Cher-ee," which was another Julie Andrews hit that also happened to be in 3/4 and in a minor key – maybe that was why. Cecil Taylor didn't hate Cole Porter. He loved those tunes, but he wasn't going to play them the way Fred Astaire sang them. I like both approaches.

Alec Wilder, who wrote the book *American Popular Song*, was really happy for jazz musicians to play those tunes. Purists often wanted them sung without improvising, but Wilder saw that as an extension of those songs, which it clearly is.[10]

Though the satirist mostly attacks what they find loathsome.
Sure. Stewart Lee has a long routine about Paul Nuttall from UKIP, where his hatred of Nuttall is expressed by the length and the repetitiveness of the routine – it's very, very funny. The things Nuttall was saying were clearly deeply racist. And Stewart takes him apart in a very funny way. But it's hard to do that in music.

Have you heard Mostly Other People Do The Killing's version of *Kind Of Blue*?
Not yet.

I gave the CD to someone who might not have heard *Kind Of Blue*.
That would be funny, wouldn't it? If they heard that version first.

You have to be reasonably expert to tell it wasn't the original. The solos seem to be note perfect, and the pianist [Ron Stabinsky] sounds like Bill Evans, but if you listen carefully . . . and the audio might not be quite authentic.
The original was pretty well recorded.

MOPDtK are great players.
Peter Evans is a really extraordinary trumpet player. Nobody's ever played trumpet like that.

Notes

1 Quoted in Cairns (2004).

2 Cairns (2004). Portsmouth Sinfonia recordings include one of the slowest recordings of Beethoven's 5th Symphony, so fragile it seems it might disintegrate:

www.youtube.com/watch?v=-JrkFh5ful8 – from vinyl album *Portsmouth Sinfonia Plays the Popular Classics*, recorded by the Sinfonia in 1973, conducted by John Farley.

3 John White, British composer and pianist, was born in 1936. In the 1960s he took part in many performances in the maverick experimental tradition by Cage, Feldman, Wolff and Cardew, and founded several small ensembles with Christopher Hobbs, Dave Smith and John Tilbury, including the Promenade Theatre Orchestra (1970–72), and Garden Furniture Music Ensemble (1977–79). He has written many piano sonatas, mainly short, one-movement works, on the model of Domenico Scarlatti. Satie is a central influence. White has produced a large number of compositions for low-tech electronic instruments, such as Casio miniature keyboards.

4 Writer Mark Sinker worked for *NME* in the 1980s and edited *The Wire* in the 1990s. He comments: "My memories of the Shropshire Schools' Symphony Orchestras (around 1975–79) are lovely rather than awful. I played double bass, a rare and much-needed instrument, so I was often included way above my skillset. The material we played was rarely exotic or demanding – the most outré composition was Constant Lambert's 'By the Rio Grande', which at least leans towards jazz. This was a door opened out of a context I found stifling."

5 Florence Foster Jenkins (1868–1944) was a New York heiress who attempted to be a coloratura soprano. Her story is interpreted in Stephen Frears' excellent film *Florence Foster Jenkins*, with Meryl Streep and Hugh Grant. As well as her famous Mellotone recordings, there are recently discovered (mercifully) silent clips of her here: https://www.youtube.com/watch?v=Hcs9yJjVecs.

6 Desert Island Discs is a long-running programme on BBC Radio 4, devised by Roy Plomley; a famous guest discusses eight favourite records they would take to a desert island.

7 The Shaggs were an American all-female rock and outsider band formed in 1968 by three sisters, Dot (vocals/lead guitar), Betty (vocals/rhythm guitar) and Helen Wiggin (drums) and, later, Rachel Wiggin (bass). Their only studio album, *Philosophy of the World*, was released in 1969 but failed to attract attention. The Shaggs disbanded in 1975 after the death of the girls' father, Austin. They're notable for their apparent ineptitude at playing conventional rock music.

8 Gramophone "Explorations," special issue p. 30, (accessed 2017) at http://www.villagelife.co.uk/code/press.html#vortex.

9 Victor Borge (1909–2000), musical humourist, pianist and conductor, born Borge Rosenbaum in Copenhagen, combined comedy and virtuosic pianism. He escaped to America after the Nazi invasion of Denmark in 1940, arriving virtually penniless and unable to speak English, but soon developed a successful act. The *New York Times* obituary comments: "Although some of his routines would not change in half

a century . . . he remained alert to the possibilities of improvisation. Once, after a large fly landed on his nose during a performance, he effortlessly cracked so many jokes about it that people afterward asked him how he had managed to train the fly to be part of his act."

10 Wilder (1972) – see p. 68.

3

Second-Generation Free Improviser

In the mid-1970s, Steve Beresford became associated with the leading musicians of what later came to be known as "free improvisation." The first generation included Derek Bailey, Evan Parker, Tony Oxley, John Stevens, Trevor Watts, Barry Guy, Howard Riley, Keith Rowe, Eddie Prévost and Paul Rutherford. Beresford was a few years younger than these players – Bailey was the oldest – and when he moved to London in 1974, he joined what later became known as the "second generation" of free improvisers. He helped found *Musics* magazine, and the London Musicians' Collective (LMC), a charitable organisation that promoted free improvisation and experimental music, replacing the Musicians' Co-op – both pioneered new approaches to the developing genre of free improvisation.[1] Beresford became involved in a wide range of projects including free improvisation, free jazz, pop, reggae and MOR songs, and music for films, dance and advertising.

The labels "free jazz" and "free improvisation" are contestable in meaning but form a useful or at least inevitable starting point for discussion. Both genres avoid explicit grooves and chord changes, aiming at maximum freedom. *Free jazz* is an American genre, arising from a particular historical moment, its politicised forms expressing Black Power. A dominant free jazz approach, found in the work of Cecil Taylor, John Coltrane and Albert Ayler, is "flexible pulse no metre" – a powerful momentum without a countable pulse, but with a residue or reminder of traditional swing. "Pulse" normally implies something more or less steady, and some free jazz – Ornette Coleman's, for instance – often had a groove. But free jazz after Cecil Taylor and Sunny Murray at Cafe Montmartre (1962) was based on a tumbling momentum or energy – what Ekkehard Jost characterises as a free analogue to swing.[2] Adam Fairhall describes it as

> an ebbing and flowing pulse, in which a solid pulse may be evident in some aspects – some free players employed quite countable individual phrases – but which often approaches a kind of constant rubato. The groups of Albert Ayler,

late Coltrane, Frank Wright, Paul Bley and Cecil Taylor from the 1960s, all employed this flexible approach to time. The result is a tumbling momentum not always present in European free music – although it often is – but which comes out of gesture, velocity of attack and energy rather than a sustained, steady pulse.[3]

Hence the terms "energy music" or "fire music." There's a rich continuum from bebop groove to free improv pulselessness, a range that skilled musicians exploit during one performance. Despite its reputation, ironically, free jazz usually makes use of compositional structure. As Fairhall comments, "It's hard to think of an American album from the '60s that doesn't have a recognisable pre-composition element. Even Cecil Taylor seemed concerned with composition, although it's often hard to tell."[4]

The movement known as *free improvisation* evolved mainly in Europe but also in the United States. Unlike American free jazz players, European free improvisers tend to be dedicated to "total" improvisation, without pre-composition. Free improvisation was a development from American free jazz, and generally avoided even a residual, flexible pulse. Free jazz tends to be expressionist, while free improvisation often involves a quieter, more reflective approach. Thus, Lennie Tristano's free recordings of the 1940s, and Jimmy Giuffre's work with Paul Bley and Steve Swallow in the early 1960s, anticipate free improvisation as much as free jazz. However, groups such as the Alex von Schlippenbach Trio, or Peter Brötzmann with Van Hove and Bennink, are formative in European free improv, despite being more expressionist. Europe has a stronger representation of musicians such as Han Bennink who can be regarded as playing something between free jazz and free improvisation – Bennink, for instance, recorded with both Eric Dolphy and Derek Bailey.[5]

A leading figure in the development of free improvised music in Britain, and Europe, was guitarist Derek Bailey – who became a major influence on Steve Beresford. His impact is discussed at length in Chapter 4. Bailey began playing jazz and then free improvisation with Tony Oxley and Gavin Bryars in his hometown of Sheffield, and moved to London in 1966 to work with Evan Parker and Paul Rutherford.

A contrasting influence after Derek Bailey was AMM, founded in London in 1965 and initially comprising Keith Rowe on guitar, Lou Gare on saxophone and Eddie Prévost on drums. Other leading British first-generation free improvisers included Evan Parker, Tony Oxley, Paul Lytton, Howard Riley, John Stevens, Paul Rutherford and Trevor Watts, whose various groups included Spontaneous Music Ensemble (SME), AMM, Iskra 1903 and Music Improvisation Company. British free improv flourished as the AACM was developing in Chicago, and its inception dates from the opening of the Little Theatre Club in St Martin's Lane in London's West End, in January 1966 – the main venue for SME and other early free improvisers. Another venue was Ronnie Scott's original basement club in Gerrard Street, Soho; when Scott bought new premises in Frith Street, he allowed improvisers to play in The Old Place.

SME's *Karyobin* is a cornerstone recording. In summer 1967, SME consisted of John Stevens and Evan Parker, who invited Kenny Wheeler, Derek Bailey and Dave Holland for the group's second record date. Though they hadn't played together regularly, the ensemble's remarkable interactive empathy expresses John Stevens' "compositional aesthetic," as Evan Parker calls it. In 1997, Parker formulated Stevens' aesthetic in two "quite simple rules": "if you can't hear somebody else you are playing too loud, and if what you are doing does not, at regular intervals, make reference to what you are hearing other people do, you might as well not be playing in the group." A beautifully remastered version of *Karyobin* appeared in 2017. Martin Davidson commented in the sleeve notes that the album "announced . . . another way to facilitate group improvisation besides the Free-Jazz-without-tunes hierarchical model, or the layered approach of AMM. This paradigm became the third of the three approaches that have influenced virtually all subsequent free improvisation."

How did you get interested in playing free improvisation?
I bought *Karyobin* when it first appeared in 1968, around the time I went to uni. It was on Island – it was distributed to some extent. Bailey was the key influence.

This was the first time you heard Derek Bailey?
I'd heard probably the expanded SME, on a big old transistor radio – on Jazz Club I think, on the BBC. It was a session.

I thought this was weird, there were two people, Derek Bailey and Dennis Bailey, and they sound very similar, how could that be? But, of course, they'd got his name wrong on the sleeve.

Probably quite shortly after that, I discovered he was working with Han [Bennink]. Also early on, I got ICP4, which is a Bailey/Bennink duo.

What did you think when you heard *Karyobin*?
It was an epiphany.

There was another epiphanic moment a little while later, when I heard a record of Tibetan Buddhist music at the Horniman Museum [in South London]. I thought "Wow, you can make music that's structured like that."

BRIAN MARLEY is an arts-based writer/photographer who lives in Brighton. With Mark Wastell, he edited *Blocks of Consciousness and the Unbroken Continuum*, a book about developments in improvised and experimental musics, and is the author of a novel, *Apropos Jimmy Inkling*.

He writes:

The first time I saw Steve Beresford play was in the early 1970s. Soho Poly Theatre. A small room with a tiny stage. The line-up: Derek Bailey, Lol Coxhill and one other, probably Evan Parker . . . and Steve, of course. There couldn't have been more than twenty people in the audience. Steve, offstage and to one side, played an out-of-tune upright piano, on top of which he'd placed a brass instrument of some kind, probably a euphonium, and various toy instruments, including a ukulele-sized-guitar connected to a miniature amplifier/speaker.

The gig started well, with lots of strong interplay, but when Steve switched from piano to guitar, with the volume on the amp set to max, his manic strumming set off howls of feedback and distortion. At close quarters – I should know: I was standing right next to him, allowing for a bit of elbow room – it was a hideous racket. One by one the other musicians stopped playing. Haloed by noise, Steve pressed on for a minute or two, seemingly oblivious – ah, but was he? – to the fact that he was now playing solo. When eventually he put the guitar down, Lol Coxhill stepped forward and said, "You see, the Greater London Council won't give us any grant money unless we bring in these young musicians." (Obviously a joke.) To which a voice in the audience piped up, "That's not true! I'm here as a council monitor, to see that our money has been spent appropriately, and there's no such stipulation!" (Some people have only a vestigial funnybone.)

Strangely, for all that, it was an enjoyable gig. It was also highly instructive. Until then, because I was new to free improvisation, I hadn't realised that it was fraught with dangers – dangers that other ways of music-making don't face. Free improv can go wrong in myriad ways. At even the most fundamental level, the players might fail to establish common ground or even fruitful uncommon ground. What a fragile edifice this music is, always being built, torn down and rebuilt moment by moment, a music in which, unlike almost any other I can think of, mistakes, even major disruptions, can play a valuable role.

Over the years I've seen Steve play dozens of times, in a wide range of instrumental configurations, never again quite so disruptively but always with great inventiveness and to the betterment of the music. Composer, player, wit and raconteur – he majors on all scores.

* * *

Teatime was issued in 1975 on Incus – the label run by Derek Bailey and Evan Parker – and later reissued by Emanem with additional material. It was an important early recording by the free improv second generation, and introduced four London-based improvisers, as well as Beresford: Garry Todd (tenor saxophone); Nigel Coombes (violin, electronics); John Russell (electric guitar); and Dave Solomon (percussion).[6] The results are anarchic and sublimely humorous. As with the work of Alterations, discussed shortly, these recordings show Beresford in the guise of performance or music hall artist, hammering tinny notes from a toy piano, drawing squeals from a balloon or making bird and animal calls. On piano, he references a range of styles, from Romantic pastiche and cheesy 1930s ballads, to Cecil Taylor and post-Webern modernism.

Between 1974 and 1978, Beresford was a member of the well-named but little-recorded Three Pullovers, with Roger Smith and Nigel Coombes – when Terry Day was added, it became Four Pullovers. Beresford mainly played toys, Nigel Coombes was on violin and electronics, and Roger Smith was on unamplified guitar. They made one recording, *Three & Four Pullovers* on Emanem.

Teatime has abrupt cuts – Martin Davidson in the reissue sleeve note says he found the "brutal editing . . . very shocking at the time."
I think we got the idea from Misha Mengelberg – from *Fragments* (ICP 5), with John Tchicai. Misha would listen to the tape, and the moment it got boring he just cut it.

Garry Todd doesn't do gigs anymore?
I don't think so.[7] He's a very good saxophone player. When I first heard him, I thought "This is like Sonny Rollins playing Derek Bailey." His father Jeff was a drummer who played with Derek.

Derek and Evan made it a condition of making the album [*Teatime*] that there should be the five of us – a stipulation that resulted in some variety in the ensembles.

I was very keen on getting a record out by The Four Pullovers – I think we played with the band (minus Terry Day) opposite one of the gigs used for *Teatime*. It was recorded by Martin Davidson and issued on a very short-run cassette on David Toop's label. Decades later, Martin put it out [on Emanem].

The band had Nigel and Roger, and myself on electronics, small instruments and toy pianos, and Terry Day, playing what I think he called couch percussion – percussion instruments on a sofa, because the gigs we did tended to have sofas in the room for some reason.

* * *

A major early influence on Beresford was free improv trio AMM, founded by guitarist Keith Rowe, with percussionist Eddie Prévost and saxophonist Lou Gare. AMM's career shows the surprisingly blurred boundaries of London's mid-1960s musical scene – they performed on bills with the emerging Pink Floyd, and worked with Christian Wolff. The group began in 1965, adopting their mysterious moniker in 1966. Gare and Prévost drew on free jazz, but their hard-to-categorise music morphed into a kind of free noise. Cornelius Cardew, an associate of Cage and Stockhausen, joined in 1966, undermining the residual jazz elements; he was a member intermittently from 1966 till the late 1970s, on piano and cello. As David Grubbs comments, AMM favoured a "Cagean experimental-music tradition, even as Keith Rowe, Eddie Prévost, and Lou Gare had played in established jazz groups," and their early manager Victor Schonfield referred to them as "John Cage jazz."[8] AMM's most enduring grouping was the trio formed in 1980, when pianist John Tilbury joined Prévost and Rowe; the trio was stable for two decades, generally exploring more meditative sounds. After 2000, Keith Rowe focused on "electroacoustic improvisation" outside AMM.

AMM and Derek Bailey were the main drivers of free improvisation, forcing a move away from free jazz. Paul Bream, an early fan who became a leading promoter and organiser of Jazz North-East, comments that "the audiences that came to AMM were from a contemporary classical school, in particular John Cage and Cornelius Cardew.... AMM and SME were two distinct developments that moved closer together."[9] AMM's performances were unplanned and spontaneous. Most of their recordings have appeared on Prévost's Matchless Recordings. *AMMusic* (1966) introduced a totally original sound that many audiences found baffling; *The Crypt* (1968) established the droning, long-form music that came to characterise the group.

Born in England in 1942, drummer EDDIE PRÉVOST is integral to the history of British free improv. He began playing skiffle and then jazz – at one point he was called "the Art Blakey of Brixton," influenced by Max Roach and Ed Blackwell. In 1965, he co-founded AMM with saxophonist Lou Gare and guitarist

Keith Rowe. Prévost has also collaborated with other major free improvisers, including Evan Parker and Paul Rutherford. In addition to performing, Prévost writes and gives lectures on free improvisation, and runs his own label Matchless Records.

Born in 1940, table-top guitarist KEITH ROWE has played with several other groups, such as the Scratch Orchestra and People's Liberation Music with Cornelius Cardew, the Music in Movement Electronic Orchestra (MIMEO), and as a duo with Eddie Prévost recording under the title AMM III. He is also a painter, whose work is inspired by and based on the work of artists Paul Klee and Jackson Pollock.

Born in 1936 in London, JOHN TILBURY is an improvising pianist, but perhaps best known for his interpretation of the music of John Cage and Morton Feldman, of which he has made many recordings. He played in Cornelius Cardew's Scratch Orchestra and in AMM. Experimental composer Cardew died in 1981, and Tilbury wrote his biography, *Cornelius Cardew: A Life Unfinished* (2008). Tilbury has also performed the work of Samuel Beckett, producing recordings of the plays *Cascando* and *Rough for Radio 1*, a combination of spoken word and music.

* * *

AMM was a revelation when I heard them live. It was one of the most important performances I ever saw.

This was around the time our student band – I forget the name – supported Bob Marley on his first UK tour, in 1973. He toured universities with the Barrett Brothers, Peter Tosh and Bunny Wailer. That was one of the greatest gigs I've ever seen, and it was around that time I saw AMM for the first time, at York Arts Centre. I did make connections between Bob Marley and AMM, and one of the things was the slowness of it. All of Bob Marley's tempos were dead slow.

What did people call AMM's music?
They might have called it free, or experimental music.

I had their first album on Elektra, before I heard them.[10] Apparently they added the echo later, it wasn't the room. I found the large amount of reverb very disturbing – it was telling me that this was another sort of music than what I was hearing at the Little Theatre Club. Although people used to put lots of reverb on everything in those days – I've not heard the version that Eddie [Prévost] put out on CD, which used the original master-tapes, which is probably not reverb-y.

Lol Coxhill and I both grew to quite like the reverb.

Derek Bailey looks to be a more dominant influence on you than AMM.
Definitely. But I notice there's an interview with me about The Four Pullovers where I say my influences were a combination of AMM and SME.

Did you feel AMM was a more classical influence – in the sense of experimental composition?
No, because at that time, there wasn't much modern composition that was to do with long tones, and sustains, and things that slowly changed – except maybe Cardew's *The Great Learning*, which I probably hadn't heard then. The distinction between avantgarde and experimental music – which is almost like the difference between free jazz and free improvisation – didn't exist. It's a grey area – obviously there's no Trump-style wall between these things.

Did you feel that Bailey and AMM were diametrical opposites, in the early days of free improv?
It doesn't have to be true, but my impression is that Keith Rowe thought it was. He sat in with the London Improvisers Orchestra, and said afterwards, "There's two completely different sets of musical languages – me, and the rest of the orchestra." My thought was "What's wrong with that?" But he thought that he was distinct from the way that the LIO operated. Clearly that was important to him.

Do you think that AMM are a kind of thing apart, in the narrative of free improvisation?
If you listen to early SME pieces, sustains were common. On *Oliv*, for instance, which Martin Davidson reissued – it came out on Marmalade originally. There were two versions, a large ensemble and a quartet – it was SME with three singers including Maggie Nicols – Trevor Watts and Johnny Dyani were on it. It's pretty great. And the large ensemble uses lots of drones. It's not true that it was only AMM that touched on sustained tones. They tended not to go for the more Webernian side, that's true – maybe they were more interested in noise than Derek was, he focused on tone-colour.

So – they had a distinctive style, but there was a huge overlap.

What do you think of Keith Rowe's music?
Sometimes it's fantastic, and sometimes it's absolutely horrible – like most people's. When it works, it's brilliant.

I love John Tilbury's piano-playing, of course, but he's not always perfect.

These guys have been spending decades building a magical story around what they've done.

The name AMM, for instance – no one is meant to know what it means. Did you get much from his use of little machines and so on?
Of course, yes. I actually don't use those hand-fans.

* * *

After you graduated from York University, you put on a solo gig by Derek Bailey there.
It was a recital of probably new pieces by students. Maybe that was the first time that I met him.

Neil Lamb was studying with Bernard Rands at York University, and he wrote a piece for Derek, in the style of a Luciano Berio "Sequenza." When Derek came to York, he played Neil's piece in a programme of student compositions. Obviously now we can say "You don't write notated music for Derek Bailey." The piece quoted from blues guitarists – and it was probably alright. Neil wasn't super-pleased at the way that Derek didn't play it.

Did play it but interpreted it loosely, or didn't play it at all?
Both! There was an instruction in the score to play a blues lick and go "Whoa." And he stood up and went "Whoa!" really loudly – he hammed that bit up, and really didn't do any of the rest.

After all the compositions, he played some free improvisation – it said in the programme, in italics, that "Derek Bailey will play some improvisations" – after the proper music, this furniture music.

I've been working with Honest Jons on three double LP releases [released late 2017], and one of the things we've discovered is a tape of these improvisations.

So that's how I got to know Derek.

The second time he came to York, maybe a year later, it was part of a concert series organised by myself and Martin Mayes – it was Derek and Han Bennink. That was mind-changing, completely amazing.

You'd heard them, but hadn't seen them before.
Right. The ICP records didn't have much in the way of dynamics – what I hadn't appreciated from the records was the physicality of Han. He came out on stage and played one hit on the snare drum, and about six people walked out. It wasn't amplified, but he's a very powerful player. People hadn't heard a snare drum played loudly before.

We also had Peter Brötzmann and Fred Van Hove, and Evan Parker and Paul Lytton.

Several years later, for one gig, Derek appeared in a trio with me and my younger brother, Pete, who plays piano, lap-steel guitar. He used to play violin as well, and accordion.

Derek Bailey and the two Beresfords.
Yeah. There were two pianos at the Unity Theatre, London, so we both played piano and Derek played guitar. My brother played in one of the tributes to Lol [Coxhill], in September 2012 – with his band, The Herbert Spliffington Allstars, named after a fictional character in a Prince Buster song.

After I left York University, I came to London briefly, in 1971, but it didn't pan out. It was to play piano in an experimental folk band, and I was living with some junkies in a bedbug-infested flat in Finsbury Park. So I went back to York, because it was cheaper, cleaner, easier to get around. We formed the trio I mentioned, Bread and Cheese, with Dave Herzfeld and Neil Lamb, who was interested in Berio and free improvisation.

We did a lot of vocal stuff – we'd been listening to Berio a lot, and he was a major influence. I think the first gig we did was probably really great. The more we practised the worse we got. Dave Herzfeld wanted us to be a jazz group, which wasn't my idea. Dave had studied with Elvin Jones – though that might have meant he'd just had a thirty-minute lesson with him.

"The more we practised the worse we got" – that's something you generally find, hence your hostility to practising?
The reason I can't answer that is that I never rehearsed a free improvisation group. The nearest I got, I suppose, was with [improvising acoustic guitarist] James Malone. When he came on the scene, he used to say, "Can I come round to your house and play with you?" In that situation you do build up a relationship with a musician, and that could be called rehearsing.

That definitely helps, and I'm not discounting that.
So free improv was the first of your own music that you did.
Definitely.
Was it called that then?
I think it was called free music, or free improvisation.

I was increasingly commuting to London on the midnight coach, on Friday night. I got to know Derek Bailey a little bit, John Stevens and Evan Parker.

I played at Ronnie Scott's for the Musicians Coop, with Dave Solomon.

I had my first espresso ever, at the Bar Italia, and spaghetti that didn't come out of a can – this was all new to me. It was completely thrilling to be playing at Ronnie Scott's.

Ronnie didn't like free improvisation. But he said, "I don't like the music you play, but you can have the club [the new place] on a Sunday night," which was great.

What is the main difference between first- and second-generation free improvisers?
We were younger.

Five years.
But in those days, that was a big difference – between twenty-five and thirty.

You had models, and they didn't.
Absolutely. I think if you look at Evan [Parker], he was absolutely committed to Coltrane, that was his model. Of course, he doesn't play like Coltrane, but you can hear Coltrane in him.

You didn't have a jazz model.
I liked jazz a lot, I grew up with jazz. I prefer to play free improvisation, but the music I listen to most is jazz. But nobody in the university, even the jazz musicians, would tell me how you play it.

If they had, you might have become a more conventional jazz musician.
That's interesting. If somebody in 1969 had said that you don't play a G triad, you play a B and an E, then I might have become some tedious bebop player – rather than a tedious free improviser.

You recently had a reunion with guitarist Ian Brighton, who was a contemporary of yours.
Ian Brighton was one of the first guitarists to sound like Derek Bailey – around the same time as John Russell. But then he took thirty years out, and didn't play. Now he's come back. I think he sounds really good.

I didn't play with him in his earlier career because he was with a particular group of people with a very serious attitude.

Your trio with Ian, and Trevor Taylor on percussion and electronics, is called The Kontakte Trio, presumably after Stockhausen.
Yes – I wouldn't have named anything after a Stockhausen piece, except as a joke. You can hear that Stockhausen is an influence, though not on me.

You said in an interview that the problem with the Musicians' Collective was that most of the musicians didn't think music was fun. People were using it as a talking shop.
Certainly some of them were.

In the days of the LMC [London Musicians' Collective], Max Eastley and I decided that because there was nothing about this music on the radio – which is generally still true – we were going to make a radio show. We wanted to get interviews with different free improvisers, but when we interviewed one leading figure, he gave us ninety minutes about how it's impossible to talk about music – which is obviously ridiculous. This made us so depressed, we gave up the idea of the programme.

It's particularly hard to write about free improvisation. If you were reviewing a Michael Finnissy record, you could talk about what it was inspired by, and when he wrote it – and that gets round the problem of talking about what notes are being played and why. Those questions are really hard, I appreciate that. Talking about music is hard, and you can see that in a lot of music writing, the writer sort of avoids doing it.

The first wave of rock 'n' roll writers who were academic, were really relieved when people said that the kind of trousers you wore, and the album-cover, are important – and, of course, they are important in pop music, maybe in all kinds of music. But they are easier to write about. The way that writing on popular music became more sociological is fine – but it kind of gets the writer off the hook.

It's quite a common view that it's impossible to talk about music – is that meant to apply to other art forms as well?
It doesn't apply to any art form.
Some musicians don't want to – or can't – talk about music. Obviously, you don't want to criticise other musicians that you might come across in a working situation.
Yes.
And there used to be the feeling that you didn't want to give away your secrets.
There was. Early on in free improvisation, there was a feeling that everyone was protecting their corner. But as more people began to play this music, there was the recognition that it wouldn't be possible to do this, because there would be half a dozen others, overlapping with you. And now nobody has that attitude.

I think it was inherited from the jazz scene.
What about a related issue, which Lester Young was very disturbed by – imitators. Would you say you had imitators?
It's not very likely – I can think of one or two people who seem to have thought "That's a nice idea, I'm going to try and do that." I think that's fine.

Coltrane and Charlie Parker were endlessly imitated – though it's very hard technically just to sound like Parker, or Coltrane.

Thinking again about the LMC, the musicians who don't find music fun, might be tortured artist types.

No doubt! You can say that again.

You must have some sympathy with that. Lee Konitz was criticised for his introversion or reticence, on occasion, in performance, and that is because of insecurity and doubt. You have those issues, but they don't affect you in the same way?[11]

That's probably right. The problem comes from expecting the rest of the world to service your insecurity and doubt, and to constantly placate it.

Guitarist MIKE COOPER (born in Reading in 1942) co-founded the Blues Committee, an R&B group, and, as a contemporary of John Renbourn and Bert Jansch, played folk blues. In the 1980s he alternated between blues and avantgarde jazz, and in 1987 released the 10" LP Aveklei Uptowns Hawaiians, with guitarist Cyrille Lefebvre, and sidemen including Lol Coxhill, Steve Beresford, and Max Eastley. It showcased Cooper's growing obsession with Polynesian music, which informed his playing in subsequent decades. His trio The Recedents with Lol Coxhill and Roger Turner was founded in 1982.

Mike Cooper writes:

> *My first meeting with Steve was at the LMC. I was on my way out and stopped at the "merch table" – a counter covered with various publications and DIY news sheets. I helped myself liberally to a handful or more and chatted briefly with Steve who watched me with a perplexed look as I exited, not realising I was supposed to pay for some of them – he was a charmingly shy person, too shy to shout "Oi mate!" I liked his style as well – raincoat, Doc Martins and National Health glasses.*
>
> *A concert at – I think – Goldsmith's College in London with Tristan Honsinger sealed my admiration, when he walked into the concert space and emptied a suitcase of toys, objects, junk and other ephemera into the bowels of the grand piano, much to the amusement of the students and the horror of attendant lecturers. This was followed later by a chase around the room culminating in a symphony of whoopee cushions which were placed on a line of chairs along the back wall of the performance area.*
>
> *His musical abilities and obvious disregard for musical genre and anything and anyone pompous enough to suggest that musical behaviour be anything otherwise have always endeared me to him.*
>
> *Anyone involved in the free improvisation scene in Europe who would agree to participate with me in a project of Hawaiian music has my never-ending gratitude, and Steve is amongst them.*

Notes

1. *Musics*, 1975–79, discussed in Toop (2016), pp. 132–3 – Ecstatic Peace's complete facsimile edition of the cooperatively run late 1970s journal appeared in 2016. Clive Bell's history of LMC is found here: http://www.variant.org.uk/8texts/Clive_Bell.html
2. Jost (1994).
3. Personal email communication, 2018.
4. Personal email communication, 2018.
5. On the difference between Free Jazz and Free Improv, see Barre (2015), pp. 45–7.
6. Guitarist John Russell was born in 1954 in London. Since the 1970s he has focused on free improvisation, on acoustic guitar; in the mid-1980s he founded the enduring free improvisation concert series Mopomoso, with Chris Burn.
7. He had to put his playing to one side when his wife Carol developed MS.
8. Both quotations from Grubbs (2014), p. 112.
9. Email to author, 2019.
10. *AMMusic 1966*, on Elektra Records UK.
11. Sadly, Lee Konitz (1927–2020) died while this book was being completed.

4

Derek Bailey

The most important influence on Steve Beresford, as he began his career as improviser, was guitarist DEREK BAILEY (1930–2005) – an influence that's endured. Bailey's grandfather was a professional banjo player, and his uncle was a professional guitarist. He began playing jazz in his hometown of Sheffield, and in the 1950s and early 1960s worked as a guitarist in every kind of musical situation, including clubs, dance halls, radio, TV and recording studios. He moved to London in 1966 to pursue free jazz with Evan Parker and Paul Rutherford, then helped to incubate what would become free improvisation. Important early groups were Joseph Holbrooke and The Music Improvisation Company, and he founded the record label Incus with Tony Oxley and Evan Parker in 1970. Bailey performed internationally – solo, in duos and in small ensembles. He inaugurated Company in 1976, a flexible organisation of improvising musicians; the event ran till 2002, featuring rotating personnel from Europe and the United States, and musicians both with and without experience in improvised music.[1] Most events were held in London, but also in New York, Marseilles and Japan – Beresford participated in some of these, as he relates in Chapter 5.

As Steve Voce comments, "Bailey had an uncompromising philosophy that involved exterminating music that he had already played. It led him rigorously to move on from one group of musicians to the next: he believed that familiarity bred predictability."[2] However, his musical belligerence might be toned down in the gentler company of such musicians as Tony Coe or Steve Lacy, resulting in beguiling partnerships. And the jazz influence was not entirely eliminated; for instance, "Paris," the opening track of *Aida* (1980), has swinging rhythms that could only come from a one-time jazz player. Bailey became an authority on the theory and practice of improvisation, through his book *Improvisation: its Nature and Practice in Music*, and the resulting Channel 4 TV series *On the Edge* (1989–91). In the book, Bailey describes free improvisation as "non-idiomatic improvisation" – though as Simon Rose comments, "a kind of generic free improvisation has developed, leaving doubt about the idea of a non-idiomatic improvisation."[3] This is an issue that Steve Beresford takes up in our conversations.

When I started playing piano, there were all these grumpy old dance band musicians who'd got to know seven hundred standards in every key, and could play them at any tempo. That scared me off being a jazz musician – which was what it was intended to do. Actually, Derek did know all those standards in any key. There was this thing where you played medleys, you'd go from one song to another, and I found that totally impossible. It's an absolutely standard thing that those bands did, and I've never been able to do that, I just don't know the tunes that well.

Derek had a long background of playing absolutely conventional music in the pit orchestra of [BBC series] *The Good Old Days*, in the studio of *I'm Sorry, I'll Read That Again* and *Morecambe and Wise* – and in pit orchestras and music halls and the West End. He was a very good reader. He'd done it for years very well and had made a good living out of it.

I think it's a fantastic ability. Derek, because he was of that age, that generation, could do all that stuff. Then he totally rejected it. Of course he referred back to it, not just on those records, *Ballads* and *Standards*, but in various other ways. If you saw him with Han Bennink, Han would usually do something so silly that Derek would have to play a ballad like "Laura." or something. So Han could get Derek in a position where he'd have to do that. That was way before the Tzadik records. I think they're great records, particularly *Standards*. But it's not like Derek never touched a tune until he did those records with Zorn. Derek's approach was to create a new language for guitar, which I think he did, that was based on absolutely different organising principles to Western II-V-I [tonal] harmony and that kind of stuff. The sleeve notes to *More 74* [Incus CD60] by Alex Ward are superb in terms of that, I think he had some really great things to say about it.

What was his attitude to the day jobs? It wasn't "Sod it, I'm here making a living from this"?
No, it wasn't.
He enjoyed the craft?
I think he enjoyed it very much, and he always liked musicians who were craftsmen and women. That's one of the reasons he liked Lee [Konitz]. Lee is a genius, clearly. Derek admired people who had lots of chops and fulfilled the

brief of whatever the music was. But at one point, he decided he didn't want to do that anymore.

Did he talk to you about that career?
Yes. He was in the pit orchestra for Morecambe and Wise. They made it a point of honour that every night they would tell one joke, a different one each night, that made the musicians laugh. Derek had great admiration for Morecambe and Wise.

Derek worked for the Kray Twins – I just read an interview where he talked about this. It was with a singer who was very good, but who never really worked outside organised crime, at a place called Phoebe's [in Hackney] – when I knew it [later] it was a dub club. I was playing with The Slits at the time, and they would go and dance there. Before it was Phoebe's, it was owned by the Kray Twins, and Derek used to play there.

The Krays loved their old mum.
And they loved celebrities – dress designers, aristocrats, people who would never be outed as gay because they were too posh, and so on – and celebrities loved them. It's the glamour of crime – you see that in the Cotton Club. People like a bit of rough. They ran the clubs – that's very traditional. Most clubs have got some dodgy purpose, like money-laundering.[4]

Could he play jazz like Jim Hall?
Yes, of course he could! He loved Jim Hall. Certainly he was horrible about jazz sometimes, and he did say that more commercial situations, like a dance band, were freer for him than playing jazz. Though maybe he only said things like that to wind people up – because he did do that![5]

Could you tell when he was trying to do this? Did he try and wind you up?
Yes, he wound everybody up.

Were you ever taken in?
Probably. He would say everything with a straight face and never let on.

Like Paul Merton?
No, it's more of a northern thing. The porters at York University would say things like "No, you haven't booked this practice room; no, you can't use it," when you knew damn well you had booked it.

So, it was a joke?
It was a joke but they would just never admit it – it was left hanging in the air and you would go off and not get your practice in, because you couldn't be bothered to go through this routine. Paul Merton has a straight face when he says very funny things, but that's not quite the same as a wind-up.

There was the Dutch gig weekend, with the ICP [Instant Composers Pool] – it must've been the early 1970s. Michael von Biel was there, and AMM. I did a duo with Derek and he drove my stuff – I used a lot of stuff in those days, like a euphonium and a toy guitar. . . . He had a van so he drove them from London to Holland. But then he said, "By the way, I'm not driving your stuff back." Why would you do that?

And he didn't?
No. Because I just went "Oh, that's fine," and, of course, it wasn't fine at all. I was really annoyed. Keith Rowe agreed to take the stuff back. There were two guys who created the template for free improvised guitar, and one of them drove my stuff to Holland, and the other drove it back. So I thought that was rather nice.

He was trying to work out whether you would be savvy that it was a joke?
It's like I said – it's left hanging in the air. I took it as being serious and made other arrangements, because if it was a joke, it was really annoying, and if it wasn't a joke, it was even more annoying.

Derek and Keith can both be difficult in their own way, but I'm sure I can as well.

On Derek's "In Joke (Take 2)," on *Lot 74*, he calls it free music – he's playing guitar, and giving a potted history of improvisation, it's very funny. So even in 1974, he was taking the piss out of nostalgia for improvised music by making this like a sort of reminiscence and getting everyone's names wrong – he calls Han Bennink "Harry Bentink," and Willem, "Willem Breuker from Kattenneuker." "Kattenneuker" means "cat fucker" in Dutch. It's a total piss-take of nostalgia, I think.

When you had a birthday, Derek might send you a cassette of him talking and playing guitar – Incus put some of them out. They consisted of Derek delineating things that happen to your body as you get older, taken from Simone de Beauvoir's *Old Age*. Certainly the one for Evan was, and that's when they were friends.

* * *

Klangfarbenmelodie

Timbral and dynamic variation is key to understanding Bailey's work, and an improbable influence on him here was Second Viennese School composer Anton

Webern. Webern isn't a familiar figure in the pages of jazz and improv histories, but Derek Bailey, with fellow free improv pioneer John Stevens, became obsessed with Webern's techniques for varying timbre, known as *klangfarbenmelodie* (literally, "sound-colour-melody"). The term was coined by Webern's teacher Schoenberg, for whom the timbral transformation of a single pitch might be equivalent to a melodic succession – thus tone-colour could be a structural element in composition, along with melody, harmony and rhythm. Bailey also followed Webern in using extreme dissonance, such as tritones and flat 9ths. Undermining diatonic harmony, he created a new freedom of pitch relations based on the string's natural sonic, vibrating properties. Bailey's Webern-influenced guitar language involved command of harmonics – he avoided a uniform tone by playing the same note in different places on guitar, and in different ways, articulated with virtuosic precision in dazzling runs. Acute control of dynamics as well as timbre was involved.

Derek was very influenced by Webern.
Massively. He got the Robert Craft boxed-set of the complete Webern from the library and taped it, and played it every day. It drove his landlady mad. I think he transcribed Piano Variations for guitar, and also wrote some pieces that were clearly influenced by Webern.

There's that idea, which is very Webernian, that every pitch should have a different colour – so a lot of the time, his line doesn't sound conventional. He'd be using octave transpositions and harmonics and different ways of playing the notes, to colour the line. That became part of Derek's basic style. Equally, then he'd wind you up by playing lots of open strings, which people try to avoid. When I play guitar, I think "Oh my God, I'm playing open E, oh shit." I try not to play open strings. Derek would do just that.[6]

The sound of his guitar is constantly in flux. There are many ways of creating notes on a guitar – some pitches can be found on several different strings and also played as harmonics, a few even behind the bridge. Derek was writing a book about improvisation on guitar, it's in a box somewhere in Downs Road [where he lived], somebody should put it together. "How to play an entire chromatic scale in harmonics," and so on.

Webern's idea to make a line out of different timbres – it's *really* exciting.

The point about exploiting a variety of timbres – did Derek stress this was important?
I don't remember him saying "people don't understand the importance of *klangfarbenmelodie* in my music."

There are many other things to say about his playing, but if you haven't grasped that, you haven't started to understand what he's doing.[7]
That's right.
But the Webern connection still seems improbable – a dance-band musician from Sheffield, with a passion for the Viennese modernist.
But this is a man escaping from that setting, and looking around for material that he could do something with.

Obviously the idea of twelve-tone improvising is utterly ludicrous.
There was the record by David Mack, of twelve-tone improvisation.
I know that record, because Shake Keane's on it – with a chang-a-dang rhythm section. Improvising a tone-row is not only really difficult, it's also kind of pointless.
Merle Hazard portrays a Country and Western singer whose dad was an atonal composer.[8]
Merle Hazard's is a very funny spoof, but Eugene Chadbourne managed to make a record that in itself is just very good music [*There'll Be No Tears Tonight*]. It's "free improvised Country and Western bebop," and it is very funny! Obviously it's about genre – but if you could listen to it with "clean ears," it would still sound great.

I did a record with Eugene and Alex Ward – *Pleasures of the Horror* (Forced Exposure Records). We play some songs about monsters. It took an enormous time to put it out. It's only on LP.

* * *

Jazz and Free Improv

The issue of the relation of jazz and free improvisation is a difficult one. We pursue it here in connection with Bailey's career, and at greater length in Chapter 8.

Derek comes out of jazz, and as we discussed, his late albums of standards shows his continuing mastery of jazz material.
Of course – he played in dance-bands. But he was really mean about jazz musicians.
Was he ever in a jazz band?
I'm not sure – but he was in lots of dance-bands.
The trio with Gavin Bryars and Tony Oxley was close to free jazz.

Yes, that's the period when Derek's closest to free jazz. He was listening to Jim Hall, and Gavin was besotted with [Bill Evans' bassist] Scott La Faro.
Gavin said that if you listen to all of Bill Evans' recordings, you never hear anything that sounds like a mistake or slip.[9]
In terms of playing piano – it's pretty well impeccable.

Derek always said the 32-bar pop song is a strong form, and if you're going to improvise you've got to have something as strong as that. You could see his strength, this is why [the album] *Carpal Tunnel* is, for me, incredibly painful.[10] He thought when he made that record that he had Carpal Tunnel Syndrome, but in fact he had Motor Neurone Disease [which he died from]. It's terribly painful to listen to because Derek was such a strong player physically and psychologically. You saw his face age ten years when he played, because he was so intensely into the music.

He loved Samuel Beckett. All those guys, Evan, John Stevens, Derek, were obsessed with Beckett – Derek did actually look a lot like him. All those creases – you could see the amount of concentration that went into the music, and also the strength. His strength as a player, physically and in terms of the way he made musical statements, was all to do with creating a really different language for guitar.

How would you compare Lol Coxhill's approach to improvisation to Derek's? Lol didn't disavow jazz in the same way.
Derek put a big full stop next to his period of being a session musician, reading music, studying Webern. After that, there was no playing notated music. He was happy to play with people playing notated music, as long as he was allowed to do what he does.[11] I thought that was a good strategy for Derek – it's not something I would recommend for everybody.

I think his idea of "non-idiomatic improvisation" made sense as a strategy for Derek – it doesn't make sense as a way of life for every musician. In fact, he created another idiom – a productive, amazingly flexible idiom that you could move in and out of. You definitely don't build up a way of playing by exorcising every idiom that you're familiar with.

"Non-idiomatic improvisation" was a way for Derek to move forward – as someone who had been immersed in being a good conventional musician. It was a strategy, not an ideology.

Wasn't it an ideology? Didn't he think others should do it?
I think it got expanded massively. He certainly didn't say "You've all got to play like this."

You don't like ideologies?
I didn't say that!

I would never say that nobody should practise. An ideology is something that's applicable to other people than you. I'm talking about *me* – I don't practise.

Han and Derek practised all the time. I just don't.

There was a famous face-to-face discussion between Cornelius Cardew and Hans Keller at the Roundhouse. I ended up on Hans's side – because Cornelius, rather like Boulez, seemed to feel that there was only one way for anyone to do anything.

I don't think Derek ever said "Everyone has to play like this." He said, "I play like this" – and clearly he had created a deliberate strategy, in which he found a new way to play guitar, that was what was so exciting about Derek.

Clearly, Derek played all the time with people who didn't follow that approach – such as Lee Konitz, who always played jazz, improvising over popular songs by people such as George Gershwin.

People said, "Free improvisation has become an idiom of itself." Of course, it has. As I said in my very sarcastic letter to *The Wire* many years ago, you can't have a new set of notes every time you sit down at an instrument. There are only so many ways of playing a violin.

Derek practised incessantly. He never stopped practising. So did Han Bennink.

How did Derek practise?
There should be a whole book about that. I think Derek practised by improvising. I'm sure there was a time, in his jazz days, when he practised standards, but also when he taught. His students included John Russell and Roger Smith.

What did Derek listen to?
I don't think he listened to very much. At one point, it seemed, he only had a couple of records, Billie Holiday and [rapper] Ol' Dirty Bastard.

That's very interesting. There seem to be artists who listen to everything, and those who just listen to their own work.
You're trying to make him sound solipsistic now.

I just mean some musicians are not so passionate about hearing a wide range of music. I think there are artists who are really focused on their own work, almost to the exclusion of anything else – and those who are eclectic, with amazingly wide interests. Derek was one of the former, you're one of the latter.
I think most free improvisers have got a very wide range of tastes. Evan Parker has. He played in the Charlie Watts big band. And Kenny Wheeler's big band – Kenny was very important to Evan.

Derek was passionately interested in playing music.

Did he go to gigs?

Occasionally you'd see Derek at a gig – I'm trying to think where.

You've described the moments in a free improv performance where nothing of interest was happening, as "roughage."

[Laughs] I think Derek was trying to get rid of roughage. I remember him saying about one musician, "I like the way he never stops playing, even when he doesn't know what to do – he just gets quieter." That would be roughage. But sometimes, roughage is the most interesting thing.

Lennie Tristano used to talk about "filler material." Roughage is necessary as part of a diet.

How about *Echtzeitmusik* (*Real-time music*) where you might play one note in an hour. That one note had better be pretty damn good! Or is the silence a form of roughage? Isn't it funny, no one does that anymore, it's gone. Does Radu Malfatti still play music like that? [**AH: Yes, apparently.**]

AMM's best silences were fantastic. When they fall into a silence, it's a very exciting, tension-filled silence. The problem is if you have that as a necessary part of your performance, it might not be that exciting. Obviously it can become a cliché.

In the music you play, are there accompaniments?

Sometimes – it depends what I'm doing.

When I worked with Francois Carrier – obviously free jazz has the kind of organisation roughly like a jazz group. As a piano-player it's hard to avoid being an accompanist, on some kind of level, with that music.

But not in free improvisation?

Of course, it's like that sometimes. The flexibility of roles is very important, but that was one of the things about Alterations, that we did end up with certain hierarchies at certain points in the music. But those hierarchies were constantly in flux.

Whereas in free jazz the roles tend to be a bit more fixed.

They tend to be a bit more fixed, which isn't to say that's boring.

Do you think that's a problem for listeners to free improvisation, that the roles are more open?

I think it can be, definitely.

* * *

An Aesthetics of Imperfection (Part One)

The "aesthetics of imperfection" emphasises spontaneity, disruption, process and energy over formal perfection. The term was coined by Ted Gioia, and associated by him with improvised music. However, it can be argued that it applies to all musical performance.[12] For many readers, "imperfection" can't be a positive value. But "imperfection" isn't the opposite of "perfection." It is like misremembering or misunderstanding – which involve remembering or understanding, and so are not cases simply of *not* remembering or understanding. Imperfection presupposes background order, functionality or even perfection, not the pursuit of disorder or anarchy. Its key defence is that there is something wrong with the thoroughgoing pursuit of perfection. This is something which Derek Bailey – and Steve Beresford – are keenly aware of. Discussion of the question is continued in Chapter 8.

If you're working with very strong players such as Derek or Han, you can sometimes paint yourself into a corner. I remember a duo record which John Stevens and Derek Bailey made after they got back together – they didn't play together for quite a while. John bumped into me in Portobello Road and said, "Steve, you've got to help me – Derek wants to put out this record and there's this terrible moment where he stops and I'm playing a really stupid sort of funk riff. Suddenly I'm playing a drum solo and it's really clunky and useless." John was distraught about this.

So I listened to the recording and it does sound a bit odd – it's the wrong kit to play funk on because it's a tiny kit. From John's angle I could see why he didn't want it out – but actually it's fine. And overall, that record is totally amazing – it was released as *Playing* (1992).

There's an interaction between these two musicians that's exciting on a microscopic level. Then suddenly there's this semi-comic drum solo, where Derek is perversely not coming in even though John's a bit lost.

Of course, if John had thought of it, he could just have stopped! But you get caught up in it, and think "Oh God, I've got to play a drum solo."
Derek hung him out to dry.
Yes, he could be quite mean.

I was at Diwana [restaurant in London] with John Zorn and Buckethead, guitar-player. This was the first time Buckethead had been out of California.[13] He was asking, "Can I do anything I want?" And Zorn said, "Yeah, but be careful – Derek does things. You'll think it's finished, but he'll continue past the point that's a good end – he knows it's a good end but he's not going to stop there because he's that kind of player."

Zorn adored Derek, as one of the greatest musicians he's ever played with. But that didn't mean he didn't see what Derek was doing.

Combativeness is not a major aspect of free improvisation, but it is an aspect.

It's a matter of not allowing someone to relax into their comfort zone.
Comfort zones can be very annoying. Nowadays I really like the Tony Coe–Derek Bailey duo disc, *Time* (1979) – but when it came out, I thought it sounded like two people passing each other slices of cake. Obviously I love both of those musicians. They were both heroes of mine, and I was disappointed. But now I can hear other stories in it.

What you said about John Stevens reminded me that there are musicians – like Miles Davis apparently – who always choose the take that doesn't have mistakes or fluffs. There are varying attitudes towards leaving things in that maybe aren't great.
Yes, there's a great range of attitudes. Ellington's record with Coltrane isn't perfect – the best bits are amazing, and the worst bits are kind of embarrassing. Duke was a one-take guy, and Coltrane wanted multi-takes. They mixed the rhythm sections up – Sam Woodyard clearly doesn't know what to do with Coltrane, but he's a fantastic drummer.

You must get that range of attitudes in improv too.
Absolutely.

John Stevens would have been very happy to have that passage edited out.

That's not a very improvisatory attitude.
It happens all the time.

The problem with Derek is that the more he knew John didn't like that record, the keener he would be to put it out.

But Derek would surely recognise that some things didn't work.
Yes, he'd think "This didn't work, let's put it out.."

That's the most extreme aesthetics of imperfection.
I know.

Though it depends what you mean by "not working."
Maybe he wouldn't use those words.

Are there recordings that Derek released, that were kind of perverse because they didn't work?
This is awkward to talk about – but probably the Derek Bailey/Steve Lacy duo record, *Outcome* (1983) by two of the most assured musicians I've ever heard. It's

very odd – both sound really unsure of what they're doing. And on one [other recording] that will be nameless, absolutely nothing happens. Derek could put out records that were just pointless.

He didn't have a very high estimate of the record as an artefact.
That's right. David Grubbs, in his book *Records Ruin the Landscape*, compares Derek's attitude with Cage's. There was that similarity in their attitude to records.

Presumably for Derek, a record that wasn't worth putting out was one where there wasn't enough provocation or challenge.
The duo with Tony Coe seems an entirely unprovoking record.[14]

* * *

The Instrument

Bailey's resources were essentially those of a dance-band and jazz guitarist of the late 1950s. On electric guitar – strictly, semi-acoustic guitar with a magnetic pick-up but hollow body – he used a volume pedal to produce extreme dynamic changes within rapid sequences of notes. Given that an acoustic guitar doesn't sustain like an electric, a non-stop flow of new material seemed even more imperative – and as part of his timbral technique, Bailey had great facility in finding the same pitch on different strings, as a stopped tone or a harmonic. For acoustic work, Bailey used a 1936 Epiphone Triumph, a large guitar with a large sound. It's debatable that semi-acoustic guitar and electronic devices afford more timbral variation than large acoustic guitar – as Beresford comments, "The problem with electronic devices is that they all sound electronic."

Derek Bailey played the acoustic and semi-acoustic guitar. What's the difference between these instruments?
The original, acoustic guitar was amplified by guitar body. A semi-acoustic guitar has that to some extent – it has F holes. But it has metal strings – the pick-up is a magnetic one that picks up the vibrations of metal strings.

There has to be a mic that picks up vibrations either from the air, or the body of the instrument.

There are many ways of playing an electric guitar. Carol Kaye played bass guitar with a pick – that's quite unusual, it gives you more attack.[15] Most bass guitarists use their fingers – Larry Graham with Sly Stone was the first to do that, slap and pop. Wes Montgomery played electric guitar with his thumb, perhaps his fingers as well. But most electric guitarists use a pick.

Derek always used a pick.
Yes – in fact, he made his own. He used the pink material that dentists made false teeth from – it's very strong.

What's distinctive about the semi-acoustic guitar is that it's not solid – it still has some resonance in the body. It's a hybrid.

Did Derek play solid-body electric?
I don't remember him playing one – I think he did in his period playing in the pit, because he could practise during the show without making any sound. To my knowledge, he didn't play solid-body electric guitar after his commercial career.

Most jazz guitarists play semi-acoustic; rock guitarists tend to play solid-body electric.

So when people talk about electric guitar, in jazz and improv, they mostly mean semi-acoustic. Isn't the Webern influence more apparent on electric?
Derek occasionally used a fuzz-box. When he had a stereo set-up, he had two volume pedals so he could move the sound from one speaker to another – I certainly saw him with this. Later he bought a Danelectro fuzz-box – it was 1950s-style retro, cheap, and rather beautiful.[16] I don't really like the visual aesthetics of the rock 'n' roll kit.

You can get more timbral variation with electronic devices.
That's a big issue. The problem with electronic devices is that they all sound electronic.

I think it's really debatable whether you can get a bigger variety of sounds out of an electric as opposed to acoustic guitar. There are pedals with all sorts of possibilities, and all kinds of noises – but in most people's hands they all sound like electronics.

Jon Rose comments that, with Derek, "The structures and forms derive almost completely out of the business of playing the guitar." That's reminiscent of Steve Lacy's comment, "The instrument – that's the matter – the stuff – your subject."
I'm sure lots of musicians would agree with that.

Did Derek agonise over electric versus acoustic?
Not to my knowledge.

Martin Vishnick, who plays with the London Improvisers Orchestra, has written two books on extended techniques and avantgarde music for Spanish guitar, the basic acoustic guitar.

Freddie Green would have been playing a bigger acoustic guitar, metal strings with a pick, to cut through the band.

I would say Bill Frisell is much more interesting on electric, but I've heard him play acoustic.

* * *

Bailey's Influence

Bailey is a complex figure, and his example was essential for the work of guitarists as diverse as Fred Frith, Elliott Sharp, Bill Frisell, John Russell and Mary Halvorson, as well as musicians across the spectrum of improvised music.

What did you make of Ben Watson's biography of Derek?
Everything Derek says is extremely illuminating, often very clever, often very funny. Most of what Ben Watson says is none of those things.
He's a critic who has fearless honesty.
Really? There's a bit where Ben starts talking about Tony Oxley's use of the 18-beat bar – triplets, and triplets over the triplets. Then Ben says, "On this record you can hear Tony Oxley using his 18-beat bar" – but it's free improv, there's no bars!

Inventing completely imaginary scenarios, basically creating a fantasy world, and then complaining that people don't conform to it – that's what Ben Watson does. His passion was so often expressed in such negative ways, like screaming at Peter Brötzmann during a gig. If Brötzmann wants to play a bit less than fortissimo at certain points in the set, I think he should be allowed to without people shouting at him. Ben's saying "No, you've got to be the figure in my fantasy. You can't do anything else, you're not allowed to change what you're doing or grow as a musician." I think that's a huge problem in music criticism. I'm not suggesting Ben Watson's the first person to have had these problems. Perhaps he expressed those contradictions more nakedly.

Was it Brecht who said, "An artist's responsibility is to uncover contradictions"? You can't blame people for living a contradictory life. Everybody's living contradictions. The problem is that people want art to be free of those.
What do you think was Derek's influence?
He influenced John Russell, Ian Brighton and Roger Smith directly, including by teaching. And more obliquely, Bill Frisell, whose sound is in a constant state of flux

And others, obviously, in his attitude to improvising.
The list would go on forever, I think.
Are there free improvisers who *aren't* influenced by him?
I'm sure there are. The influence is filtered down, so I'm sure in some cases it's like a homeopathic cure by now.
Are there players who are resistant to very dominant influences, like Bailey, or Evan Parker? Because that is an attitude.
If you were an early generation free improvising musician, it would be very hard to get away from their influence.
Are there Lee Konitz figures – Konitz resisted the dominant model of Charlie Parker?
I expect there are. I know exactly what you mean – Konitz came so quickly after Charlie Parker, and had such a different approach to the instrument.

I can't right now think of a Lee Konitz figure in free improvisation.

* * *

Work with Percussionists

Some of Derek Bailey's most rewarding albums were duos with percussionists – Han Bennink, John Stevens, Tony Oxley. Even among these, *Dart Drug* with Jamie Muir stands out. Recorded and released on Incus in 1981, it's a challenging yet strikingly beautiful recording – a stunning display of Muir's percussion artistry and invention, which matches the guitarist's rather percussive approach. Muir's unique kit included bells, gongs, chimes, woodblocks and many sound-sources hard to determine – peeling masking tape, maybe, or scraping saucepan lids across a brick wall. As he commented in an interview: "I much prefer junk shops to antique shops . . . in an antique shop – it's all been found already; whereas in a junk shop it's only been collected."[17]

One of Derek's greatest records is *Dart Drug* with Jamie Muir.
Jamie and Derek both have a strong feeling for dynamic levels – a sound can hide in another one, especially with someone like Jamie.
Jamie Muir retired from music to become a painter. It's sad that someone who created *Dart Drug* could just give all that up – it's unlikely he's a greater painter than he is a percussionist.
People have different trajectories. Perhaps his drumming would not have been as good if he hadn't also painted.

I think most people of my generation would have got *Music Improvisation Company*, with Evan Parker, Hugh Davies, Christine Jeffrey and Jamie Muir (1970), because it was easy to find [on ECM]. So I think it was very influential.

There are several Derek Bailey recordings on ECM. There's a duo record with Derek Bailey and Dave Holland, *Improvisations for Cello and Guitar* (1971), recorded at the Little Theatre Club. Someone added reverb that doesn't really work – Martin Davidson, needless to say, has the original recording without the reverb. It's a record that ECM has almost disowned, I think – it's only on CD in Japan.[18]

ECM have moved away from free improvisation. But I'm a fan of them, just as I'm a fan of Marks & Spencer and Pizza Express.

Don't get me started on Pizza Express!

Notes

1   Simon H. Fell (1959 –2020), who worked extensively in the Bailey/Incus archives, commented by email: "What constitutes a Company Week – as opposed to a Company event – is not cut-and-dried. There were 'classic' Company Weeks, which are what most people are referring to, and occasional Company events. The 'classic' weeks were organised by Derek (and his partner Karen at least for the later ones, and various other helpers) from scratch – they organised funding, venue, publicity, invited the musicians and programmed the event. These are the events which ran in London (with occasional regional and overseas outgrowths) until 1994. However, during (and especially after this period) there were other occasions where a third-party promoter or venue would undertake most of the funding, venue, publicity and other administrative organisation, and invite Derek to curate a series of performances with musicians of his choice. These were often described as 'Company' and would sometimes be as long as a Company week. Derek used the term "Company Week" with some leeway here, sometimes changing his mind along the way."

Simon Fell continues: "Peter Stubley – a good source regarding Bailey – in the *Oxford Dictionary of National Biography 2005-2008* identifies New York 2001 as 'the last "Company" event'. It certainly was a Company Week type of event – except that Derek didn't undertake the funding and admin work – and musically it was classic Company. It was clearly labelled Company by both Derek and Tonic, and in the publicity. Bailey himself identifies, in Watson's biography, a further Company Week at Tonic in 2002, although his description of the event sounds markedly different from the usual Company Week methodology." (See chapter in Shoemaker (2017), and discussion in Watson (2013)).

2   Derek Bailey obituary, *The Independent*, 29 December 2005, at https://www.independent.co.uk/news/obituaries/derek-bailey-520911.html
3   Rose (2017), p. 21.
4   The Kray brothers – criminals who had showbiz connections. Their career is discussed in Pearson (2015).
5   "I didn't personally like [Ornette Coleman's] stuff – I didn't like it then and I don't like it now" (https://richard-scott.net/interviews/derek-bailey/). He adds that "jazz is about getting a certain atmosphere, a kind of fantasy element . . . and I don't think free music deals with that at all . . . it's not going to dump you in 42nd Street in 1945, it's not going to put you in some kind of flamenco bar."
6   According to classical or standard technique, open strings should be avoided because they disrupt the flow of the line – the sound of an open string note is different from that of a fretted note.
7   Julia Miller refers to "Bailey [incorporating] the concept of *klangfarbenmelodie* into an improvised guitar language." Jon Rose's blog describes Bailey undermining the tyranny of the diatonic chord, creating a new freedom of pitch relationships based on the string's natural sonic qualities.
8   www.youtube.com/watch?v=gzodB0Sp6ZI
9   Email to author, 2019.
10 Bailey's last solo album, recorded in 2004 and released in 2006 on Tzadik.
11 As on Steve Lacy's album *The Crust* (Emanem).
12 Gioia (1988); discussed in Hamilton (2020), and Hamilton and Pearson eds. (2020).
13 Buckethead, born Brian Patrick Carroll in 1969, near Disneyland in Southern California, is a multi-instrumentalist whose main instrument is electric guitar; he performs with a KFC bucket on his head, and an expressionless white mask. His work crosses many genres; he has collaborated with Bill Laswell, Bootsy Collins, Iggy Pop and Mike Patton, and was a member of Guns N' Roses, 2000–2004.
14 Discussion of the aesthetics of imperfection continues in Chapter 8.
15 Los Angeles-based session musician Carol Kaye, born 1935, played bass on around 10,000 sessions, including classic recordings from The Monkees' "I'm A Believer" to The Beach Boys' *Pet Sounds*. See www.bbc.co.uk/programmes/b05nk25s.
16 https://en.wikipedia.org/wiki/Danelectro.
17 From a 1972 issue of *Microphone* magazine, quoted in Bailey (1993), p. 96.
18 Bailey also appears on *Improvisations* by Globe Unity (1978).

5

Company Week 1977 + The Dutch School + Alterations + White String's

The late 1970s was a crucial period for Beresford's music, starting with his appearance at Derek Bailey's Company Week in 1977. In Company Week, Bailey fulfilled some of the characteristic aims of free improvisation, putting together groups of musicians many of whom had never worked with each other before. Leading participants in 1977 included American free jazz players such as Anthony Braxton and Wadada Leo Smith, with whom Beresford's relations proved problematic. The final Company events were held in 2002.

Beresford's participation upset some of the less Dada-inclined participants, as Ben Watson describes in his biography of Bailey:

> At Company Week 1977, Steve Beresford's interpretation of freedom – very much in the vein of the performance art antics introduced by Gavin Bryars – didn't suit the high seriousness of the AACM delegates. On the first night, during the third act – a quartet with Coxhill, Bennink and Altena – Beresford poured water from a hot-water bottle into his trumpet, and paddled in the resulting puddle. He then set fire to a piece of paper.[1]

As guitarist Eugene Chadbourne recalled:

> I was talking to a lot of those guys, so I get this report: "Well there was this one guy who was a *complete* lunatic, don't ever play with him," I remember Leo [Smith] saying. "He doesn't have his musicianship together." That was Steve Beresford. . . . I don't like anyone to tell me what to do. . . . So I thought, I'll play with Steve Beresford if he bothers those guys that much.[2]

The upshot is described in Chadbourne's semi-fictional contribution on Rollo Cissgee, below.

In 1977 Beresford was one of the founding members of Alterations – the highly influential quartet which introduced aspects of popular music, and electric instruments, into performances of free improvisation. In addition to recordings with this group, a landmark Beresford album from the period is *White String's Attached* with Nigel Coombes, from 1979.

You became closely involved with Derek Bailey through Company Week. You were a member of one of the earliest editions in 1977, and performed at one of the later London events, in 1994, with The Shaking Ray Levis and Roger Turner. Why did Derek call it "Company"?
It's one of those nothing names – it's perfect, because it can mean just being with someone, or a large multinational organisation.

Some musicians at Company 1977 had reservations about your contributions.
I don't know, they wouldn't tell me.

They were polite.
Leo Smith and Anthony Braxton are charming gentlemen.

Braxton has a fantastic sense of humour. You know he's obsessed with Monster movies?

And he writes crazy compositions for inter-galactic forces.
I think it's following on from Sun Ra. Because Sun Ra never cracked a smile when he talked about being from Saturn. He talked about how he went into the Supermarket of the Omniverse, and saw the most beautiful socks, but they were three million dollars.

The point is, you do this with an absolutely straight face. The level of put-on is quite complicated.[3] There's an element of that with Braxton.

But he didn't like Dada.
Well, he didn't like what I was doing.

Because he wanted what he thought was musical substance.
I imagine that would be the argument.

I got on very well with those people later.

They were confused by your thoroughgoing lack of seriousness?
I don't think they were confused – they were very clear that they were hostile. They thought I was rubbish. But you must remember that no one ever said anything at the time.

They thought you were mocking their seriousness. But were you?
No.

But you could understand why someone might think that.
Yes.

You don't have a thoroughgoing lack of seriousness, do you?
Maybe I did in those days. I may have got more serious.

I don't think I was very good. I think I was playing really badly, especially on keyboards. So it wasn't that I didn't get my free jazz chops together, but that I didn't have any chops of any description.

There was a lot of running about and not playing piano, and Han Bennink set fire to some paper on his hi-hat.

They didn't like that either.
No, but Han clearly had his chops together – he clearly was and is an amazing drummer, who'd worked with Eric Dolphy. So, looking back, I think they had a point.

* * *

Born in 1954, guitarist EUGENE CHADBOURNE has had a career in rock and improvised music. Influenced by the Beatles and Jimi Hendrix, he started on electric guitar at age eleven, later focusing more on acoustic guitar. He initially studied journalism, but moved to Canada, following those who were avoiding the Vietnam draft. Returning to the United States in 1976, he released his debut album, *Solo Acoustic Guitar*. Chadbourne also began working with John Zorn and guitarist Henry Kaiser. He has also collaborated with Derek Bailey, Camper Van Beethoven, and They Might Be Giants, and was a founding member and frontman of Shockabilly. He writes the following memoir:

> "Rollo Cissgee"
> (From "DREAMORY" by Eugene Chadbourne; House of Chadula, 2015)
> Author's note by Chadbourne: I can't provide any information as to how this pseudonym was arrived at. Nonetheless, because of the nature of the anecdote, I am willing to admit "Rollo Cissgee" is based on Steve Beresford. Otherwise the names are changed to protect the innocent. The policy in *Dreamory* was to use only real names when people appeared in dreams, and apparently I don't dream about Steve very much if at all.
>
> LONDON, 1977
>
> *A shift to lodgings house-sat by multi-instrumentalist Elvis Tavid came up the next morning – closer into London, a mansion full of dark rooms and exotic drapes. As part of the moving process I was to take my instruments into the London Musicians' Collective near Hampstead Heath. I could leave everything there for the upcoming gigs and be done with schlepping.*
>
> *I was told to call Rollo Cissgee to let me in, he would have the keys.*

The name was familiar from programs I had seen for The Agency, a large-scale improvisation event coordinated by Tabitha Towers. An international collection of musicians would improvise in various configurations. Most of the people I had heard of – however, there was for me the new name Rollo Cissgee, playing "piano and toys."

At these events, who played with whom at each set was sometimes a plot hatched by Tabitha, sometimes the people he invited were allowed to suggest configurations, sometimes it was done at random.

For one infamous Agency event, sixteen musicians showed up but the first two guys played for two hours and then everyone went home.

A few weeks after this event took place, two of the Americans that had been involved warned me about Cissgee. I was in the habit of calling to talk about what they were doing and to drop hints that I was available, for any and all projects.

"All the cats are cool over there except for Cissgee," the great multi-instrumentalist and composer Tony Axeton had told me. "He isn't serious."

Normally I would hang on to every word Axeton said but in this case he reminds me of girls breaking up with me, perpetually asking "Why can't you be serious?"

Meanwhile, mellophone and metallophone genius Freddie Cruhuru aka Freddie Lingerell said, "Stay away from Cissgee. The cat's musicianship isn't together."

Once again I was conflicted since Cruhuru, even more than Axeton, seemed a genuine guru to me. I was already in the habit of writing down his provocative comments: "I can't play and listen at the same time . . . ." "Water . . . think about it." "The only people that can really follow me musically are my children." "If it is rigid, it will break."

On the phone Cissgee and I set a time to meet at the LMC and then he asked, "Do you fancy a play?"

I agreed without hesitation, although anxious about what I was doing, defying the suggestions of people I regarded as authority figures, such a typical pattern with me, following me into this new world in which I was trying to make a name for myself, to get everyone to like me and think I was really talented, a visionary even. These interactions with people were turning into a hike down a dark hole back into high school, for instance, I was friends with both Thor and Reeve but the two of them could not really combine, each thought the other was an asshole.

Now it was going to be me in the middle of Axeton, Cruhuru and Cissgee.

The latter arrived with a suitcase full of toy instruments as well as unrecognizable objects and the music began with him opening the suitcase and dumping all of *its contents on the floor. We played at such a rapid pace I felt constantly out of breath, even though I was not playing an instrument requiring lung power above and beyond mere survival.*

We improvised for something like twenty minutes. I must have changed between the dobro and the prepared 12-string at least forty times, imitating the antics of virtuoso woodwind players from the Axeton school.

The difference between the way they carefully picked up and strapped on a sopranino saxophone and then an alto clarinet and a bass flute for various textural changes and then ever so delicately replaced it on its stand or in its case, and the sloppy way I dumped the guitars back and forth, clunking and generating random noise in the process, was amusing in itself. I noted in my diary that it would also appeal to those who liked the clatter of drunken stagehands.

* * *

Born in 1942 near Amsterdam, HAN BENNINK is a drummer and multi-instrumentalist, notable for his original style and use of ordinary objects as instruments. Through the 1960s, Bennink accompanied visiting American jazz musicians such as Sonny Rollins, Wes Montgomery and Dexter Gordon. He was a member of Eric Dolphy's quartet on his final album, *Last Date* (1964), alongside regular partner, pianist Misha Mengelberg. Bennink is a multi-instrumentalist, playing saxophone, trombone, trumpet and many other instruments, particularly in a trio with pianist Fred Van Hove and saxophonist Peter Brötzmann. He attended art school in the 1960s, and sculpts with ordinary found objects, as well as designing much of his own album artwork.

MISHA MENGELBERG (1935-2017), Dutch pianist and avantgarde pioneer, was born in Kiev in 1935, son of pianist and conductor, Karel Mengelberg, who was himself the nephew of the great conductor Willem Mengelberg. Misha studied at the Royal Conservatory at The Hague, and in the early 1960s formed a quartet with Han Bennink; their first album was live at the 1966 Newport Jazz Festival. In the late 1960s the ICP label [Instant Composers Pool] was initiated with a recording by Mengelberg, Bennink and saxophonist Willem Breuker. The group broke up in the 1970s, with Mengelberg continuing the ICP Orchestra, while Breuker formed the Willem Breuker Kollektief. Mengelberg later collaborated with Evan Parker, Derek Bailey, Steve Lacy and Franz Koglmann.

I had the first Han Bennink and Misha Mengelberg record on ICP. ICP records were very cheap, I think 15/6d – I believe they were getting a grant, subsidised by the oil revenue. So I had most of the early ICP records, which I liked enormously. I thought all improvising pianists played like Cecil Taylor – then I heard Paul Bley's *Touching*, and Misha's "Where Is The Police?". Han was playing something with bamboo – I think an anklung – in a completely different tempo. They were playing tempos, but different tempos – I loved that. I quite liked the boxiness of the recording.

I loved Misha's playing from the first moment I heard him.

I guessed you'd be soulmates.

Well, certainly he was very supportive. He put me on, on the Holland Festival, solo, way back – in the early 1980s. That was amazing!

I find his playing funny and beautiful at the same time. It's highly allusive, but you're not quite sure what he's alluding to – that's one of the most exciting things about it.

Misha was interested in failure. He made a piece for a celebration of the Concertgebouw – a vitrine that contained mice. The vitrine was divided in two by cardboard resembling the front of the Concertgebouw. There were little metal doors in it. At a certain moment, the doors opened and the mice could go into the other half of the vitrine. Then the doors shut and Mozart was played to the mice, several times faster than normal. The mice very quickly ate all the cardboard. Misha liked that a lot.

Misha is one of my great inspirations. I've never laughed so much as when I was watching Han and Misha. I think they're one of the great comedy duos, like Laurel and Hardy, or Morecambe and Wise.

They were the pianist and drummer on Eric Dolphy's *Last Date*.

That's a great session! Dolphy gave him a really difficult tune to play, so Misha wrote a really difficult piece called "Hypochristmutreefuzz" and gave it to Dolphy.

Misha and I got on very well.

Maybe he recognised you as the British player with the most affinities to his own approach.

Each member of Alterations had affinities with Dutch music – Terry Day with Maarten Altena, Peter Cusack studied in Holland for a bit. We all had a great interest in the Dutch improv scene.

Alex Maguire and Steve Noble's duo was clearly influenced by Han and Misha.

Did you ever think of moving to Amsterdam?
Yes, vaguely. I don't think I could quite have . . .

All the guys in the ICP Orchestra were really good sight-readers. And I'm not, really. It wasn't something that hugely excited me.

Doggedness is one of Misha's great values. He's one of the most dogged piano-players I know. Misha and Tony Oxley – two extremely stubborn people – were playing at Company, I think at the ICA. They were doing this endless very unproductive duo that was torture for both of them, but of course they wouldn't stop. What stopped it was Derek's very small dog – it ran on stage, jumped into the grand piano and barked. The dog saved everybody!

Misha and Han were massive influences on me, obviously. Misha thought of free music as soup, and Steve Lacy talked about how you went into it and took out a piece of cucumber or whatever. Misha was making perfectly coherent references to Mozart – he knew that repertoire intimately. That was a small Dutch obsession – the Willem Breuker early record had a parody of Mozart. The early Dutch player-composers – not Han of course – were into Mozart a lot.

In fact, that ICP record, there are so many weird things. Misha plays a VCS3 on it – a very early British synth. He didn't really feel very comfortable with electronic music.

They had a very strong Fluxus influence – that also had a big effect on [free jazz saxophonist] Peter Brötzmann.

* * *

The best-known and most influential group that Beresford was involved with in his early career was Alterations. The inspiration came from Peter Cusack (guitars), who created the quartet with Beresford, David Toop (flutes) and Terry Day (drums, percussion). It existed from 1977 to 1986, though it was named Alterations only in 1978. They performed throughout the UK and Europe, and released *Alterations* (Bead, 1978), *Up Your Sleeve* (!Quartz, 1980) and *My Favourite Animals* (nato, France, 1984). Two live albums appeared after they broke up, *Alterations Live* (Intuitive Records, Denmark 2000) and *Voila Enough!* (Atavistic, USA, 2002). Notes on the cover of their eponymous debut LP indicate the range of sounds they embraced: "lovely waterfowl noises, accompanied by reggae piano"; "Bosun's call and two dog whistles, with flapping binliner"; "SB fantasises about Cecil Taylor on toy piano"; "TD's Phil Spector bells"; "A euphonium tune with mistakes."

In his remarks for the Café Oto website, Carl Bergstrøm-Nielsen aptly comments that "The great discovery of Alterations was that musical styles and idioms are there to be played with." The group explored popular and unpopular music of many periods, and included increasing numbers of electric instruments in their live performances. Response to their work was often uncertain, however. During the interval of a 1977 performance, a perplexed and apologetic manager at Brillig Arts Centre, Bath – named after a word from Lewis Carroll's nonsense poem "Jabberwocky" – offered the audience their money back.

Alterations re-formed in 2016, when Blanca Regina helped curate an Alterations Festival, with exhibitions, talks, workshops and performances at London's Cafe Oto and University of Westminster.[4] The recreated group has a strong visual art element – performance as theatre. Given its use of ephemeral objects and non-musical instruments, Blanca Regina, on whose label their disc appears, regards the performance as mixed-media.[5]

Born in London in 1949, DAVID TOOP is a composer/musician, author, academic and curator based in London who has worked in many fields of sound art and music. He has recorded Yanomami shamanism in Amazonas, and appeared on Top of the Pops. His books include *Ocean of Sound* and *Into the Maelstrom*; *Rap Attack* (1984) was one of the first books about hiphop. His first album, *New and Rediscovered Musical Instruments*, was a collaboration with artist Max Eastley; recent albums include *Dirty Songs Play Dirty Songs* (Audika). His curated exhibitions include Sonic Boom at the Hayward Gallery, London. He has been a member of The 49 Americans and The Flying Lizards, in addition to collaborating with Steve Beresford, John Zorn and Evan Parker. He is Professor of Audio Culture and Improvisation at London College of Communication. His autobiography *Flutter Echo: Living Within Sound* (Ecstatic Peace) appeared in 2019. He comments [email 2018]:

> Free improvisation is so lacking in sustained discourse, scholarship, even the public record of journalism, that it's hard to register changes that naturally occur over a musician's lifetime. I've been listening to Steve for something like forty-five years and working with him in many diverse contexts since 1977 or even before. The changes of which I'm conscious are dramatic, to my mind extremely interesting, yet I've never heard them discussed anywhere. One of the first times I heard him play was in the Three Pullovers and he had a kind of needling presence. Everything was small, frantic, insistent, deliberately a bit abject. He seemed to grow from there into wildness. He upset people, notably other musicians, because they hadn't the wit to understand that he was throwing out questions and at the same time building

a language. The comedic, which became a powerful element of that language, distracted them from the intellectual foundation of its usage as a strategy. There were questions about class, race, technologies and how certain styles of music and musicking could be deployed to reinforce dubious political positions or violence of one kind or another. Age has a mellowing effect, or so the cliché goes, but I think much of that wildness, chaos and absurdity has been internalised. It remains but at a subtle level. The fact that he has matured into a player of extraordinarily beautiful piano goes largely unrecognised, largely because he seldom performs in contexts where judgements are passed on relative merits. The thing I notice these days is the acuity of his ear, the way he can identify, instantly heighten and develop whatever material – whether dull clunk or stratospheric melody – another player is hurling into the melee. Of course, this near supernatural skill is made possible by a highly specialised virtuosity nourished by experience and a dedication to the music. Ultimately it depends upon sensitivity in abundance.

Born in 1948, PETER CUSACK is a musician, researcher and field recordist with a strong focus on environmental sound. His projects include *Sounds from Dangerous Places* which took him to locations such as the Chernobyl exclusion zone, and *The Favourite Sound Project* that explores people's interest in everyday sounds. During 2011–12 he was artist-in-residence for DAAD (German Academic Exchange Service), looking at the relationship between sound and urban development for the project *Berlin Sonic Spaces*. With an interest in improvisation, Cusack has collaborated with musicians and groups including Alterations with Steve Beresford, Terry Day and David Toop.

TERRY DAY is an improvising multi-instrumentalist, painter and visual artist, and poet. He studied at the Royal College of Art in London, and in 1955 began improvising on drums in a duo with his brother Pat, forming a trio in 1960 that included Russell Hardy. Day has collaborated with many musicians, and been a member of the People Band, London Improvisers Orchestra, and Ian Dury's Kilburn and the High Roads. As well as drums, his instruments include piano, cello, mandolin, saxophones, and bamboo reed flutes; he's also worked with dancers, poets, painters and other visual artists. Terry Day writes:

I first heard Steve in a duo with Dave Solomon on drums and was struck by his craziness, his irreverent attitude towards improvisation and performance. What a relief it was to hear someone from the next/second generation making music unrepressed by the Purist ideologies of the first generation, which have held sway over the various genres of improvisation to this day. Steve would have sat in well with the original People Band which included in its repertoire all forms of music, and was inclusive and spontaneous. This inclusiveness of all forms of music in a performance was later explored by ALTERATIONS, which Steve and I were members of, along with Pete Cusack and David Toop. Prior to Alterations, Steve and I were members of the FOUR PULLOVERS, by which time we had assembled an array of instruments and toys between us.

Within an Alterations performance, I liked it that Steve and I had fun, and could clown about. (The seriousness of the Purists is that to have fun and clown about – to enjoy one's talent – is considered not to be "ART." How sad is that!) I also find that the purist-minded, although very accomplished musicians, tend to make music within very narrow conceptual genres, and therefore do not explore the full range of their instrument, stifling their potential. Steve is a breath of fresh air and does not fall into this repetitive mode of improvisation that has been prevalent since its inception in the mid-60s.

Steve has always encouraged me when I have had musical doubts, especially about my alto saxophone playing which didn't go down well with some musicians. Steve would always insist that I brought it to gigs. After I had been thirteen years out of the game of improvisation due to health problems, Steve was the first to invite me to "Come and recite a poem" with the London Improvisers Orchestra in 2000. I asked him "Can I play my bamboo reed pipes too?" "Sure," he said – and then he encouraged me to do a CONDUCTION with the orchestra.[6] Every time I play with the orchestra, he is always complimentary of my lyrics – Steve calls them POEMS – which at times is me just shouting my head off over the NOISE/volume of the orchestra which I'm trying to conduct. Steve also checks out a lot of gigs, music and musicians, which is admirable. I'm glad that he exists in the world of improvisation – it would be a dull place without him.

Peter Cusack formed Alterations in 1977 – and it was re-formed in 2016. That's not the first time that a group has existed for ten years, then re-formed thirty years later.
Give me an example of another group.
Iggy Pop and the Stooges.
I don't think it's like that at all. Rock 'n' roll bands expect you to be just in that band – they're a bit shocked if you have other projects. Alterations has never been like that – its members have their own projects, and we liked the way that these filtered into what we did with Alterations.

David Toop and I were producing Frank Chickens, and hiphop acts, and so on. It certainly wasn't a band that demanded a 100 per cent attendance record, because we didn't have that many gigs, or that much money. So it can't really be compared to a rock 'n' roll band.

Is there a place for nostalgia – for an early era of free improvisation?
I don't think the music of Alterations is much to do with nostalgia for a tradition of free improvisation – though I'm not against nostalgia per se.

Some writers have commented that Alterations seems more serious now, than the first time round. Music writer Richard Cook commented that "Until I saw Alterations play, most improvised music had seemed to me to be an inflexibly serious enterprise."[7]
That's nice to hear. But I don't think it's entirely true. There were always people who were capable of being side-splittingly funny – as I said, the duo of Misha Mengelberg and Han Bennink was a brilliant comic achievement.

We didn't go onstage with the intention of making people laugh. If we do, we're very happy about it. I think there's lots of funny things that happen in that music. The transitions are often very funny – something can be murky or threatening, and then turn into something ridiculous. I don't sing many doo-wop songs, but then I don't have a falsetto anymore, to sing them in.

Perhaps the loaned material from other types of music is less obvious now, but it's still there.

[Improviser] Rhodri Davies thinks that Alterations is your key group.
He's right. It survived for nearly ten years, and it was about the fact that there were four very different people in it. I remember a night when we were put up by the guy who was the first manager of The Beatles, before Brian Epstein – Allan Williams. His wife said, "You're a music group, and there are four of you . . . ." I think a light bulb went off in her head about parallels with The Beatles. She would have been less than impressed if she'd actually heard us!

But I realised that many of the improvising groups I like are a bit like The Beatles, in that each person in the band has a very strong personality. I couldn't imagine before Alterations started that I'd be working with David [Toop] so much, because we're very different people. Terry [Day] I'd worked with before, in The Four Pullovers – but certain things that happened in Alterations were post-Four Pullovers musically.

If you look at the first [eponymous] album on Bead, the white album, we're using small toys a lot, and small instruments – and not a lot of electronics. The second album, which David [Toop] put out, uses bass guitars and early drum machines – it was getting louder, but the dynamics were more varied. We were using stuff that most free improvisation groups didn't use – in terms of instruments, and things we played on them.

For instance, we played riffs. I love riffs, I'm a huge James Brown fan and I listen to dance music a lot. But in an improvised music session riffs can often be disabling – some of the worst jam sessions I've been on have featured a bass guitarist who thinks "This sounds like chaos, I'd better play a boring riff and then it will sound completely coherent." But I think we used riffs in an enabling way.

Stylistic pluralism was another contrast with earlier free improvisation – and your montage-like approach.

We were aware that we weren't playing like other groups. You could look to Cage or Ives – who was another big influence on me – for that idea of simultaneity.

The Topography of the Lungs, for instance, had a very strong style. It sounds like they'd sat down for months and discussed what the music would sound like – of course, they hadn't, they just played. That was another way to go – where the music had an incredible strength and clarity.[8]

You said that the group had four strong characters, and you didn't always get on. But when you play, is it as if the differences don't exist?

There was an interview that NME did with John Stevens, John Martyn, Danny Thompson and Paul Kossoff, who did a fantastic record *Live In Leeds* – the interview is hilarious, and involved violent threats to the writer. And they made the most beautiful, delicate music. I think with Alterations, some of those differences got played out onstage, and that was good.

In Alterations' recent album *Void Transactions*, the presence of non-musical sound-producers forces a re-evaluation of the role of traditional instruments.

Definitely – that's one of the things that's most clear. It involves an effort to play very high notes on saxophone, but if you do that with a balloon, it's dead easy – to get a high squeaky note requires just a small finger technique. The non-musical instruments put into perspective the kind of sounds we get from musical instruments. But there's lots of other kinds of relationships between instruments and non-instruments.

The first album is much more to do with instruments on the floor – we have more tables now, I don't know why. People just started bringing stuff, and it got incorporated – very early drum machines, and bass guitars, things that you don't normally have in improvised music. We tried it, and it seemed to work – so we just brought more and more stuff, and influences from other things we were doing.

We certainly use less stuff than we used to, partly because we don't have a van to drive boxes of stuff around. The presence of cardboard boxes, and violin bows to use on them, is not such a big thing now.

How did it get the name "Alterations"?
That was my idea. I loved the idea of being in a band with "-tions" at the end, like The Temptations. And then I noticed that virtually every dry-cleaners had a sign that says "Alterations." And I thought "This is great – we're playing music but altering it."

Everyone plays what you call "objects."
I think we say that so that it covers everything we might have forgotten about – things not designed to be musical instruments.

There's a Casio organ in there – is that you?
Yes, and it's a Casio MT68, in case you need to know. There were a couple of early hiphop records that used presets from MT68s, and I think they sound great.

In the coda, when David Toop plays rock guitar, it sounds like kazoo – is that Terry Day?
I don't remember a kazoo. It could be Terry – some of his pipes can sound like kazoo.

The kazoo is a mirliton. It's not really an instrument at all – it doesn't make a sound itself, it just responds to pitches. It's a piece of paper, dry paper not toilet paper – a membrane that vibrates when a sound goes through the instrument.[9]

What is the role of field recordings? I assume Peter Cusack would switch one on at some point – there's nothing added in post-production.
That's right, it's just mixed.

Do you go along with David Toop's explanation of the title *Void Transactions*? "Improvisation is always close to nothing . . . as a monetary transaction within a functioning market, there is nothing much to speak of. No sale, as they say."
Compared to Lady Gaga, that's clearly true.

You had a respectable audience at Café Oto.

We were discussing Jamie Muir, who appears with Derek Bailey on that remarkable album *Dart Drug*. You played with Muir in other contexts, you said, including Alterations.
Jamie sat in with Alterations when Terry couldn't make the gig, and played superbly – I remember saucepan lids being scraped across a bare brick wall.

Jamie, David Toop, Mike Giles, Viv Albertine and I had a short-lived group inspired by Nigerian Juju music. We played grooves that we made up on the spot.

Jamie was a man of contradictions. I found him hard to work with. I certainly greatly admire his work with Derek, and Music Improvisation Company. I went to see him with King Crimson at York uni, a band I would normally run away from.

* * *

Guitarist DAVID BROWN (aka candlesnuffer) has been involved in the Melbourne avantgarde, art rock/punk rock scene since the mid-1970s. His solo project "candlesnuffer" melds opposing compositional streams, notably electroacoustic methods with noise and rock, and develops a vocabulary of tiny acoustic sounds, enlarged outside their normal context. His vocabulary runs from rock bass through experimental guitar to sound art, and he recently completed a PhD on the use of electroacoustic compositions in a public hospital Emergency Department. He has collaborated with Chris Abrahams, Philip Samartzis, Tony Buck and Magda Mayas, and was a long-time member of improvising trio Pateras–Baxter–Brown.

My point of discovery with the music of Steve Beresford was through the group Alterations. I picked up their nato LP "My Favourite Animals" on a regular jaunt round Melbourne's import record stores. It was at one of these stores that I'd already stumbled upon my first record on the French label nato – which I think was "Godard ça vous chante?" [nato 634, 1986], a tribute album to French film director Jean-Luc Godard. That record had caught my attention through the participation of Arto Lindsay, who I'd discovered along with No Wave, my idea of real punk music – and most likely through the participation of John Zorn and the allure of his intense, genre-bending cutup music. The Godard album sent me on a pilgrimage, for a few years, to nose out all the nato releases I could find.

I think "My Favourite Animals" [nato 280, 1984] was the second nato LP I happened on. It took me a number of listenings to unravel the gist of Alterations and connect with the group's sensibilities. Through repeated listening, "My Favourite Animals" pulled me in with its irreverence, humour, stylistic disparities and somewhat beautiful smartarseness. The music touched me, while demonstrating an "anything goes" approach where openness on all levels was promoted. Pastiche, overt references, piss-taking, call and response, serious technique, theatrical gestures and the spirit of cabaret were all inherent, and segued coherently. Throughout the crazy, wacky, almost random mixture were further elements, often keyboard-based, from both Beresford and Terry Day – including melodic interjections providing a soft glue that adhered the loose but muddled whole, a filament-like umbrella of harmonic references.

The other conspicuous glue-like component across the LP's fifteen tracks is a relaxed engagement in spaciousness that reveres the moments of silence interspersed throughout – moments that engender expectation. This engagement in sonic spaciousness was new to me in improvised music – Alterations' music was free of some of its usual formal templates. Missing for example were: elongated dronal periods, passages of overt intensity along with reliance on periods of sustained and repetitive building toward crescendo and fall. "My Favourite Animals" also blurred distinctions between composed and improvised music. The group's methodology allowed them effortlessly to meld genres while engaging in live playing within the studio – leading to music of responsive interjections, where refined listening procedures and harmonic knowledge allowed whimsical genre quotation. It added up to an unprecedented and unique listening experience.

* * *

"White String's Attached"

Like most people, I thought it was "With Strings Attached."
The sleeve notes say that the title is from a double misprint on a Joseph Szigeti record issued in Japan. I was influenced by those Mao Zedong records you used to get, like a big Communist red flag and lots of Chinese writing. We reproduced a section of the sleeve notes to the Szigeti record with the misprint, so it says "White String's Attached" rather than "With Strings Attached." Also there's a grocers' apostrophe in "Strings," which shouldn't be there.

With Strings Attached is a Joseph Szigeti biography – it's one of those generic titles of a biography of anybody that plays a string instrument. We dedicated the record to Chic and Szigeti, because I was listening to Chic a lot at that time.

Chic were the best disco group ever – Bernard Edwards, Nile Rodgers, Tony Thompson, a fantastic rhythm section. They used a small string section as well. That's where I got the word "schmear" from. It's a Yiddish word, when you have a *schmear* of cheese on your bagel – so by extension, the movement on violin, that very fast, downwards gliss on disco records. "Good Times" by Chic has a schmear on it. I was fairly obsessed with Chic, I learnt all the bass lines on bass guitar.

How did *White String's Attached* come about?
Nigel Coombes was the violinist in the Spontaneous Music Ensemble, with Roger Smith on guitar. That was the longest-surviving Spontaneous Music Ensemble – I loved that band. Again, it could be quite accidentally very funny, but also very intense. Our quartet the Four Pullovers began around that time.

Nigel is a huge fan of nineteenth-century Romantic classical music, so when we did gigs as a duo and there was a piano, I played piano, and this duo evolved.[10] In the sleeve notes, Nigel says that it's not a surprise that these two instruments sound as if they hate each other. Beethoven gave up writing violin and piano sonatas after only ten sonatas – although that's actually quite a lot. In fact, we did another record, much later, for Martin Davidson, called *Two To Tangle*. Nigel and I get together every decade or so and do a few gigs.

We're probably due for a reunion. Other people have said this, but you find that you play in a certain way with someone that you don't with anybody else. For instance, I play duos with Satoko Fukuda, who also plays violin, and I've thought maybe I can do some of that stuff I do with Nigel, but it never works. It doesn't sound convincing.

Satoko went to the Yehudi Menuhin School and did all the proper classical things. I think she was living in Brighton, and saw an advert "Come to the workshop and play free improvisation." So she got into the free improv scene there. Generally we play as a duo – there's something incompatible about violin and piano, and it's nice to exploit that. We've recorded a lot, but nothing's been released.

Do you think violin and piano playing together is inherently problematic?
No. I can put violin into some very awkward situations, in a way – or a violinist can. I can't play quarter-tones, really – except maybe by sliding things on the strings, which is very inaccurate – and they can. It's not a very attractive combination of instruments, but that's OK. Richard Pinnell has a very thoughtful blog, The Watchful Ear. He saw my trio with Okkyung Lee on cello and Peter Evans on trumpet, and said he wished there hadn't been a piano.[11] I thought, "You just want everything to sound the same, don't you?" People tend to want an unbroken consort. There was a process in reductionism or lower-case music, where instruments were expected to relinquish their characteristics to the point where they were not recognisable. Sometimes that resulted in them sounding quite similar to each other, whatever they were built to sound like.

Some people have lost the idea of an instrument that's instantly recognisable as what it is. Obviously there are groups where all the instruments sound like something else rather than what they are, which is absolutely fine – but I think it's also fine for piano to be clearly a piano. You can meet the historical baggage of piano head-on, or you can find other ways to work with it – like Magda Mayas, an amazing inside-piano player.

It's not the combination. It's the fact that piano is an instantly recognisable sound.

Eddie Prévost recently made a record with Jenny Allum [*Penumbrae* on Matchless, 2011], where I believe they only use bows – the sounds of Jenny bowing a violin and Eddie bowing a gong overlap quite considerably. That's a sort of unbroken consort: an ensemble of instruments that can easily be mistaken for each other. Instruments in the same family – violin, viola and cello – are an unbroken consort; trumpet and piano is a broken consort.

Notes

1 Watson (2004), p. 215. Beresford denies that he set fire to a piece of paper.
2 Watson (2004), p. 216. He continues: "Bailey put [Braxton and Smith] together with [Han] Bennink, and Bennink was kind of lampooning them. They were playing this very serious-sounding thing that sounded like a composition and he got out this tenor sax and got in between them, towering over them, starting to play 'Misty' with this honking tone . . . Derek was creating this mini drama, this mayhem . . . he likes to see people under pressure, he fiddles with people's expectations."
3 Like the porters at York University discussed in previous chapter.
4 Café Oto is a leading alternative music venue in Dalston, East London. It seems to be spelled both Café and Cafe, so we have taken the liberty of being inconsistent ourselves.
5 *Alterations* is discussed in Toop (2016), pp. 131–2 – while they were playing at the Palais des Beaux-Arts in Brussels, a group of art dealers walked across their performance area, resulting in an aggressive stand-off.
6 See Chapter 8 for a discussion of conduction.
7 *The Wire* 10, 1984.
8 *The Topography of the Lungs* by Evan Parker, Derek Bailey and Han Bennink, was recorded in 1970 and became the first release on the Incus label; it is a landmark recording of free improvisation.
9 *Britannica* says: "Mirliton, pseudomusical instrument or device in which sound waves produced by the player's voice or by an instrument vibrate a membrane, thereby imparting a buzzing quality to the vocal or instrumental sound. A common

mirliton is the kazoo . . . Mirlitons are also set in the walls of some flutes (e.g., the Chinese *ti*) and xylophone resonators to colour the tone. The mirliton is one of the few membranophones (membrane instruments) not sounded by percussion."
10 See Chapter 12.
11 The trio recorded *Check for Monsters* (Emanem, 2009).

6

Saxophonists: Evan Parker, Tony Coe and Lol Coxhill

There are three key saxophonists that Beresford worked with in his earlier career – Evan Parker, Tony Coe, and the late Lol Coxhill. He began performing with them in the 1980s, and they've been formative influences on his musical development since then.

Tenor and soprano saxophonist EVAN PARKER, born in Bristol, West of England, in 1944, is one of the leading exponents of free jazz and free improvisation. He moved to London in 1966 and began an association with guitarist Derek Bailey, as a member of The Music Improvisation Company 1969–72, and was the co-founder of the Incus record label in 1970. He subsequently played in ensembles including the Globe Unity Orchestra with Peter Brötzmann and Alexander Von Schlippenbach. Since 1980 he has played in a trio with Barry Guy and Paul Lytton, and in 1990 assembled his Electro-Acoustic Ensemble, a group exploring live electronics in the digital era. Evan Parker writes:

> *My first contacts with Steve were when he was still a student at York University. He arranged quite a few invitations for various of us on the London scene to come and play there. In return the Musicians Co-operative invited Steve to play on one of our Sunday night concerts at Ronnie Scott's. He brought a trio with bass and drums which as I recall played well in the tradition of current modern jazz, except that at a key moment in their set Steve broke off playing and produced an inflated artificial flower in a pot from inside the piano, showed it to the audience and said, "Nature . . . ," then sat back down and carried on playing where he had left off. This was the shape of Steve to come.*

* * *

With French horn-player Martin Mayes, I presented improvised music at the Sir Jack Lyons Concert Hall, at York University.[1] It was a nice hall. We presented Evan Parker and Paul Lytton. I think that was the first time I met Evan. There was a jam with them at some point, in which I played, and also Dominic Muldowney on organ. Evan said, "Who's that nutcase playing the organ?" By that time I was commuting to London from York, and playing with the Portsmouth Sinfonia – then I would go to the Little Theatre Club. My peer group were John Russell and Nigel Coombes, and we went to the Club.

Then Evan and I did Company at the ICA in 1977.

Do you want to spill any beans about Evan?
I wish I could. About [the split between] him and Derek [Bailey], obviously resentments had been building up. I imagine it was something like – they're on tour, they finish the gig, and somebody says, "Oh, you don't mind sleeping on the floor, do you?" and Evan says no and Derek says "Yes, I do fucking mind. I want a bed." I think it was the conflict between Derek's awkwardness and Evan's willingness to compromise for a good gig, his diplomacy.

Sometimes it's difficult when you're doing a gig for someone who hasn't got enough resources. I'm not saying either of them were unreasonable, although they both could be unreasonable at times, clearly, in slightly different ways. They are both quite stubborn, and they're both sensitive artist types in their own strange ways.

Evan didn't appreciate the Dada aspects of your performance.
No, he hated it, as did many people at Company.[2]

Yet you ended up playing in one of Evan's regular groups. The album *Foxes Fox* was recorded in 1999, by accident – I mean, the group was formed by accident.[3]
[laughs] Oh, look, we're in a recording studio, what a surprise! And here's a piano! . . . What happened, I think it says in the notes, was that I went to the Vortex – the old Vortex, which we still sort of miss, in Stoke Newington – to see Evan with John Edwards and Louis Moholo, who are three of my favourite musicians. John had just come back from New Zealand, and had amoebic dysentery. He played great, of course, as always, but he was not well, so he went home, and I played the second set.[4]

Afterwards Evan said "Steve was really good, he didn't use any balloons or do anything stupid. . . . Let's put a quartet together," which I was thrilled by, of course. I was very, very happy to do that.

You said he calls everything he does "jazz." Did he call this jazz?
He didn't tell me we were playing jazz. He didn't say, "OK boys, play jazz *now*!"

If he had you'd have done it differently?
No. I talked to Mark Sanders, because sometimes he would be in this band instead of Louis [Moholo]. Mark said to me, "You play much more jazzy in

this band than, say, Veryan Weston does when he plays with Evan."And I said, "Yeah, well, I grew up with jazz." I still listen to huge amounts of jazz. I just don't think of myself as a jazz musician, I don't have the chops, I don't have the knowledge. If you asked me to play an over 300 bpm [beats per minute] version of "All the Things You Are," I would fall apart almost instantly.

Was there a time when you could have done?
No, never!

At half the tempo?
Possibly half the tempo [laughs] – a quarter of the tempo.

Luc Houtkamp asked me to do some songs, from *Signals for Tea*.[5] We got Michael Vatcher on drums, and a really nice bass-player – and Piet Noordijk, the famous Dutch alto-player. We did "All the Things You Are," and I said I'm not a jazz pianist – and afterwards, Piet said "Yes, you are." He thought I did an OK job – that's nice to know.

You love songs, but you don't want to explore them in the way that a jazz improviser like Lee Konitz does.
I think I have a completely different relationship to songs than Lee does. I love his relationship. These are great tunes.

[Improvising pianist] Achim Kaufmann has done one album of songs and standards – it was so good, I wrongly assumed he had a double career, as a free improviser and as a songs-player. So maybe you're neglecting a hidden strength.
Well, if someone wants to pay me, I'll do it!

I don't think of myself as a jazz musician, but I'm certainly a jazz fan. The *Foxes Fox* group is the same line-up as the John Coltrane Quartet, or dozens of other bands – saxophone, piano, bass, drums. In fact, it's interesting that when you mix a group like this, which has a clearer relationship to more conventional music, then you can't put everything on an equal level, it just sounds weird. You do need saxophone out front. Your ears just can't deal with it, it sounds like a flat recording. If it was a less conventional line-up . . .

If it was trumpet it would be the same?
Yes, a horn with a rhythm section.

A violin?
I think you'd still hear it, because it's piano, bass, drums. It's a conventional line-up for a rhythm section. It's very difficult to get completely away from that. I don't think we mixed it exactly like a jazz record, but you have to reference that in the way you mix it.

Obviously the title is ambiguous, because "Foxes" can be a noun or a verb. Also it can mean "foxed" – slightly shop-soiled. It's a book-sellers' term.
Did *Foxes Fox* change people's perception of you as an improviser?
Not particularly. I don't know why people wouldn't know I did that, because there was lots of stuff before that. I don't really think what I'm playing there is free jazz, particularly.[6]

* * *

British percussionist MARK SANDERS, born in 1960, works mainly in free improvisation, and also theatre, dance, contemporary classical and conceptual art situations. He has working groups with Nicole Mitchell, Elaine Mitchener, Trevor Watts, John Butcher, Elliott Sharp, Pat Thomas and Rachel Musson. His long-standing duo with Sarah Gail Brand featured on the BBC's The Stewart Lee Show, and in the film *Taking the Dog for a Walk*. They also have a group featuring Steve Beresford and John Edwards. His own group StaggerLee Wonders uses Black Radical poetry and prose. He writes:

> *Steve is a walking encyclopaedia of music. When I first saw him play with The Slits at a wonderful festival of left-field rock music at Alexandra Palace, he was running around the big outdoor stage playing an encyclopaedia of instruments. There was so much to take in. As well as Steve, The Slits were their brilliant anarchic selves, with the excellent Bruce Smith on drums – I'd been hoping to see Budgie, the drummer on "Cut," one of the soundtracks to my youth.*
>
> *Then a few years later I saw him perform with Derek Bailey in a tiny bar in Hackney on even more instruments, including a euphonium and various toys. He moved between the instruments, setting off a clockwork or battery-operated toy, then deftly stepping over instruments to get to the euphonium. A few notes blown and he's off towards the melodica.*
>
> *Watching this I felt distracted by the hilarious vision of this cool cartoon character dancing round a tiny space, then I closed my eyes to listen and was taken by how well the music worked. When Steve started playing in Evan Parker's group Foxes Fox, many of us including [fellow pianist] Keith Tippett were knocked out by Steve's beautiful free jazz piano-playing. He'd kept that a secret for a long time!*
>
> *I'd played many different styles of music working with Steve in his composing and MDing [Musical Directing] days, with people like Tony Coe, Lol Coxhill, Chris Laurence and Alexander Balanescu. Steve's encyclopaedic knowledge of all styles of*

music meant he knows how to put an eclectic ensemble of musicians together and make great music. Have I said "encyclopaedia" too much?

* * *

Evan Parker had a great story about Numar Lubin, the Russian opera singer who ran the Nimbus label, famous for their very high quality classical records. Numar had lived in Paris in the same block as Sidney Bechet, so he would hear him play every day. Finally Numar, who got on very well with him, asked, "Sidney, do you mind me asking about your practicing routine? I've noticed you play scales and arpeggios, and you play well-known tunes, and then you play some stuff at the end that I can't identify." And Sidney Bechet said, "I'm trying to play birdsong; for me this is the highest form of music." That's fantastic.

We made a record for Sidney Bechet, called *Vol Pour Sidney*, on nato. Lots of people contributed to it. Evan's idea was that Numar Lubin would tell this story in his beautiful Russian accent and Evan would make noises on soprano that were like bird sounds. This never happened, unfortunately, but it was a lovely idea for a three-minute piece.

I think Sidney Bechet would call trying to sound like a bird "practice," or perhaps "research."[7]

* * *

Born in 1934 in Kent, TONY COE has had a career as a clarinettist, saxophonist and composer. He was a part of Alan Hacker's chamber ensemble Matrix, and has worked with many well-known jazz musicians, including Count Basie, Dizzy Gillespie and Stan Getz. His group with Lol Coxhill and Steve Beresford, The Melody Four, made its first recording in 1982, and its last in 1988. He has worked on film soundtracks, playing saxophone for Henry Mancini's *Pink Panther* theme, and has composed his own scores, including a chamber orchestra piece for Marie Epstein's silent film *Peau De Peche*. In 1995, Coe won the Jazzpar Prize, a major Danish jazz prize awarded to artists between 1990 and 2004, and in 1998 received an honorary doctorate from the University of Kent.

Your group with Tony Coe and Lol Coxhill in the 1980s, The Melody Four – why did you give the trio that name?
Because we loved the idea of a trio called The Melody Four. It was originally Jean Rochard's idea, he ran nato Records and Chabada Records. These labels

were named after his two cats, who were both named after American Indian chiefs. Nato was quite contentious, and Chabada was big, fluffy and cuddly. Chabada [the label] began with a single made by myself, Tony and Lol Coxhill, that included "La Paloma." That was the first time I met Tony.

Actually there were four people in the Melody Four originally – Jean Rochard's father, Yves Rochard, played violin. He was a very active member of the community of Chantenay Villedieu, a tiny village near Le Mans.

The original Melody Four were a vocal group of Ivy League-type white men, who made saccharine recordings of gospel music.

I discovered an album by that very conservative 1960s white gospel group, way after we started the Melody Four. I knew that that would happen. "The Melody Four" is a spectacularly uninspired name for a band – that's why we chose it.

I'd never met Tony Coe and was anxious about playing with him. I knew he was a phenomenal jazz musician, though I later discovered earlier he'd been a classical clarinettist. Conservative jazz musicians had terrified me by telling me I should know eight hundred standards in every key, and be able to play them at ludicrous tempos and segue from one to another. I couldn't do any of that. They said "well, you'll never be a jazz musician," so it kind of decided me not to be a jazz musician. I'd heard so many joyless post-bebop groups, where you really did feel that playing jazz was following a set of rules. But Tony wasn't one of those players. All he wanted was for you to have your own sound on the instrument.

He's from Canterbury – that's very important. I think of him as a mystical anarchist. His dad, George Coe, ran a dance-band around Canterbury. He told me, "When [Tony] was 12, he played the Mozart Clarinet Concerto in Canterbury Cathedral," that's what he was most proud of. Then Tony took up alto and played with Humphrey Lyttleton, and sat in with Duke Ellington. He is an amazing musician – he's also very interested in Boulez, and wrote some twelve-tone ensemble pieces. His sound is like Paul Gonsalves filtered through Debussy and Schoenberg. Count Basie loved him, Duke Ellington loved him, he played under the baton of Pierre Boulez – what more do you want?

Does he still play? The last gig mentioned on his website is 2012.

I wish he played more. He's an amazing saxophone player. He should have got an MBE, he should have had a knighthood – for God's sake, the guy's a genius. Recently he's been ill, and anyway usually prefers playing quiet duets with highly competent piano players in unexceptional pizza joints, and pubs.

That reminds me of encountering that fine guitarist, the late Louis Stewart, playing Carluccio's in Dublin to noisy diners – so unjust.

I remember hearing Tony Coe's group Zeitgeist at the Camden Jazz Festival.

Tony was a friend of Alan Hacker, the classical clarinettist. He did serial jazz with Bob Brookmeyer and the Danish Radio Big Band. There was a crossover with contemporary classical – the Maxwell Davies, Harrison Birtwistle sort of area.

Tony Coe is a total master. He was a good orchestrator, and had a real interest in modern classical music. It's frustrating that when people talk about saxophone players, they don't know about him. Tony has his own voice, as well as being able to play exactly like Johnny Hodges – he has an incredible craft. He is an amazing reader.

Tony has self-belief. I don't know why he isn't playing at the Vortex regularly. **His album on Incus with Derek Bailey is a neglected classic.** [Derek Bailey / Tony Coe, *Time*, Incus Records / INCUS 34 (1979)]

Beboppers would ask "Why are you playing with Derek Bailey?", and he'd get furious. He had this intense defence of the principle of freedom.

* * *

Saxophonist LOL COXHILL (1932–2012) was born in Portsmouth. As a teenager in the late 1940s, he organised club sessions that mixed live music and recordings of musicians including Miles Davis and Dizzy Gillespie. He briefly served in the RAF, before returning to work with jazz ensembles and visiting US musicians. In the late 1960s he was a member of Delivery, and of Kevin Ayers and The Whole World; he worked in duos with David Bedford and Steve Miller. From the 1970s, Coxhill performed internationally, and collaborated with Tony Coe, and the Spontaneous Music Ensemble. He was a member of The Recedents with Mike Cooper and Roger Turner, between 1983 and 2012 – as Cooper put it, "scandalously under-recorded, underpaid and under-employed we continued to groove." Coxhill also worked in film, theatre and television. An eloquent obituary from The Association of Musical Marxists commented that "Lol was there at the origins of practically every worthwhile style of Anglo pop – Ska, Bop, Hippie, Improv, Punk, Noise – but peeled off as soon as the movement came to be about fame and money rather than playing."

You had a close affinity with Lol Coxhill.
I produced the double-album *Spectral Soprano* on Emanem – the tracks are all archive. A guy who worked in Mole Jazz wanted to do a retrospective album of Lol, and a friend of Lol's put some money in.[8] We did lots of picture research – the pictures are fantastic. We included some old, crackly acetates.

One of Lol's first gigs was with [r 'n' b vocalist] Rufus Thomas, who practically invented rock 'n' roll – he did "Do The Funky Chicken." He was from Memphis, and made fantastic records. Lol was in his pickup band that toured England.

Lol at that time was playing tenor with Tony Knight's Chessmen, whose uniform was chequered – there's a picture of them, with Tony Knight, who was dressed in armour, sitting on a horse! I think it was in Denmark Street – this was the early 1960s, I'd say.

Could Lol sound like a tough, bar-room tenor?

I would say yes. He was a great r 'n' b player – greatly appreciated among old school Jamaican musicians. In bebop vein, I always said he sounded like a more lecherous Bud Freeman.

Lol was a showman – but not a bar-walking showman. He was fearless as a stage-act. He was a good actor, but he was always Lol.

When I was living in York after university, Lol came up several times. It took him a while to remember my name, but then I'm like that with people myself. I didn't know much about him at that time. He probably played a solo, and then we'd jam.

Was he not particularly organised?

He was and he wasn't. Famously, he once showed up for a gig a year early. But that's easily done, isn't it!

Lol was naturally a very funny person.

Lol by name, LOL by nature.

Most musicians are funny, in my experience. Paul Lytton and Max Eastley can tell very funny stories. Lol was a great raconteur. He was very conscious of his image. He liked getting dressed up, and he liked posing. He was in a few movies, like the Sally Potter movie *Orlando* – I think that's her best movie. He was also in a short she made called *London Story*. There's an element of Jacques Tati in his performance there.

He was a bit remote with people?

He was vaguely friendly, because he wasn't that good with faces. There was a sort of vagueness – certainly when I was just an ex-student from York playing piano.

I just read a piece on a Scotland Yard unit called the super-recognisers, employed to recognise people on CCTV. Lol was *not* a super-recogniser.

He was extremely benevolent – everyone loved him. Sometimes he would enjoy doing something that shocked people, like being rude or offensive – but it was never malicious.

Lol was never a part of the showbiz thing in the way that Derek had been. He never sat in a saxophone section with the Northern Dance Orchestra.

He was a showman as an MC.

Of course, he was. But he was never like Kenny Wheeler or Tony Coe – you'd switch on Cilla Black on a Saturday night, and there was Kenny Wheeler, in the orchestra.

They had commercial careers.

Lol was never a super-efficient reader like those guys. That's what you had to be – it was a real craft.

Lol took an oblique approach to all musics.

And to life.

Yes, absolutely! That oblique approach was very flexible, in terms of moving into different genres. He could play Palm Court favourites with the Johnny Rondo Trio, go on tour with The Damned, and then sit in with a ska band – and play with a Dixieland band, and play free improvisation.

He would be gently, affectionately subversive with a Dixieland band?

Yes, but it was organic subversion. Not like a teenager going "Yeah, I'm going to take the piss out of these people by playing feedback all through 'Strutting With Some Barbecue.'" I mean "organic," because that was what Lol was like. It came naturally to him.

He was naturally oblique, and sometimes that took the form of subversion.

He *loved* New Orleans music.

But he might take a different view to those who are trying to recreate it commercially, and not particularly effectively.

Exactly, no doubt.

I remember Lol giving me a bell, and saying "You've got to come and hear Harry Gold, he's playing in the crypt of the church just off Clerkenwell Square."[9] Lol had played there with The Recedents at some point. This was so wonderful, it was perfect Lol. It was a little local event – a festival or something, probably introduced by the vicar. There were ladies bringing tea and cakes, and saying "Ooh, thank you."

Harry was around ninety at the time. He played bass saxophone – he was possibly shorter than his instrument. Maybe that was the first time I heard the bass saxophone. He didn't do a lot of blowing, because he was very old. It was fantastic to see him. Lol loved that – he could see the funny side of it, but he liked Harry Gold, and he loved Dixieland very much.

Lol had an incredibly wide musical scope. He was a big record collector – unlike Derek, as we saw.

You worked with him in The Melody Four, which we discussed, and The Promenaders.

The Promenaders were born on Brighton beach. Max Eastley, Paul Burwell, Terry Day, Lol Coxhill, David Toop and I were playing the Brighton Festival. I think Alterations played there too – various permutations played free improvisations in small rooms in Brighton Art College, and on the beach.

We decided to busk through some popular songs – which of course Lol was very good at, no one else was. So it became this strange group – soprano saxophone, euphonium, two one-string fiddles, an acoustic guitar, a drum-kit and sometimes a cello. We played "Sleepy Lagoon" – the Desert Island Discs theme – old Albert Ayler tunes, Prince Buster tunes, 1930s pop songs.

We weren't thinking that we'd attract the proletariat, we just thought, "As we're on the beach, why don't we do things vaguely associated with end of the pier entertainment – though we won't play it like they'd play it on the end of the pier."

That was the nearest we got to bringing our music to the people.

That band played quite a lot, actually. Nigel Coombes sat in a few times on violin.

Notes

1 Martin Mayes comments: "We got quite a number of improvisers to perform at the Music Department – one of them was Evan Parker, who described the university as a 'holiday camp'. I also remember one concert with Peter Brötzmann and Fred Van Hove. Bernard Rands introduced us to graphic scores from the US – a very short stop away from free improvisation" (email communication, 2017).
2 As discussed in Chapter 4.
3 *Foxes Fox* was recorded in July 1999; the Vortex gig was maybe a year earlier.
4 John Edwards, born in 1964, began playing bass in 1987, and became a mainstay of the free improv scene from the 1990s onwards. He works with Evan Parker, Paul Lovens and the LIO, and has collaborated with Sunny Murray and Paul Dunmall.
5 The 1995 album discussed in Chapter 10.
6 The contrast between free jazz and free improv is discussed in Chapter 9.
7 http://search2.downtownmusicgallery.com/lookup.cgi?item=2007_05_10_12_29_12
8 Mole Jazz was a record store in King's Cross, North London, since closed.
9 Harry Gold (1907–2005), British Dixieland saxophonist and band-leader.

7

Piano, Toy Piano, Toys

Beresford now discusses his relationship with piano, his main instrument – and with substitutes, including the toy piano. He was an innovator and early adopter of toy piano, as Adam Fairhall discusses in his essay at the end of the chapter. We look at the problem of obtaining a good instrument for gigs, the difficulties of buying good toy pianos and the motivations behind his exploration of toy instruments. He considers the little instruments, mechanical and electronic, that he also includes in his performances. We examine the influences of Dada and related artists, including Kurt Schwitters, Robert Rauschenberg and Joseph Cornell, and conclude by discussing toys, such as whistles and duck-calls, as favoured by John Zorn.

You're primarily a pianist.
I think so, yes. I've played a bit of organ as well, but I never thought of myself as a keyboard player particularly.
There are some musicians who happen to be pianists.
I'm very fond of arranger's piano – I really like Gil Evans playing piano, or Carla Bley. You can learn a lot from people who don't have piano as a main focus.
Would you say that as a pianist, you were more influenced by classical than jazz tradition – because nobody could, or would, give you jazz lessons, and you had classical tuition?
I got to [British piano examination] Grade VIII. And I had lessons at university, and did a recital. My piano teacher there thought I was an idiot – though maybe he thought everybody was.
The only musical career he could imagine anyone having was as a classical pianist.
I would imagine so. Probably everybody thought like that. The idea that you could spend the next fifty years playing free improvisation – who with any sense would have suggested that?

But you've done it. Does that strike you as amazing?
Completely ridiculous.

Obviously I haven't existed off the enormous profits from free improvisation alone.

What piano do you have?
I just bought a Zimmermann baby grand – a cheap-ish East German instrument from the mid-1970s. The piano-tuner, who's also called Steve, discussed how far the key should drop down – you're looking at a tiny sliver like a cigarette paper. Concert pianists are obsessed with absolutely tiny things about pianos.

That might be so that they can play with confidence more freely.
Absolutely.

And certain pieces of music have very precise requirements.

Piano is a symbol of Western high art – it's an expensive thing to have. You need a house that's big enough, you need to keep it in tune, it can't be somewhere damp or cold – it's high maintenance. And then the music typically played on piano is associated with nineteenth-century harmonic logic or has that kind of function – orchestral transcription and so on. Before Cage, Henry Cowell worked inside piano – then prepared piano took away the element of pitch, or at least correct pitch.

One of the aims of piano is to have a beautiful uniformity of sound from low bass to high treble – that's hard to achieve.

As a pianist you're always making do because unless you're Alfred Brendel, you don't have a bloke with three Steinways in the back of the truck who turns up at the gig and puts them all in the hall and asks, "Which one do you want?"

That becomes part of the positive experience of the gig – you're discovering a new piano.

You appreciate a good piano.
Oh God, yes. There's a new piano shop in Gray's Inn Road called Peregrine's Pianos. They've got pianos with carbon-fibre action, made by tiny companies. The main room has a Fazioli. I recorded a solo disc on one a few weeks ago, for Martin Davidson's label, Emanem. But I've since had a big block about putting the CD out – something to do with a lack of enthusiasm for listening to my own solo playing.

The Fazioli is fantastic, a really amazing piano. The first time I played one, I played a duet with Neil Metcalfe, the flute player – we were supporting Charles Gayle at the Red Rose.[1]

It was a broadcast so they got the Fazioli in, because Charles plays piano. I love his piano playing, it's fantastic. It's nothing like Cecil Taylor, it's more like Bud Powell – quite fractured, not really full on. He might do that [Cecil Taylor] style, but not when I heard him. It's sometimes based around a Billie Holiday song or something, though you might not be able to recognise it.

Are you agonising over whether the new disc is a complete album?
I haven't played it for a year or so.[2] I don't really like what I'm doing on it. There's a lot of records where I don't like what I'm doing. I think I'm getting less and less confident about making solo records.

Martin Davidson recorded it, it's his label. He has a simple but effective recording system – he's the engineer. We recorded some of it at the Vortex.

It's almost impossible, it's so solipsistic – trying to make decisions about releasing a solo recording. You just want someone else to decide.

What does Martin think?
He doesn't have that kind of role really.

John Zorn is exactly the opposite. He'll reject stuff that you think is great, but go crazy about stuff you think is terrible. In a way I'm fine with that.

I can't think of anybody I could play it to, to get their opinion.

I suppose I don't want people to say "Yes you're right, it's not very good." You see, I'm not very secure about it. It's like a thesis that a student hands in, and you say, "Why didn't you show this to me before you handed it in?" It's because they didn't think it was very good that they didn't show it to me. But a thesis is a lot less personal than music.

All art is personal.
Yes.

You're not sure, so why not put it out?
Then I'd be sure because everyone would say "You're right, it's crap."

Except that they won't – there are always people who can't hear what's going on, and will say it's great even if it is crap.
You're right.

* * *

Toy Piano

Beresford is known as a proponent of toy piano – a niche product with a minor but unassailable place in experimental genres. John Cage pioneered its use, with his *Suite for Toy Piano* (1948) and *Music for Amplified Toy Pianos* (1960). Despite the instrument's apparently limited expressive capacity, a repertoire has developed. Composers such as George Crumb and Mauricio Kagel have composed for it, and pianists such as Phyllis Chen, Margaret Leng Tan and Bernd Wiesemann have developed its possibilities. As well as Beresford, improvisers who perform on it include Chris Burn.

The toy piano is not really a scaled-down piano, but a relative of the xylophone and glockenspiel, its hammers hitting metal rods instead of strings. It began to be mass-produced, with other toy instruments, in the later nineteenth century. The Schoenhut is the Steinway of the toy piano world. Improviser Chris Burn distinguishes between the baby pianos that he plays, and toy pianos: "Most baby pianos are diatonic, and only have white keys with the black keys painted on. I do have a Disney baby with 'black' keys – bright blue, in fact – but they are fixed and for visual effect only. The keys on the babies are very narrow and it requires a lot of care not to play two notes at once." Toy pianos such as the Schoenhut generally have a chromatic keyboard, though on earlier Schoenhuts up till around 1920, black keys were painted on. The toy piano is a scaled-down version of the adult piano, which a young child might play as a stepping stone to a full-sized instrument; the baby piano is for very young children to mess around on.

John Cage is a constant point of reference among toy and baby pianists. In *Conversing with Cage* edited by Richard Kostelanetz, the composer explained that his works just before the *Suite* of 1948 had been for prepared piano: "I wanted to find a way of writing for unprepared or normal instruments . . . the place to begin would be with the simplest aspect of the piano, namely, the white keys . . . the black keys on toy pianos are merely painted on. . . . I tried to write in such a way that these [white] pitches, which were the most conventional, would become new to my ears." Cage continued: "I wanted to approach each sound as though it were as fresh as a prepared piano sound. . . . Actually, the *Suite* . . . can be played on any keyboard instrument. I like the sound of a toy piano very much. It sounds like a gamelan of some kind."[3]

During the late 1970s, Chris Burn had begun looking at Henry Cowell's piano music and early Cage-prepared piano pieces. He became intrigued by the varieties of tone between different instruments, the fact that the focal point as a performer is tiny, and the often monochrome sound of each instrument. "The best way to play the *Suite* is to strip away conventional pianistic mannerisms such as might be applied to a piece of Chopin," Burn adds. "Play it straight without any subjective involvement, in a mechanical way as far as possible."

How do its proponents respond to the objection, why use such a limited, child-like instrument? For Chris Burn, "As in just about any other form of art, limitations can be inspiring, you can use the boundaries to define your work.... The child-like quality of the instrument clearly appealed to Cage." There's an incongruity, as when an adult goes back to primary school and sits at the small desks and chairs. Margaret Leng Tan sees the instrument's limitations as a strength, not a disadvantage: "It is restricted in its compass and dynamic range but then, so is the harpsichord and clavichord. Marcel Duchamp, the Dada artist, said 'Poor tools require better skills'. This is the challenge facing the serious toy pianist." She continues: "With the quality instruments that I have and twenty years of dedication, my boast is that any articulation and nuance I can create on the adult piano I can do on my toy pianos, and the same goes for virtuosity!"[4]

What made you start playing toy piano?
It was mainly because lots of places didn't have pianos, so you had to have something else. Even now there are gigs that don't have pianos.
Or decent pianos.
Well, that's the other issue, of course. I don't mean the working men's clubs, I wouldn't go into a working men's club and play a toy piano – that wouldn't work. Upstairs at The Engineer, which was opposite the old London Musicians' Collective in Gloucester Avenue, in Camden, they didn't have a piano. But I had a collection of toy pianos and other instruments, which I schlepped there. That was the birth of the Three Pullovers – or The Four Pullovers, depending how many of us there were. It was to do with me *not* playing piano, specifically.
I've just been listening to a recording by Margaret Leng Tan.
She's Ms Toy Piano. If you look at the score for *Suite for Toy Piano* by Cage, which is her party piece, it's a really nice piece – there are ridiculous things like quite radical dynamic markings, and you can only do dynamics a little bit on toy piano. She plays the top-of-the-range toy piano, of course. The Schoenhut is the professional's toy piano.
What does that mean? It's for Brendel's children?
It's better made, it's in tune. It has pretty well adult-sized keys. It's made for rich kids – a bit like those Steiff teddy bears. They were the original teddy bears, and now a Steiff teddy bear would cost you a hundred quid. Schoenhut were the first toy piano manufacturers. There's lots of toy pianos, there were good ones from China and East Germany.

Someone pointed out that Schoenhut means "nice hat."

Why play toy piano rather than electric keyboards?
Because electric keyboards were too heavy, and I didn't have the money for one. To get a toy piano, you just went to a toy shop. Now it's hard to buy toy pianos in toy shops.

Can you get them in equal temperament or spectral tunings?
[laughs] Of course, they go out of tune a bit. They're basically a plastic hammer that hits a metal rod.

Chris Burn, Tania [Chen] and I performed John Cage's *Music for Amplified Toy Pianos* at a gig in Shoreditch [in 2010] – Tania and I also performed *Indeterminacy* with Stewart Lee. But the toy piano thing was never a major element for me – Chris is much more expert. He takes stuff super-seriously. He made a record of Henry Cowell's music, and studied very hard. Chris is a fantastic piano player and a really good trumpet player as well – he was very much part of the New London Silence thing at that time.[5]

* * *

CHRIS BURN, born in Epping, Essex, in 1955, is a pianist, trumpeter and composer. He studied music at Surrey University, where he met and began a lifelong friendship with saxophonist John Butcher, who was studying Physics. Burn began in jazz and contemporary classical music, but from the 1980s, free improvisation increasingly became his focus. He formed the octet Ensemble, and also performed solo, almost exclusively "inside" piano. He performed Henry Cowell and John Cage, and played at Tate Modern for the opening of the Switch House, including a one-hour piece by Butcher. Burn writes:

> *For many years I ran Mopomoso at the Red Rose with John Russell, and often had the pleasure of listening to Steve perform in several small group settings – duo, trio, quartet or maybe solo. We would give him a large table and he would spread out his selection of electronics, toys, various paraphernalia and often a baby piano or two – like myself, he has a couple of Wuyi [baby pianos]. He explained to me that he would always buy the cheaper electronics, as ultimately all electronic items would go wrong. But I am sure he takes delight in the lo-fi qualities of the cheaper instruments.*
>
> *Again, at the Red Rose, in the 1990s, I programmed a set with myself, Mark Sanders and Phil Durrant. For this concert I borrowed a celeste, and called the group Music for Strings, Percussion and Celeste [after a piece by Bartók]. I had the celeste for about a week in which time I was able to familiarise myself with the touch and character of the instrument.*

I noticed when I played a low F# and Eb, I felt a mild sense of surprise, and could not work out why. Then one day, while playing the celeste, the doorbell rang – the very same F# and Eb. (I remembered reading about Varèse's "Ameriques," where the New York audience sniggered at a high piccolo note which was the everyday sound of a whistle from a Hudson river boat.) This got me thinking about sound and memory, and specifically the ways we connect with the sounds made by toy pianos.

Listening to Steve's recording from 1975, on <u>Not Necessarily "English Music,"</u> I find myself immediately connecting with sounds made by a push-along toy I had as a child. Whether Steve has this relationship with toy pianos or indeed toys and memory I don't know. I have yet to ask him.

* * *

You've played organ too.
I just dragged out my Casio SK1 again, which I hadn't played for a long time. It was to do Helen Petts' new film *Space & Freedom* [2018] – she wanted lo-tech samples of whistling, and I thought a Casio SK1 is perfect.[6] It's mainly a piano score, but with little bits of Casio. Then I thought "I really like this, so I'm going to use it again."

A Casio organ is a home entertainment centre?
It's going in that direction.

The Casio SK1 came out at a time when people were making ludicrously expensive and complicated samplers for use in the studios, and the SK1 takes about ten seconds. You turn it on, press "sample," and it goes "ping" when you've made the sample.

Do you know the keyboard that Veryan Weston plays on his album *Crossings* [2020] – the M-Audio Keystation?
Most keyboard players don't know most keyboards. Why would you have a go on every single keyboard that's around? It would be mad.

There's lots of keyboards that don't have their own sound – the Keystation is a midi controller. "Midi" is just a process to get the note you want – if you hit a D sharp with such and such power, it will transmit that information to a box that has the sounds of a million different instruments in it.

Veryan is interested in polyrhythms and rhythmic modulation.
He does amazing things with rhythms – with Trevor Watts' Moiré Music he became very adept at it. You can do rhythmic modulation, so that the beat seems

to have moved. Veryan is a great virtuoso at that – five in the left hand to seven and a half in the right, and so on.

He toured churches around Britain, playing tracker-action organ with Hannah Marshall and Jon Rose.

You played a tracker-action organ at the Huddersfield contemporary music festival [in November 2019].
Tracker-action organs are mechanical. You can get all sorts of wonky sounds out of them, by half-pulling out the stop – which you can't do with an electric church organ, in the same way.

You made a piano trio recording – three pianos – with Veryan Weston and Pat Thomas.
Veryan comes down to the LIO sometimes, and he'll play piano on some pieces, where I conduct. If he's using electronics, it's always controlled by a keyboard. He plays inside piano only occasionally.

I've heard him play standards with Harry Beckett – that was a while back.

Some of my favourite records are piano trio records, like *Money Jungle* by Duke Ellington, Thelonious Monk, Bill Evans – and the piano player is central. I never wanted to be in that situation, it was so scary. A few times I tried it, I thought I played really badly. [Bassist] Joe Williamson said, "You and Roger [Turner] live quite close to me, why don't we form a trio?" I thought it worked quite well. That's probably the most consistently lyrical thing I do.

Who are your favourite improvising pianists now?
Liam Noble – I like his playing in completely improvised contexts, especially with Ingrid Laubrock and Tom Rainey. I was really blown away by their first album.

For a while it felt like Liam would never play in a free improvisation context – I think that's what he's best at.

For a long time, he was Bobby Wellins' pianist, and he's worked with singers.

It seems to be best for Liam to be in a group that works a lot.

I think Cor Fuhler is amazing – a Dutch pianist who also plays his invented instruments. He lives in Australia now.[7]

Of course, I love Misha Mengelberg. Paul Bley was a huge influence. I love Fred van Hove with Brötzmann and Bennink. I love very early Don Pullen with Milford Graves – he was a bigger influence on me than Cecil Taylor. I like Cecil playing standards, like Cole Porter. I also like his Blue Note records.

I love his recording with Coltrane, and Kenny Dorham.
I love that period of Cecil, with Buell Neidlinger. Cecil had a very distinctive rhythmic approach.

What about younger pianists?
I like Elliot Galvin – his jazz playing is admirable, but I like his free improv playing the most. He avoids just about every cliché of free improvising pianists.
There must be some charlatans in improvised music, as elsewhere.
Of course. But charlatans – people who have an enormously high opinion of themselves, and get by on chutzpah – can sometimes be interesting, musically. Misha Mengelberg had a very good saxophone player in his band. Misha said to me, "I have him in my orchestra for two reasons. Number one: nobody likes him. Number two: he only plays clichés."

* * *

Toys

At the moment I'm trying to finish an article for Zorn's *Arcana* – I'm sort of enjoying it, it's on little, inconsequential things.[8] About little pieces of cardboard that come in useful when you're using electronics, and how you respond to small things in particular instruments. Mark Sanders, for instance, had been trying to find the right cymbal for decades. His mum found a mouldy old cymbal in the garage, and he tried it and it's the one. It's a bit like Schwitters – in fact, a lot like him.
And Robert Rauschenberg.
And Joseph Cornell. He had boxes with ballerinas, astronomical maps, pictures of Lauren Bacall, parrots, all those things he used [in his glass-fronted "shadow boxes"]. I do like that kind of art.

Jean Tinguely is a great inspiration to me. These funny machines, that were also very beautiful.[9] I think it's that combination of something that's supposed to explode and doesn't. I'm hoping that's true of the world at the moment.
Tinguely's machines are mostly too frail to be operated.
I don't know . . . I saw a show not long ago. The little early ones are good, they have a lot of mechanism just to move a feather.
Like Heath Robinson.
Yes, though I don't think Heath Robinson ever made anything – he's more of an illustrator. His designs are totally useless, or their purpose might be very minimal like licking a stamp.
How do you acquire the toys that you play?
I go to shops and buy them.

I've made it a point of etiquette, not to go and look at people's stuff. I might say, "I love the sound that Magda Mayas gets out of the piano," but I won't ask how she gets it. I have to find my own way, to get those sounds. Or I might find other sounds.

Of course, Pat Thomas might phone me up and urge me to check something out. But he might back away from something, if I'm using it. He uses the new Theremin – which is by the way very good value, and a pretty amazing instrument.

Martin Mayes has a portable telescopic alphorn – and it's not cheap.

It's fantastic. I did ask him about it – the price is insane.

They sell well in Switzerland.

I imagine that would be their biggest market.[10]

What features of toys attract you?

The very small pan-pipe that I have, which probably cost about fifty pence, has a label on it that says "Kazoo." An instrument with a wrong label on it that tells you it's another instrument, would definitely attract me immediately.

So, cheapness is one thing.

Sometimes I buy something that turns out not to make a very interesting noise.

What kind of reaction do you get, when you play toys?

I think that now, most audiences know what they're getting.

Steve Lake wrote in a review – this was decades ago – that I was "silly, absurd, fumbling, wishy-washy, petulant and weedy." I did a PR sheet with reviews on it, and included his description. When I bumped into him at Moers, in Germany, and told him, his wife said that I was really cruel to use it! *[we laugh]*

I have a vast collection of toys. But I can never find the one I need, so I'm always going for second best. But then the whole musical concept is about making do. And of course the toys go wrong, and break, and batteries run out and I haven't got that kind of battery with me . . . . So the whole thing is a struggle.

TOP TIP No. 2: Always bring spare batteries.

Is there a connection with Levi-Strauss's notion of "bricolage"?

I'm happy to be seen as part of that tradition.

The challenge is partly to maintain antique technology.

Well, technology always goes wrong.

But when it's cheaply made, it goes wrong more.

Yes, you're right.

That's an attraction to you.
Oh yes. Though I'm always happy to use the latest technology – I'm not saying that old technology is better than new technology. But I do think that laptops in music are a problem, for all sorts of reasons.
But you're less likely to want to get a toy from Hamleys, which is very lavish.
It's on Regent Street – it's huge, and very crowded. Although they're meant to be a posh toy shop, they don't actually stock toy pianos, for instance. Obviously these have had their place taken by little Casios and things. But people still do make quite beautiful toy pianos that aren't that expensive, and I think it's ridiculous that Hamleys don't stock them.

So I slightly resent Hamleys (a) for being much too pleased with themselves, and (b) for not stocking the stuff they should be stocking. Their toy musical instrument section is very disappointing. They should be doing some up-market toy pianos, really.
You could be a consultant in this area.
I'd love to be a consultant.
They're missing out on a marketing opportunity.
I totally agree.

So I'm more likely to be going to a Pound shop.
You're often popping in to check what they have.
Oh yeah, all the time! Tiger have just got little rubber beetles that vibrate – you can put them on drum-heads, and piano-strings. You can use one to create quite a convincing roll on the snare-drum.

The main problem is that they are so small, they fall into pianos – Tania Chen is always losing them. But the new ones are three inches by two, they're not going to fall into a gap. Yes, they're toys.

Tiger are a chain of cheap shops from Scandinavia – like a pound shop, but more self-consciously eccentric.

Pound shops also have things that really don't work, like a key-chain that has stuff like bubble-wrap – pseudo bubble-wrap, it keeps on popping. These shops are where failed products go to die.
You're celebrating the ordinary.
My God, yes – absolutely! There's a wonderful George Melly documentary where he walks round Portobello Market, saying "This is real-life surrealism."
It's a Walter Benjamin concept.
Of course. He's right. I still find Portobello Market very inspiring.

Melly wasn't the world's greatest jazz singer, but he was a really great writer about art. I would see him around Portobello Road.

* * *

ALEX WARD comments on the power of the visual in Beresford's instrumentarium. Ward is a clarinettist, guitarist and composer based in London, a major figure in British improvised music. His involvement dates back to 1986, when he met guitarist Derek Bailey, and became a regular participant in Company events. He works with free improvisers such as John Edwards, Dominic Lash, Thurston Moore, Joe Morris and Steve Noble, and belongs to groups including the Duck Baker Trio, and This Is Not This Heat. He leads his own ensembles including Forebrace, and Items 4 & 10, and plays guitar, sings and co-writes for avant-rock duo Dead Days Beyond Help. He also co-runs the label Copepod Records with Luke Barlow. Alex Ward writes:

> *I first met Steve at the 1988 edition of Derek Bailey's annual Company Week. Its remit over previous years – a group of roughly ten musicians playing in a variety of combinations – was suddenly expanded to include around thirty billed musicians and several unannounced guests. I believe Steve was one of the latter, and the somewhat carnivalesque atmosphere engendered by the quantity and variety of characters seemed to be encapsulated by the main instrument he brought with him – a large and colourful electric organ with a variety of hand-cranks and levers. It gave the impression of something as likely to have been invented to generate electricity as to be powered by it. Even before Steve played, looking at this instrument set my imagination into overdrive as I tried to predict what might be the audible product of such an entity.*
>
> *Over the subsequent thirty years, the more I have seen Steve perform the more I notice the deftness with which he employs and manipulates the expectations that the sight of a sound-producing object – including, of course, objects not at all likely to be thought of as such in their everyday usage – may produce. Whether he is expertly summoning coherence from a tableful of implements that, from appearance alone, one would never imagine to find collected in one space, or equally expertly unravelling the customary sonic voice of the standard concert piano into a multiplicity of tongues as likely to bicker or cross-talk as to join in unified utterance, Steve grasps the power of the visual in performance. It serves both as a captivating dimension of his work in itself, but also as a sly tool of misdirection for anyone foolish enough to think they might be able to keep up with the true audio magic underway, with anything less than their full wits about them.*

* * *

So your love of pound shops isn't just about the everyday, it's about the bizarreness of some of their products.
Oh yeah! Tiger is more self-conscious about its bizarreness. They used to do more musical instruments – they had a really nice melodica, a diatonic one that looked like a plastic clarinet. It was amazingly good value – I should have bought more of them, but I thought "They'll always be around," and now they aren't. The bugs haven't been around for three years now, and I'm running out of them. These get mentioned in my piece in *Arcana*.[11]

I did have a duck-call. And I had a little Audubon bird-call, which uses a brass piece inside a wooden recess – you put rosin in.

Is there a range of these?
Are you kidding? You've never seen John Zorn in his *Classic Guide to Strategy* period. Not just bird-calls – animal-calls, too.

Mostly they're variants of a metal reed in a tube. The classic Acme duck-call is the brand of J. Hudson & Co. Whistles Ltd., Birmingham. I can recommend a visit. They are *the* whistle-manufacturer.[12]

I did a residency there with Hayley Newman and others, culminating in a concert, and I absolutely loved it.

I got to play the only remaining lion-call. It was made for the British Army in Burma in the Second World War, in the belief that Japanese soldiers would be frightened. It's a long copper tube with a metal reed inside the mouthpiece, what looks like an air-filter, and a kind of bell, like a brass instrument. It has a wah mute on a little chain, and it really does sound like a lion.

Hudson's have a kind of museum?
They have a glass-fronted cabinet, with whistles and bird-calls. They serve you Vimto and biscuits.

Duck-calls are used to attract ducks, for shooting.
Yes, absolutely. One of my strangest experiences was going shopping with John Zorn when he was obsessed with animal-calls. We went to every gun shop in central London. This was the early 1980s. He did a gig at the ICA – the *Classic Guide to Strategy* with bird-calls that I just mentioned. I loved it but apparently the promoter was not impressed.

What's wonderful is that in Wile E. Coyote and Road Runner cartoons, when Wile E. gets a package with the new bomb, it always has "Acme" on it. It's great that the duck-call has the same name.

Acme invented the police whistle. Up till then, policemen had rattles. They did this experiment on Clapham Common, and the whistle could be heard a mile away.

They do all sorts of whistles.

Do policemen still have them?
You'd have to ask a policeman!

They made a killing from the film *Titanic* – Kate Winslet blew an Acme Thunderer Whistle that was salvaged from the real Titanic. On the back of that, they sold thousands of Acme Whistles As Blown By Kate Winslet.

Beresford and Toy Piano

By Adam Fairhall

Steve Beresford's use of the toy piano is well known. The instrument is often cited as part of his arsenal of toys and objects, and contributes to a notion of Beresford as a kind of creative bricoleur, alchemising fascinating music from "found" sources. The toy piano is not just a found object, however. Over the past three decades, and mostly in the field of contemporary classical music, it has become the focus of albums, articles, concert series, academic conferences, composition competitions, commissions and performers' careers. Beresford started using the instrument in the 1970s, after Cage had introduced it to avantgarde music with his *Suite for Toy Piano* (1948), but well before the instrument became a mainstay of contemporary classical music culture. So Beresford's position is that of an innovator, an early adopter. Several years ago, as a budding player of toy piano myself, I was keen to hear what Beresford was doing with the instrument at an early stage of its performance tradition, and keen to compare his work to the field of contemporary composition for toy piano which has blossomed since.

However, there is little readily available recorded evidence of Beresford playing solo toy piano in his early period. Fortunately, in 2001 the academic journal *Leonardo* issued a double CD, curated by David Toop, of British experimental music from the 1960s and 1970s, including a previously unissued track of Beresford playing toy piano. The track, entitled *Toy Piano* and donated by Beresford himself, was recorded in Charing Cross Station in 1975, in a "Record Your Own Voice" booth. The machine, akin to a photo booth, produced single-sided records of an unusual and small size. Beresford notes in *Leonardo* that the record's handwritten label includes the phrase "before gig in Greenwich," and that he started using toy pianos because of the lack of real pianos in the "tiny rooms" he was playing at the time. The recording, therefore, represents a tantalising glimpse of Beresford's toy piano work, at the time of those initial tiny room gigs.

The first thing to note when listening to *Toy Piano*, after hearing recent recordings of toy piano music by classical performers such as Margaret Leng Tan and Phyllis Chen, is that the timbre of Beresford's instrument is highly distinctive. Many classical performers – including Tan and Chen – use Schoenhut toy pianos, often their "concert grand" model. Indeed, Schoenhut endorse dozens of classical performers. Their pianos have a bright, ringing sound, produced by plastic hammers and a particular quality of tine. (A tine is a metal rod that the hammers hit to make the sound.) This orthodoxy in instrument choice lends a timbral uniformity to contemporary classical toy piano performance – occasional uses of other models, preparations and extended techniques aside. Such uniformity may be desirable in a music in which a composer writes for an expected sound, prior to the involvement of a performer. However, Beresford's sound reminds us that improvised music has no such requirement, and that individuality of tone is valued.[13] The ring of Beresford's piano does not sustain in the manner of a Schoenhut; his piano has an attack, full of inharmonic overtones, which dies quickly. Toy pianos have often been referred to as "gamelan-like" by music critics – a very arguable point – but in the case of Beresford's *Toy Piano*, the complex attack and fast decay is perhaps more reminiscent of some types of African xylophone music. This lends the sound a mixture of familiarity and exoticism from a Western perspective, almost as if we are hearing a field recording of a non-Western folk music.

It is not just the timbre of Beresford's toy piano that contributes to this effect; the very lo-fi analogue sound, including the constant background sound of vinyl scratches, is instantly familiar to collectors of folk music records from the 1920s and 1930s – the background noise is almost at the level of a 1920s Paramount 78. This is in keeping with Beresford's intentions, as he writes in the accompanying notes:

> I envisaged showing up with an acoustic guitar and recording a pseudo-blues that I could pass off, because of the inevitable scratches and low fidelity, as an undiscovered 1930s blues classic.[14]

The musical content, too, evokes the folkloric. The playing begins by oscillating between two pitches a major third apart, and proceeds via a series of small musical cells or groups of notes, sometimes arrived at by introducing a note or two to the previous cell, and sometimes by jumping straight into a new group. The music is non-melodic, with cells often shared between the two hands in figuration. The reduction of pitch materials in individual cells and the frequent single-note figuration recalls the music of many non-Western tuned percussion traditions.

Yet there are also aspects that point to an avantgarde mind, one familiar with twentieth-century compositional techniques and the practices of first-generation free improvisation. Various tempos are set next to each other, there are moments of independence between the hands which result in rhythmic counterpoint, and clusters are used, amplifying the inharmonic dissonance already found in piano's overtones. The piece is palimpsest-like, an intertext, in which the traces of disparate musics can be heard.

The track is only one minute forty-eight seconds long, and a lot of that is just crackle. And yet its impact on me has been considerable. The timbre of the recording and the tone of the instrument mix with the playing to create a sense of an imaginary folk music. Even my initial discovery of it on YouTube recalled the way in which field recordings previously only available to contemporary Western listeners via university archives can now be found online, without the context of liner notes or catalogue texts, as unfamiliar, free-floating codes to be deciphered. The notion of the toy piano as a way of connecting creatively with non-Western musics has not been ignored in contemporary classical composition, but Beresford's *Toy Piano* is more convincing, unshackled from the context and requirements of the concert hall.[15]

Notes

1 An established venue for free improvisation, and for comedy, in Finsbury Park, North London. It closed in 2008.
2 As of this writing, the disc has not been released.
3 Kostelanetz (2003), p. 69.
4 Quotation from Hamilton (2015), available at https://www.rhinegold.co.uk/international_piano/toy-story/.
5 See discussion of Echtzeitmusik in Chapter 8.
6 http://home.clara.net/helenpetts/helenpetts.com/space_%26_freedom.html. The film is discussed in Chapter 11.
7 Sadly, Cor Fuhler, born 1964, died in July 2020.
8 *Arcana* is a series of books, edited by John Zorn, in which musicians write on music.
9 Swiss sculptor Jean Tinguely (1925–91) was a pioneer of kinetic art. He produced abstract spatial constructions with electrically powered mechanisms that could

be set in motion by the viewer; their popularity arose from their wit, charm and unpredictability. His later work was influenced by Fluxus as well as Dada.
10 https://swisscarbonalphorn.net/en/
11 Beresford (2017).
12 www.acmewhistles.co.uk/
13 For a critical discussion of the values surrounding tone and technique in classical and improvised music, see Hamilton (2000).
14 Beresford (2001), p. 99.
15 My own toy piano work, an attempt to develop in an idiosyncratic way those qualities I found in Beresford's *Toy Piano*, can be heard at https://youtu.be/wPWxEod7Gu0, "Adam Fairhall at ABc No-Rio," and Fairhall (2019).

8

Jazz, Free Jazz, and Free Improvisation

This chapter takes up issues in the aesthetics and philosophy of free improvisation, referred to in earlier discussions. We look at the contrast between free jazz and free improv, and the "aesthetics of imperfection" that arguably underlies improvised music – how imperfectionists value a spontaneous response to the contingencies of the performing situation, while perfectionists favour a planning model. Topics covered include "faking," spontaneity in improvisation and composition, preparation – Beresford, like Paul Bley, is a non-practiser – the relation of jazz and free improvisation, conduction, invented instruments, lower-case music, and the song-based material of jazz.

We begin with the topic of *conduction*, the focus of one of Beresford's most important and enduring projects – the London Improvisers Orchestra. The LIO originated in the 1997 Contemporary Music Network UK tour by the London Skyscraper ensemble, directed by Lawrence "Butch" Morris, using his "conduction" technique, in which an improvising conductor used prearranged signs and gestures. In 1998, some participants – notably Steve Beresford, Evan Parker and Ian Smith – agreed to develop the work begun on that tour, exploring the areas of conduction and free improvisation. Monthly concerts began in 1998 at the Red Rose Theatre, and the name "London Improvisers Orchestra" was adopted. The LIO has been documented on Emanem, Psi, Kukuruku and LIO labels. Conductions can be by any member of the orchestra. Regular members have included Harry Beckett, Alison Blunt, Adam Bohman, Lol Coxhill, Terry Day, Sue Ferrar, Sylvia Hallett, Caroline Kraabel, Tony Marsh, Neil Metcalfe, Rachel Musson, Adrian Northover, Roland Ramanan, Alan Tomlinson, Dave Tucker, Phil Wachsmann, Ashley Wales and Jason Yarde. Guests include Jaap Blonk and Leo Smith. Monthly concerts have been held at Cafe Oto, Iklectik in Waterloo, St Mary's in Stoke Newington, and occasionally elsewhere, including Kings Place and Amsterdam's Bimhuis.[1]

Conduction

"Conducted" is the verb for both conduction and a conventional orchestra. With the LIO [London Improvisers Orchestra], is your conduction the equivalent of a compositional score? To what degree do you prepare it – do you freely improvise along with the orchestra?
I don't prepare it at all. But we use signals, and we have to tell new members what they mean. So it's prepared on the level of "This means 'sustain,'" and so on. The composition is collective, and I see the conductor as another member of the orchestra. I think it's OK if people don't do what I ask them to do – it's a question of negotiation. It's the same as me playing something on piano, and maybe hoping someone will respond. But that's all negotiation within improvised music.

Not all conductors feel like that – I know that Butch Morris didn't. He was very clear that you looked at what he was indicating all the time, and you followed his instructions.

He was always the sole conductor. With the LIO, anyone in the orchestra, and some people not in the orchestra, are welcome to do a conduction. For instance, Ashley Wales of Springheel Jack does conductions, but he's not in the LIO. His conductions are very different from everybody else's. He loves doing that, and he's great.

Butch Morris had a gesture for "Develop what you're playing." I was talking to John Butcher afterwards, who said, "There's more than one way to develop a phrase." Butch Morris's ideas were not super-unusual, in terms of how an idea should be developed. Robin Hayward was working out a new way of playing the tuba – and he would say "I'm developing this idea in my own way," which might involve having three minutes of silence. That might not be how Butch saw development.

Interestingly, some of the people least happy with Butch's conduction were those who were most used to being directed – coming from a classical tradition. I assumed they'd be perfectly happy to have someone waving a baton at them.

It's odd that Butch Morris should have that rather classical, prescriptive attitude.
Well, we all have different bits of different things in us. Butch clearly liked conducting. He apparently had a large collection of biographies of famous conductors, and enjoyed seeing himself in that role. Herbert von Karajan didn't conduct without a score – obviously that's a huge difference. But there were other relationships that Butch retained from that tradition.

* * *

"Faking"

How far does the audience understand what improvisation involves? Some people are astonished there's no score – and then conclude that without a score, it's "made up as you go along."
There'll always be people who are upset that you're improvising, because they thought you were playing a piece of composed music, and so you've been tricking them. AMM had that problem – someone would come up afterwards and say, "You had that worked out didn't you – it can't possibly be improvised." It happened to me with my first improv band, Bread and Cheese. [Composer] Dominic Muldowney, who was at university with us, came up and said, "You've been rehearsing that for months, haven't you?" And we said, "We really haven't." He was furious that we were – as he thought – pretending.
It hadn't occurred to me that people would regard "being improvised" as a negative thing.
I think Dominic Muldowney thought we were lying, that's why he was annoyed.
I would have thought that most people would be impressed to discover that something is improvised. "Making it up as you go along" suggests "You haven't done your homework."
Yes. [Vocalist] Shelley Hirsch told me she did a gig in New York, I think with Ned Rothenberg and Elliott Sharp, very experienced guys. These Italian people in the audience said, "We loved what you did tonight, we want you to come to Rome for a month, and work on another piece like that." But, of course, it was completely improvised!
According to Dominic Muldowney, you were "faking."
Well, there's about three different meanings of that.
Isn't a Fake Book so-called because "faking" originally meant pretending you could read music?[2]
In the 1970s, I had a gig playing a horrible electric keyboard, at a venue called "The 1520 Rooms," down St Martin's Lane. It was supposed to be like Henry VIII's court – we had to wear leggings and so on. There were lots of blue-collar days out – they ate syllabub.[3] They liked me there because I had a few clichés from early keyboard music – I'd got the Fitzwilliam Virginal book, and I switched the keyboard to harpsichord sound and played lots of bare fifths and things – not really Henry VIII, but within a hundred years or so.
You were faking in the original sense of the term here?
Yes – ersatz early music.

Tudor-style free improvisation.
They were misremembered Tudor-style keyboard pieces.

No one else even tried to play music that had anything to do with Henry VIII's time, they just sang folksongs.

I also backed this singer/comedian – his voice was somewhere between Tony Hancock and Richard Burton, a total "actor." We didn't have a set list – he'd just go "I . . . " and I'm supposed to know which song it is. So it was hell working for him.

The venue might have had some connection with organised crime.

* * *

Improvisation as a Compositional Method

Improvisers have long been disadvantaged by arts funding bodies, with their bias towards composers. Victor Schonfield, one of the most important promoters of new music from the 1960s onwards, recalled the Arts Council setting up the Contemporary Music Network [CMN] in 1971 – a touring network for jazz and contemporary composition. Estimable though that organisation was in many ways, he commented that

> They were rigid . . . You had to invent a non-existent composition that you were going to rehearse for. They wouldn't accept that music could exist if it wasn't [paper] composed. AMM was the real breakthrough. It was an improvising band but because it had Cornelius [Cardew] in it, it was accepted as suitable for the big concert halls and for receiving grants at the festivals.[4]

CMN existed until 2008, and though Sound and Music was meant to take on its role, it was never really replaced. However, Sound and Music do allow that improvisation is a compositional method, in contrast to the work of *paper composers*, who produce scores.

"Improvisation as a compositional method" involves

(1) Spontaneous composition
(2) No repetition of the composition – rejection of the work-concept, a *fixed and repeatable* composition.

As Tony Buck of The Necks comments,

> it's no longer a dichotomy of improvising and composing – it's all composing, and improvisation is a methodology for composing, just like serialism, or rhythmic interlocking. I'd argue that [free improviser] Steve Beresford

did compose a piece of music, he just did it there and then – and he's not interested in doing it again.⁵

To describe improvisation in this way is to assume a broad sense of "composition," as the creation of pleasing artistic structures – as opposed to the narrow sense, of desk-composers in music producing notated works. Brian Olewnick commented that

> Often in recent years, [Keith Rowe has] opined that one can't truly, freely improvise. His own performances are often structured, even if that structure is obscure. . . . He was playing with Christian Fennesz and he was pretty sure, having spent the day with him, that Christian was going to do a strong, surging performance, so he quite consciously structured his to be very quiet. . . . After he played a solo set on the 10th anniversary of 9/11, he asked me if I recognized the structural reference. . . . He thought that it was obvious (!) that it was based on Shostakovich's 8th String Quartet.⁶

I'd assume that for commercial reasons, music publishers might not like improvised music.
They might like it personally! But publishers don't make that much money out of contemporary composers, and I'd imagine they're not happy about a festival like Huddersfield featuring people who are not signed to *any* publisher – because this is an important showcase for New Music composers. There's only a certain number of hours' music that can be presented, and if [improvisers like] John Butcher or David Toop are taking up that time . . .

There are certain august institutions, Sound and Music for instance, and the Hamlyn Foundation – thank God for them! – who now use the word "composer" to include free improvisers. I think that's perfectly kosher – in fact, they use the term "paper composer" to cover "classical" composers.

Improvisation *is* a compositional method. I don't have any problem with that.

Until fairly recently, the Arts Council wouldn't give funding to jazz musicians who hadn't written a suite.
Under Milk Wood by Stan Tracey is a fantastic record – there was a genuine inspiration by the literary material it was based on. An amazing band – Bobby Wellins was extraordinary on that record.

But basing a set of pieces on a work of literature became a cliché very quickly – people felt they could stress the Englishness of the source-material, and produce something you could have on at your local small-town arts festival, and it wouldn't scare anyone away.

Windmill Tilter is a great suite – by Kenny Wheeler, written for John Dankworth's band.

* * *

Spontaneity as a Value

Do you think people want spontaneity in a performer?
The problem in presenting spontaneity is that you can't guarantee there'll be epiphanic moments.

What can improvised music do, that composed music can't?
That's a good question. There are certain things that happened last night [in Newcastle, with Sarah Gail Brand and John Edwards, October 2016] that you couldn't notate and probably couldn't rehearse – unexpected things. It's a totally different feeling.

One great advantage of improvising is that beautifully timed things can happen. John Stevens had a piece "Together Untogether." He had a tiny drum kit, and the rule was "The moment you play at the same time as the other person, that's the end of the piece." When I heard them, he and Trevor Watts stood in silence for a really long time, with their eyes closed – and then they both played at exactly the same moment, so that was the end of the piece! Trevor was quite annoyed.

So you can get the most phenomenal timings with improvised music. Even if you'd been making eye-contact, it still wouldn't be that tight. And, of course, it has a flow, a grace, a naturalness – if it's good – that's very hard to achieve in paper-composed music. That's a huge advantage, and I think some people would resent that in a way.

A lot of rehearsing in paper-composed music is to do with making it flow – making it feel spontaneous and natural. In a way, that's why Webern's great, because it *never* feels spontaneous! It's funny how much of an influence he had on improvisers like Derek Bailey and John Stevens – they both adored his music. John really loved Webern's Saxophone Quartet.

Wouldn't the greatest interpreters succeed in giving the impression that a performance of Webern is spontaneously created?
Well, perhaps there are different types of flow, or continuity.

There are misconceptions on both sides. Many classical people think improvised music is "made up as you go along" – it's random. And many improvisers think that for performers of paper-composed music, it's "reproduced automatically from the score." In fact, both should aim at spontaneity.

Well, there can be [incomprehension]. But not with the people I work with, coming out of contemporary classical music – it's really changed.

A lot of improvised music is unspontaneous. I was listening to Oscar Peterson's album *Walking The Line* from 1970, where the profusion of licks is amazing.

And ridiculously fast tempos.

It can be exciting.

I get bored pretty quick with Oscar. I like him accompanying Fred Astaire, and I like his singing – he sounds a lot like Nat King Cole. They say he made a deal with Nat, that he wouldn't sing, and Nat wouldn't play piano. It was a joke, of course. Nat made some great late piano records. He's absolutely one of my favourite piano players.

   Oscar Peterson is a virtuoso piano player.

He's just not a virtuoso improviser.

Exactly. I tend to like people who play less – like Teddy Wilson. But I love Fats Waller. My dad had a couple of Waller's records, "Viper's Drag" and "Alligator Crawl." Sometimes I think he's my favourite piano-player. Also, his bands were beautiful.

In the Ellington Orchestra, you'd work out your solos, then go on stage and deliver.

Are you sure about that? That's certainly true of the Glenn Miller Orchestra. Duke did 330 gigs a year so they probably did repeat themselves, because that's an enormous number of gigs. They'd play "Take The 'A' Train" every single night at least twice, and Johnny Hodges would do "Jeep's Blues."

If Konitz was in that band he wouldn't, out of principle.

But Konitz was never in a band that did that. He was with Kenton, and Claude Thornhill . . .

And Birth of the Cool.

That band only did half a dozen gigs in total – but I'm talking about a band that played two sets a night.

   There were stories that Harry Carney couldn't sleep in a bed because he was so used to sleeping sitting in a coach, you know. So, they stayed up and played a great deal.

Harry Carney and his colleagues didn't practise their solos to note-perfection, but they developed a rough outline. With modern jazz, things changed – the "high art" players felt that this wasn't what you should do.
Coleman Hawkins' "Picasso" was recorded in 1948, but he'd been working on it for years. The idea of a totally unaccompanied saxophone solo was quite extraordinary. I think that was probably mostly worked out, but it's high art and I think there was always that aspect [in jazz] – Bix Beiderbecke's "In A Mist," for instance.

Louis Armstrong listened to Italian opera – though I guess that wasn't really high art for him.
Louis, I think, saw himself principally as an entertainer. It just so happened that he was a genius and an amazing trumpet player.

Was there a point when you realised you were committed to improvisation? Was the fact that the music was improvised, always a big thing about it?
It must have been at some point in the three years after I left university. I was committed to free improvisation, but not to the exclusion of everything else.

Were the people you were working with particularly committed to being spontaneous?
Certainly Bread and Cheese were very concerned with being spontaneous.

To the extent of worrying about excising things you've done before?
I think we started thinking like that quite early.

Jeremy Vine tells an amazing story about Boris Johnson's alleged "improvisations," which turn out to be virtually identical. He pretends to improvise – the audience is being manipulated.[7]
He's selling a persona. The number of people who are going to bust him for saying the same thing when he's pretending to make it up is very small. Is it exactly the same? Stewart Lee does enormously long sets of pre-worked-out material – and he does have something written on his hand, to remind him of what the next bit is. He's always got things written there.

How much can you have written on your hand?
Not much!

> TOP TIP No. 3: *"Don't worry about being wrong, just worry about being uninteresting" (Whitmer).*[8]

I think that's a pretty good tip.

You obviously are not someone who wants to be perfect.
[Beresford laughs]

I'll change that slightly – you're someone who thinks that perfectionism has drawbacks.
"God Only Knows" by The Beach Boys is near perfection I think.

* * *

RACHEL MUSSON is a saxophonist, improviser and composer living in London. She is involved with a variety of improvisation projects, including the trio Shifa with Pat Thomas and Mark Sanders, a nonet I Went This Way featuring composition and spoken word, and other collaborations with improvisers in the UK and internationally. Rachel's recordings can currently be found on 577, Iluso, Weekertoft and Babel. Here she discusses Steve Beresford's spontaneous approach to improvisation:

> *The rich London improvised music scene owes much to Steve Beresford. A founding member and enthusiastic stalwart of the London Improvisers Orchestra, he appears across the capital in different line-ups and on different instruments – partly due to the varying availability of pianos and partly due to his enthusiastic ransacking of charity shops for second-hand toy instruments. He's a gig-attendee who graces so many events, it's hard to believe he hasn't got a twin brother in the cause. Steve makes me think of a laughing Buddha, someone in touch with depths of musical (and other) knowledge and understanding that only comes from a lifetime of application – and at the same time a levity and light-hearted touch that locates a hidden and often comic depth in whatever situation he finds himself in. Steve is like that to play with. He will entertain whatever aspect his playing partner (or partners) choose to bring, whether it's supporting a mawkish melody, or engaging in a similarly obsessive exploration of a gnarly sound – then he'll toss a wind-up toy beetle into the inside of the piano to take matters out of everybody's hands and let chance do its work. I love playing with Steve. I never know what will happen or where it will go, but I know he will bring the broadest of musical palettes and cut the set short before my, or anyone else's, ego becomes over-invested – and usually, with a twinkle in his eye, turn to chat, food and maybe a glass of wine.*

* * *

Preparation

We haven't talked much about preparation.
My preparation consists of buying train tickets when necessary, and packing [toys and small instruments] in that box. That's it.

You're like Paul Bley.
Yes, he was really against practising.
But when you're doing a piano gig, of free jazz, you've got to keep your chops in shape?
I never consciously do that. Generally, I don't play unless there's an audience.
You have a piano at home.
I might work out a chord, or try and work out how a tune goes – but I don't practise the way a classical musician does.
Or like jazz players like Lee Konitz do – "preparing for the spontaneous effort."
If you play music the way he does, it makes sense to practise. When I saw Konitz with Derek [Bailey], he did a solo date with Derek, and he also had some outtakes of *Motion*, [his recording with Elvin Jones] and played along with it. Which was nice – very interesting.
Have you heard Lee Konitz much?
I saw him with Steve Arguelles at the Jazz Cafe, and with Derek – I think that was it.
Don't your fingers get stiff?
Sometimes they're stiffer than others'. Maybe I'm suddenly going to get horrible arthritis, but I haven't yet, touch wood.
So you believe in total spontaneity, as far as it's possible.
No, because that sounds like an ideology. And it's not an ideology, it's just what I do.

It's not that I have a horror of practising – it's just that I don't do it.

TOP TIP No. 4: Don't rehearse your improvisations at home.

* * *

An Aesthetics of Imperfection (Part Two, continued from Chapter 4)

In pop music, I've used auto-tune in a vocal track where a note is clearly flat. You just auto-tune that. The system seems to have gone, but it used to automatically tune the melodic line, or one note, to whatever you told it, say D-Dorian. Now it seems you can't tell it to do that – that seems insane.

It doesn't have to be exactly tuned – you don't want all the notes perfectly in tune because that sounds robotic. But what people have discovered is that if you push the auto-tune, you'll get something like a vocoder. Quite often, what sounds like a vocoder is an auto-tune being pushed to the limit.

A vocoder produces an envelope around a pitch that makes it sound like a human voice – Sparky's Magic Piano, you remember that? A talking piano.

When Cher's record came out, people thought it was a vocoder, but it was auto-tune.[9]

How often would you use auto-tune on a record?
Maybe twice.
When there was a particularly glaring note out of tune, you'd correct it.
That's what it was originally for.
This is the aesthetics of imperfection – when an imperfection, or the correction of an imperfection, becomes a new device or genre in itself. Guitar feedback is another example – it began as a fault that needed correcting, and became a stylistic device.
The famous sound of guitar on "You Really Got Me" by The Kinks was supposedly accidental, caused by poking a hole in guitar amp's speaker cone.
Or Louis Armstrong supposedly dropping the sheet music, and inventing scat.
But there's always that move, in non-classical music, to an instrumental sound that's not as clean – Ellington's jungle period with the wah-wah and plunger mutes, growling through trumpet... fuzz-boxes... prepared piano and prepared guitar... the dirtiness of a cranked-up amp. Piano is the ideal for classical music, the sound has a smooth transition from note to note, a uniformity through the octaves – that's why the prepared piano was such a big gesture.
One view is that when people get interested in an imperfection, it becomes a perfection.
You're trying to put the effect in a £100 pedal that you can sell – all these things become commodities.
But you're an imperfectionist, who's always looking for new imperfections – that's why you go round the pound shops.
That's right.
An entertainer wants a schtick, but an improviser wants something new.
Yes and no. The Zoom sampler that I still use after twenty years – I haven't changed any of the samples in there for years.

Thinking about Derek Bailey's broken guitar string – people say it became a device that he used.
It was probably an opportunist moment.
 I don't remember Derek breaking strings an awful lot – but he had a very strong attack, he was a very strong man. John Edwards tends to break bass strings.

* * *

Free Improv and Jazz

How do you contrast free jazz and free improv? Free improv isn't so common in the US – it began in Britain.
Have you read David Toop's book, *Into the Maelstrom*? I think there's some good formative stuff in the United States that you definitely couldn't call jazz, even though it was performed by people known as jazz musicians.
"Free improviser" isn't a very good term – and there isn't one, is there?
No. Blanca said, "Why don't we call it spontaneous music?" – and I said "Like the Spontaneous Music Ensemble – yeah!" Obviously "free improvisation" is pretentious – but we've got to call it something. Cecil Taylor didn't like being called a jazz musician. "Improv" is worse, because it's taken from "improvisational theatre" where you improvise scenes. That's like how film critics use the word "riff" – when they mean exactly the opposite to a riff. They mean improvising, but it's not that at all – a riff is playing the same thing.
 Or "rising to a crescendo" – no, the rise in dynamic *is* the crescendo.
Why is "improvisational theatre" the opposite of improv? Because you're creating something fixed from something spontaneous?
Yes.
Like Mike Leigh, who gets his film actors to improvise, then fixes the result.
Yes.
Free improvisers want to create spontaneously – and they don't want to repeat the result of their spontaneous creation.
Yes. That's where the word "improv" came from, and to me it feels disparaging. So I think Blanca's suggestion is a good one.
 Then we don't need to get into this ridiculous thing about "Yeah, but what do you mean by free?" You're not free of gravity, and you need food, you have to book the gig, so you're not free. People say this all the time.
 People have started to use the phrase "improvised jazz."

As opposed to hack jazz?
I think what they mean is (sings), and they write it out. The point is, that's how popular music sounded in 1938, and it wasn't all jazz, but it had a swing feel. It was popular music, or swing as it was in its first incarnation.

"Improvised jazz" is a tautology – all jazz involves improvisation. I read someone referring to "tabla percussion." What else is a tabla but percussion? You don't blow it, you hit it – it's a percussion instrument.

"Schmaltz" is actually Yiddish for chicken fat. It's a strange word to use about over-sentimental music. What's chicken fat got to do with sentimental music? I don't know, but it's called schmaltz.

That suggests false emotion.
Even if free improvisation has no suggestion of swing, or blue notes, still it couldn't have happened without jazz. Seymour Wright says he plays jazz. I'm not sure – but that playing couldn't have happened without jazz.
There's no doubt about that.

I don't care what he thinks he plays – I'm perfectly happy for Seymour to think it's jazz. Seymour is a great historian of jazz saxophone – he knows absolutely everything about the instrument.

Paul Bream responded that a lot of jazz played by younger musicians today couldn't have happened without improv.
That's a very interesting angle.

The generation of Laura Jurd, Elliot Galvin and Shabaka Hutchings have very wide listening habits – they are very open to different types of music.

I think free improvisation is part of the lives of many jazz players in a way it didn't use to be.

* * *

Inventors

What's brilliant about free improvisation at this point – and it might change, it hasn't always been like this – is that the craft can be something that you've invented. Adam Bohman, who rarely plays a conventional instrument, has to devise his own techniques.[10] There are no conventional ways of playing anything that Adam plays. He bows bits of cardboard, and rubs light bulbs against record racks – there's virtuosity, but it's to do with an instrument that you can't be trained on, because you just invented it.

Other inventors are Max Eastley and Hugh Davies. Max Eastley's Arc is basically a plank with a string on it; Hugh Davies' springboard looks like a piece of garbage but – I realised as soon as I played it – is a fully-rounded musical instrument.[11]

Planks with strings on, they're invented and reinvented. One of the interesting things about Max's instrument is that it's a flexible plank.

Not Max Planck, but Max's plank.

[laughs] The pitch of the string can be changed by flexing the plank as well as touching the string, or putting a glass rod on it. So there are different ways of playing Max's instrument. I think you need a technique, on your instrument or instruments, but I think that technique can be absolutely individual. Keith Rowe, I gather, was not the world's greatest conventional guitarist, but then he put guitar on the table – which seems like a really obvious thing to do now, and of course they did play guitars on their laps in Hawaii before Hawaiian guitar was invented. Keith evolved a real virtuoso style on that instrument, which was a self-taught technique.

The cliché about free improv is that it's stuff you don't need technique to play – so it's only people without technique who play it.

There is a grain of truth in that – especially for people in related areas like dance. A lot of not very good dancers ended up working with free improvising musicians. Ballet Rambert wouldn't be very interested in them.

There's a small number of "small instruments specialists."

One of them is Douglas Benford – a very humble genius. His entirely unshowy playing of usually small instruments has a remarkable power. I think his warmth and humour have a huge effect on the players.[12]

He has a habit of putting together sometimes unexpected quartets. About a year ago [in 2019] I heard him with John Edwards, Mandhira de Saram and Hannah Marshall. It was at the Hundred Years Gallery in Hoxton, a little bar and small art gallery. I thought that was one of the most amazing groups I'd ever heard – just extraordinary. He tends to put together quartets who've never played together before.

Have you worked with Lee Patterson?

No, but I like him very much. I like the record where he burns hazelnuts and uses tiny springs out of cigarette lighters.

I don't think Douglas and Lee fit into the same category. Douglas uses small Indian harmoniums, toy glockenspiels – and sometimes he uses a small amplifier from his iPhone. So he crosses over with my approach, whereas Lee uses things that people wouldn't see as musical instruments – like Adam Bohman.

I think Hugh Davies is an inspiration to all three players. He made instruments. I don't think Douglas Benford creates instruments very much – but Lee and Adam do, and Hugh did.

Is this a more British practice? Harry Partch was an inventor of instruments.
There's an American writer and instrument-builder called Bart Hopkin who had a magazine called *Experimental Musical Instruments* – a lovely magazine.

* * *

Lower-Case Music

In the 1990s, a trend developed for very hushed improvised music with long silences – so-called lower-case music or reductionism. It was initially exemplified by Berlin musicians Burkhard Beins, Axel Dörner and Andrea Neumann, and also includes Japanese musician Sachiko M; UK musicians Rhodri Davies, Phil Durrant and Mark Wastell; Viennese Radu Malfatti and Werner Dafeldecker; and Americans Bhob Rainey and Greg Kelley.

What's your view of so-called lower-case music?
I'm not sure it exists anymore. Quite early on in that period, I saw a trio with Matt Davis, Phil Durrant and Mark Wastell. I thought they were brilliant – Matt Davis is one of my favourite trumpet players.

Another lower-case group then played and I thought "This is all the same bits, but it's not put together right." The problem with lower-case music is that there's nowhere to go if it's not working. You can't rescue the gig. If you feel you have to stay in that stylistic area, even though at that point the music is clearly not happening, there's not enough room for you to move the music anywhere else.

There was a famous incident when Robin Hayward, the tuba-player, played a slightly loud note in a piece once, and there was a three-hour discussion afterwards about it.

Rhodri Davies is now making quite noisy music – and Angharad [Davies] is using a lot less silence than she used to.[13] There was clearly a decision not to do certain things – in the manner of Derek Bailey's strategy of "non-idiomatic improvisation." I think it was another strategy that probably needed to be done to clear the air, but I don't think it was a way of life – I think everyone who played it has now realised that. But maybe there are people in Tokyo or Vienna who are still playing music that's 90 per cent silence. I haven't seen a performance like that for years now.

You mean lowercase music?

Yes, exactly. Here, they called it New London Silence.

Like *Echtzeitmusik*?

Literally, "real time music" – though all free improvisation is real time music. Anyway, it got to mean music where most of the sounds were produced in unconventional ways, and tended to be quite low volume. People didn't do anything to suggest that they were listening to each other – that was quite an important thing.

There's a book called *Echtzeitmusik* with a nice piece by Rhodri Davies in it.

* * *

Vocalists

Who are your favourite improvising vocalists?

Shelley Hirsch. I haven't worked with her much – but she's got phenomenal ears. She doesn't skirt around the issue of pitch. You can get away with never listening to pitch. But she's very attuned to it – that's really nice, having a singer who thinks "I can do something with that," rather than "I can sing over the top of that."

Would you say there are free improvisers who are not really attuned to pitch?

Yes – particularly in the singing department.

Because they're more like sound-poets?

If you're Jaap Blonk, that's ok – he has his own area that you might not want to call music, though I am happy to call it that. Sidsel Endresen's more interesting work is in this area – albums like *Merriwinkle*.

Most listeners seem to prefer vocal music, and identify with the words more than the music.

My dad didn't really like singers that much, though he was one.

I love really good lyric-writing, but it's a very hard thing to work with in a free improvisation context, for all sorts of reasons. I'm not saying you can't do it, but it's very hard to improvise linguistically and musically at the same time.

Singers have got to really perform – they have to look at the audience.

I think it's difficult – but some people can manage it.

The greatest jazz singers, I think, are the ones who really interpret the lyrics, like Billie Holiday. For Sarah Vaughan and Ella Fitzgerald, it seems, the words don't mean anything.
Lester Young famously said a saxophone player ought to know all the lyrics of the songs. Of course, he was Billie Holiday's favourite accompanist.

Although vocal music is usually the kind people respond to, I find free improv vocalists the hardest to appreciate.
I don't think you're the first person to say that. I guess it's because your voice gives away a lot about you – an insincerity, a lack of clarity, an insecurity. Maybe you don't know that, as a singer – and also the influences are very clear, very naked.

* * *

You did albums like *Eleven Songs For Doris Day* where you were singing – what do you think about your singing?
I wish I could stop! I really tried to get another singer. Later on, John Zorn did a record called *Signals for Tea*, which was basically me with Masada.

Did you say, "Do you really want me to sing?"
I said exactly that. He said "No, it's great! You gotta sing!" but I said, "Can we have someone else singing?" There's one song where I get a word completely wrong every time I sing it, and nobody noticed. The lyric sheet was right there and I sang it wrong.

You had a history as a vocalist though.
We had a soul band at university – I played bass guitar and sang some songs. I don't think I was ever much of a singer but my phrasing wasn't so bad. There was a band called Free with Paul Kossoff, so we called ourselves Expensive. We were quite consciously unfashionable – everybody liked twenty-five-minute guitar solos and we were doing three-minute Motown tunes, with three female singers who sang harmony.

Tony [Coe] sang and he was terrible, and Lol [Coxhill] – they were both marvellous in their way but they weren't great singers, so I thought I can probably do some of this. We wrote love songs for our first album, called *Love Plays Such Silly Games*. It became a tradition that the three people in the Melody Four would sing some songs. I always did "Besame Mucho," and Lol loved doing "Begin the Beguine" – a fantastic song.

Sarah Vaughan was recorded singing "chapter one," which was nonsensical, as the lyric said "chaperone." Nobody noticed and she didn't notice, and that tells you that she was singing the lyrics without any attention to what they mean.[14]

Well, yes and no. That doesn't reflect on Sarah Vaughan's entire history.

I think it's a telling example.

Sarah Vaughan was a fantastic interpreter.

She wasn't a fantastic interpreter of a lyric.

That's interesting – that's a different thing.

Her sound is beautiful. But Billie Holiday makes you believe in the tritest lyrics – somehow she makes them meaningful.

You were a reluctant vocalist, then.

That's a good way of putting it, yes.

But enough people liked it for you to do it quite a bit?

Nobody said, "Stop doing that for God's sake, it's horrible" – not to my face.

That's in your past?

I don't think I've sung for years, actually.

* * *

Notes

1 See www.londonimprovisersorchestra.co.uk/history.html.
2 William F. Ludwig, founder of drum manufacturer, commented in 1927 that because the drum part is notated, "the new jazz form is no guess work or faking. It is highly scientific." The quote is from Brennan (2020), p. 106, which discusses the term; "faking" means "deviating from the written part."
3 A once-popular English dessert, made from curdled milk or cream, sweetened.
4 Quoted in England (2018), p. 36.
5 Quoted in Hamilton and Pearson eds (2020), p. 340.
6 Email to author, 2 August 2018.
7 https://reaction.life/jeremy-vine-my-boris-story/, also found here for subscribers: https://www.spectator.co.uk/article/my-boris-johnson-story
8 Complete quote: "The idea . . . must always be kept in a state of flux. An error may only be an unintentional rightness. . . . Polishing is not at all the important thing; instead strive for a rough go-ahead energy. Do not be afraid of being wrong; just be afraid of being uninteresting" (Whitmer, T. *The Art of Improvisation*, p. 16, available

at https://archive.org/stream/artofimprovisati005713mbp#page/n11/mode/2up). See also discussion of James Brown drilling his band, in Chapter 15.

9 David Lloyd comments: "The tuning software I have can be set up to tune to any scale/mode in any key which, as Steve says, can be useful. It seems this feature – they call it 'auto-key' – is only included in the 'pro' version of Antares Auto-Tune, and has to be purchased as a separate item for the other versions. So the vocoder function has taken over as the rationale. It seems it's a marketing decision. Their largest market is the bedroom 'urban' music scene that needs that horrible sound" (email communication, 2019).

10 The Bohman Brothers are discussed in Chapter 15.

11 Max Eastley describes it as an "electro-acoustic monochord" (email, 2020).

12 Douglas Benford, born in 1961, established a music career in electronica – as an artist, and by running Sprawl events in London – until the mid-2000s when he gravitated towards live improvisation. Since then he has specialised in acoustic experimentation, including field recording and performance.

13 Rhodri Davies, born in 1971, is immersed in improvisation, musical experimentation and contemporary composition. He plays harp, electric harp, live-electronics and builds wind, water, ice, dry ice and fire harp installations. He has released five solo albums, and regular groups include HEN OGLEDD, Common Objects and a duo with John Butcher. Angharad Davies, sister of Rhodri, is a violinist working in free improvisation and contemporary composition. She has long-standing duos with Dominic Lash, and has collaborated with Tony Conrad and Eliane Radigue. She plays with Common Objects, Richard Dawson and Skogen.

14 Mark Steyn (2012): "Miss Vaughan, sight-reading without her glasses perhaps, sang 'With never a sign of any Chapter One,' which not only doesn't rhyme but makes no sense whatsoever. Yet in a roomful of producers, engineers, conductor and orchestra, not one person said 'What the hell are you on about?' Decades later, it's still there on the record."

Figure 1 Steve Beresford, euphonium and cat, by Caroline Forbes. Used with permission.

Figure 2 Steve Beresford, Tristan Honsinger, Derek Bailey, copyright Roberto Masotti / Lelli E Masotti Archivio. Used with permission.

Figure 3 Steve Beresford and Han Bennink looking snazzy, by Caroline Forbes. Used with permission.

Figure 4 Steve Beresford switched on, by Fabio Lugaro. Used with permission.

Figure 5 Company (Derek Bailey, Maarten van Regteren Altena, Lol Coxhill, Steve Beresford, Anthony Braxton, Tristan Honsinger, Han Bennink, Evan Parker, Wadada Leo Smith, Steve Lacy), copyright Roberto Masotti / Lelli E Masotti Archivio. Used with permission.

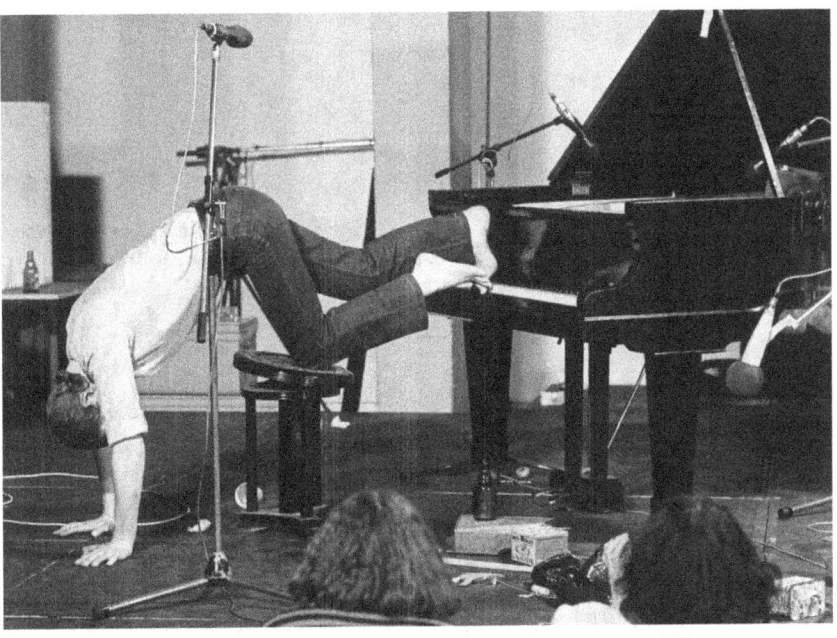

Figure 6 The Steve Beresford twinkle-toes piano method, copyright Roberto Masotti / Lelli E Masotti Archivio. Used with permission.

Figure 7 Steve Beresford and Nigel Coombes, by Caroline Forbes. Used with permission.

Figure 8 John Zorn, Steve Beresford, David Toop, Tonie Marshall, by Caroline Forbes. Used with permission.

Figure 9 Steve Beresford conducts the LIO, by Sean Kelly. Used with permission.

Figure 10 The Melody Four (Lol Coxhill, Steve Beresford, Tony Coe), by Caroline Forbes. Used with permission.

Figure 11 Alterations (Terry Day, Steve Beresford, Peter Cusack, David Toop), by Caroline Forbes. Used with permission

Figure 12 Steve Beresford on electronics, by Helen Petts. Used with permission.

Figure 13 Megaphone diplomacy, by Fabio Lugaro. Used with permission.

Figure 14 Talking to David Toop, by Fabio Lugaro. Used with permission.

Figure 15 With Satoko Fukuda, by Fabio Lugaro. Used with permission.

Figure 16 Table-top, by Fabio Lugaro. Used with permission.

Figure 17 With Mandhira de Saram (violin), by Fabio Lugaro. Used with permission.

Figure 18 With Tania Caroline Chen, recording session, by Fabio Lugaro. Used with permission.

Figure 19 Playing melodica with General Strike, by Fabio Lugaro. Used with permission.

Figure 20 Looking at Derek Bailey records, by Fabio Lugaro. Used with permission.

Figure 21 Table-top with ukulele, by Fabio Lugaro. Used with permission.

Figure 22 Stewart Lee, performing Cage's "Indeterminacy," by Fabio Lugaro. Used with permission.

Teaching Improvisation

Beresford's career as an improviser has been sustained by teaching. He taught Commercial Music students at Westminster University between 1995 and 2017, focusing on arranging and film music. We discuss that period here, and continue by looking at his approach to teaching improvised music in general, in which he was influenced by John Stevens. Beresford suggests that John Stevens was a kind of Lennie Tristano of free improvisation, in the sense of a guru or teacher, and addresses the kinds of approaches that are appropriate to the genre.

Born in London in 1940, JOHN STEVENS joined the RAF in 1958, and learned to play drums in the Royal Air Force School of Music, where he met saxophonist Trevor Watts and trombonist Paul Rutherford. With them he formed his own ensemble, which evolved into the Spontaneous Music Ensemble (SME) – an ensemble with a varying format that included Evan Parker, Derek Bailey and Kenny Wheeler. It was influential in the free improv scene – as were Stevens' workshops, in Ealing in West London and elsewhere, and his book of workshop pieces *Search and Reflect*. Stevens – along with Terry Day – realised that the standard jazz kit was too loud for this music, and reworked it to be at the same volume as other, mainly unamplified instruments. The result appeared on the groundbreaking album *Karyobin* from 1967 (discussed in Chapter 3). With other groups, he played free jazz on his bigger kit. Stevens perhaps returned to jazz in his later career – jazz and jazz-rock projects included Away, Splinters and Freebop. He died in 1994.

When did you start working at Westminster Uni?
I think in 1995. I just taught one module then – that was when it was still in what they called the Garment District, in Titchfield St. I never understood why they moved the Music Department to Harrow.
It was a gradual change in your pattern of work.
Initially I didn't make much money out of it, but then I got more teaching.

My students were taking a degree in Commercial Music – that's the name of the department. They mainly wanted to make pop records. I could help them in oblique ways. My approach is both the most traditional and the most radical. I taught score-writing and arranging. Most of them didn't read music. We ended up creating notated pieces – of course, most people use computers these days. Notation software is notoriously stupid. It will create ridiculous scores with a hundred ledger lines, for instance, and incredibly complex rhythms which obviously were not intended.

We got good results – sometimes great results.

Another module I taught was film music and composing – which was not an academic module, they didn't have to write a word about anything. They just had to produce some music in any way they wanted, to go with some scenes from films. Film music can be much more to do with intuition, but obviously there are strategies you can use. You have to step back and not be carried away by the plot.

It's a .7, so that's quite a lot of teaching.[1]

A day job, but sometimes more than that?
Something like that.

It's craft, not high art.
Exactly – music for films, pop songs, jingles, music for video games. Stuff that I've done myself, in the past.

How many people were in the department?
It seemed like a lot – I was always bumping into someone I didn't know. But they might be teaching just one course. I started off teaching the Experimental Music module – within the course there were things that weren't commercial.

"Commercial" is an interesting word to use.
They thought about it quite a lot, before launching the course.

Commercial music is music produced primarily to serve some other function, and which you can make a living from writing.
Though pop music doesn't serve another function. The course looks at the sociology, the legal side, the logistics – how you set up a gig. I love the idea of having a course like that.

It sounds like a course on the commercial aspects of music.
That might be true.

Did some students become intrigued by your work?
Oh yes, several – like Katy Carr, Jamie McDermott, and Steph Horak. Steph was quite conservative about music, then went to Goldsmith's to do visual art, and got interested in weird music – which is quite often the way.

I think visual art gives you another way into music – Morton Feldman had this.

We had a trio with Gino Robair, I think we played twice.

These are people who came to you thinking quite narrowly in terms of a commercial career, and then discovered that there are other kinds of music.
To a certain extent that's true. But Katy Carr writes quite conservative songs, they're well-crafted – though she loved the Innovation in New Music module, and I appreciated the piece she did for it. That was the first module I got called to teach at Westminster.

These people are now in music careers that don't seem to have anything particularly to do with that module, but I think it was important to them, in terms of seeing the possibilities. Maybe that's all you need to do – to point out that there's all this music that's organised and presented in a different way, outside the commercial mainstream. Most hadn't heard of any of these people, except that they knew that John Cage wrote a silent piece.

My students often had a narrow listening range. If I asked, "What kind of music do you like?" they would say, "I like everything." My response to that was "Do you like Tibetan Buddhist music?" Normally the answer was "I've never heard any," to which the answer is, "Then how do you know you like everything?"

One day I got the response, "Oh yeah, I love it – my granny is Tibetan and she plays it all the time." I totally deserved that!

When you're eighteen, you have a very narrow imagination about what music can be, so it's very important to extend your listening past the usual tropes.

That's a tip, I suppose:

TOP TIP No. 5: Extend your listening past the usual tropes.

What are your views on teaching improvisation?
What David Toop's doing at LCC [London College of Communication] is really good – a lot of interesting people come out of that. It's perfectly possible to talk about improvisation.

Talk about, or teach?
I think "talk about" is much better than "teach."

As Paul Lytton said, "Earn while you learn." And as David Toop said, "You can't teach free improvisation, but you can set up situations where it happens." You can create an environment where people try it, and you can talk about it. Eddie Prévost's workshop has been going for decades now – again, I'm not sure you'd call it teaching, more like facilitating.

Is it analogous to teaching conceptual art? Aspiring artists used to go to art school to learn the craft, through life classes and drawing. That's no longer central.
Yes.
Maybe it's partly an issue of modernism and postmodernism. Where people no longer believe in a set of rules to be learned, teaching becomes more open.
It becomes a different thing, certainly. If you really want to be a hard bop player, there are things you need to know. In classical music, the rules are to do with nineteenth-century music.

I always use "You've Really Got Me" by The Kinks as a song that immediately breaks five rules of traditional music theory. It's in parallel fifths, and goes from the flattened 7th to the tonic.

For mainstream jazz, there's a craft. You can teach jazz improvisation as Jamey Aebersold does, in his combo improvisation courses.
There's no equivalent craft for free improvisation – there's no Jamey Aebersold!
There's craft in the sense of learning to play your instrument.
But the craft develops in a different way. Perhaps it's more to do with developing a personal relationship with the instrument, rather than an approved way of playing.

David Toop used to go to John Stevens' workshops on Monday afternoons. There's definitely stuff coming from John Stevens there. I helped to get John's book *Search and Reflect* reprinted. But I found those pieces weren't really my style.

Maggie Nicols still does The Gathering, based on John Stevens' *Search and Reflect* – although she's in South Wales now. Maggie was around when John was doing those pieces, and I think she's still the best person to do them.

When I do free improvisation sessions, I don't use John Stevens' pieces. I went into the music from a totally different angle – some of his playing is so mysterious to me.

I still love his drumming.

I do occasionally do workshops, but I shy away from them these days. When I do them, I enjoy them – but I never enjoy the idea of them.

Lennie Tristano's jazz teaching was clearly didactic.
Extremely didactic. There's a bunch of really great musicians who came out of that. Probably John Stevens is the nearest thing we've had [in free improv] to Lennie Tristano.

So a teacher – in the sense in which you have reservations – is someone who says "You must do this."
It's probably just me.
You don't like the idea of teaching or being taught?
I was never very happy at school. Or at university.
Some people love to be given rules – but you're not one of those people.
I don't think Toop's students love to be given rules either.

I am doing a piece with Paul Khimasia Morgan, and video artist Blanca Regina. He just uses feedback, using microphones in the body of this old guitar, which has no neck or strings. He's a kind of virtuoso, his work is absolutely amazing – but you can't do A Tune A Day with that instrument! He's worked out his own technique – the instrument didn't exist until he put it together.

I wonder how unusual that is in the history of music.
I read a piece on experimental musical instruments, on innovation in traditional African music. There's an assumption that those instruments were always there, but that's wrong. Someone will get bored with the thumb piano, and put it aside. Then a later generation will bring it back, maybe with a different way of playing it. Things get reinvented.

Traditional instruments are usually made by the musician who plays them, as opposed to the specialists that we have. Obviously John Butcher doesn't make his own saxophones, but Terry Day creates his own reed bamboo instruments. Innovation is present in lots of musical cultures where people don't talk about it, because the music has been handed down through generations.

The conservatory tradition is relatively new.
Two friends of mine, who both come out of classical music, met. One of them immediately asked, "Where did you study, who was your teacher?" No one ever asks those questions in free improvisation.

They could do.
They could – they're very interesting sometimes.

Note

1 That is, 0.7 of a full-time position. Beresford retired from teaching at University of Westminster in 2017.

10

The 1980s and 1990s

Musicians that Beresford began working with extensively during this period included John Zorn, Otomo Yoshihide, John Butcher and Hannah Marshall. On recordings for Jean Rochard's label nato in the 1980s, he played tunes, as opposed to free improvisation. Notable albums included *Deadly Weapons* (1986) with Tonie Marshall, John Zorn and David Toop. Some of these albums featured his singing – such as *Dancing the Line*, recorded with Japanese vocalist Kazuko Hohki, and *Eleven Songs For Doris Day* (both from 1985). He also worked with Zorn on some of his game pieces. In the 1990s, Beresford produced recordings by the Dedication Orchestra – *Spirits Rejoice* and *Ixesha (Time)*. Beresford describes working with Louis Moholo-Moholo, with John Butcher and with Otomo Yoshihide on *Museum of Towing and Recovery*.

JOHN ZORN, born in New York in 1953, is a composer and saxophonist involved in a vast range of projects – jazz, experimental rock, metal and classical. Zorn studied composition at Webster College, St. Louis, and began to play alto saxophone. Though he didn't finish college, he continued to compose. His early recordings, a series entitled *Game Pieces*, were named after games including Lacrosse, Pool, Hockey and Archery. He set up his own label, Tzadik, and confronted his own heritage with the Radical Jewish Culture Series – subsequently, Jewish folk elements are found in much of his music. He's covered Ornette Coleman compositions, created the bands Naked City and Painkiller, and made several recordings of film music, including one dedicated to Ennio Morricone. He appeared with Beresford on Eugene Chadbourne's *English Channel* (1978), and on *Deadly Weapons* (1986). They performed *Cobra* in Switzerland, with Bill Frisell, George Lewis and Joey Baron, and collaborated on *Cue Sheets*. Zorn later appeared on Beresford's *Signals for Tea* (1995), with a band that was essentially Zorn's Masada, with Dave Douglas on trumpet, and Kenny Wollesen replacing Joey Baron on drums. Andrew Brenner's lyrics deal with life's vicissitudes in a witty, rather melancholic manner; Beresford sings them in a pleasant, almost conversational voice.

Deadly Weapons was a very bad, semi-pornographic movie about this woman who had enormous breasts.

That she used to suffocate men?
Exactly. And as we worked through the album, most of the titles became about film actresses. There's one about Tallulah Bankhead, and one about Jayne Mansfield. Tonie Marshall [the vocalist] was an actress and director, daughter of a famous French actress [Micheline Presle], and she was introduced by Jean Rochard who ran a record label called nato.[1]
Nothing to do with the North Atlantic Treaty Organisation.
It's an American Indian name – nato, not NATO. NATO in French is OTAN.
Organisation du Traité ... Atlantique Nord?
There you go.
   It was an interesting label.
It still exists, though it doesn't release so much. You did a lot with them?
Yes. It was tied in with a festival in Chantenay Villedieu, a tiny village near Le Mans – we played in a little chapel outside the village. I always thought nobody would come. It was completely dark – getting to the chapel, there was no lighting – but it was always packed. Quite a successful festival.
   Rochard regularly booked Lol Coxhill, Tony Coe and, one year, David Toop. I think David Toop, John Zorn and I made the trio performance first. Then Jean Rochard said okay, let's have a French actress [Tonie Marshall] involved. Tonie was a really good choice – she had a nice singing voice and was easy to work with. She was pleasantly surprised at how fast we worked, because in movies, actors sit around for days waiting for them to get the lights right, then it starts raining, and then somebody can't make it so you can't do the scene.
Where was it recorded?
At Dave Hunt's studio in White City in London. I don't think we went in with any material. Maybe some words or something. Basically, somebody would say "why don't we try this ...."
Fred Frith called it "vacuously atmospheric." It was also called "a film noir soundtrack music to a film which does not exist" – though obviously the porn film did.
I don't think there's any doubt it's atmospheric. But we certainly didn't sit down and think "Let's do something vacuous."

We didn't go in with a set of tunes or a set of intentions. [Tonie] sings one song that was already written. It's sort of a cappella, over the sound of distant foghorns, I think.

The idea of writing tonal songs, and getting someone to sing them – that was Jean Rochard's strong point, that he could invest time and money into something that looked like it wouldn't work.

You said the jazz magazines hated it – one of them said it was "chic elevator music for pseudo-leftist intellectuals," which you took as a compliment. This was an unobvious group to do this kind of project?

No, David Toop and I had done General Strike [1979–82] – we weren't against tonal tunes and metres. This was a side-project we had when we were in The Flying Lizards, based around loops and tunes. The way it was put together was unusual. We did Sun Ra covers at a time when not many people were doing them. David Cunningham made tape loops from things we'd played. We asked a few people to sit in, like singer Dawn Roberts, Lol Coxhill and violinist Maartje ten Hoorn, who were all very good. It came out as a cassette with Touch.

It was a recording band – we didn't do any gigs, till we revived it decades later for David Toop's seventieth birthday.

In 1995 you released another song project, *Signals for Tea,* **where you wrote the music and Andrew Brenner wrote the lyrics. It's a witty, whimsical set of songs, a kind of avantgarde Noel Coward, as one reviewer commented. How did it come about?**

I met Andrew on Brighton Beach when I was playing with the Promenaders. He had a T-shirt with a recipe for Chicken Surprise written on the front – the last word was "giblets," and he was known in those days as Giblet.

He had a band called The 49 Americans.[2] Their first album was a seven-inch EP, and I think each track was fifty-eight seconds long, recorded on a cassette recorder usually in the front room – you could hear somebody counting the seconds sometimes. David Toop and I both thought it was a milestone in very low-tech, post-punk songwriting – very witty, and pastiching different forms of music. I think there were four albums of The 49 Americans altogether. David Toop and I produced the last, called *We Know Nonsense* – we co-wrote songs with Andrew.

When I went on to write songs with Andrew, he would always come up with the lyric first. When I did a series of albums for Chabada and nato, with Lol Coxhill and Tony Coe, Andrew wrote at least one song per album. There were songs about the Marx Brothers, Charles Trenet, Doris Day . . . I tended to sing them. These were all ten-inch albums. Then John Zorn asked if I would like to do an album of my songs, which he liked very much. So Andrew Brenner and I wrote the songs that became *Signals for Tea*, with John Zorn and Dave Douglas.

He always wrote the lyric and I always wrote the music. Until a couple of years ago, his main gig was writing scripts for Thomas the Tank Engine – I think it's an animation. I'm not sure what he's doing now.

I did some other albums with Jean Rochard, including *Dancing the Line* [in 1985] with the Japanese vocalist Kazuko Hohki, and lyrics by Andrew Brenner. This was about fashion designer Anne Marie Beretta, which became a high-budget project for Banlieues Bleues, the festival in the Paris suburbs. There was some serious money, so we had a catwalk show without the catwalk – with Tony Coe, Alan Hacker and a couple of drummers. We could rehearse, and we went and hung out in Anne Marie's atelier. We wrote a series of songs, some of them instrumental, some of them with words, around her and her clothes.

* * *

KAZUKO HOHKI is a London-based artist, singer, theatre performer and director. She was born in 1952 in Tokyo, and moved to London in 1978. She founded Japanese cult-alternative pop group Frank Chickens with Kazumi Taguchi in 1982, which released five albums and toured worldwide. She has been involved in making theatre since the late 1990s, fusing storytelling with multimedia, film and animation. She has published four books in Japan about her life in London, and her aesthetic centres on semi-autobiographical themes concerning her life as an outsider. She writes:

> *I arrived in London from Tokyo in June 1978. I was 26 years old. England was the first foreign country I had ever visited, though I felt I already knew it well as I liked many English things, especially English children's books, which I read a lot while growing up in Japan. When I arrived in Heathrow holding my freshly made passport, I felt as if I was entering a magical world – but at the same time I felt surprisingly at home.*
>
> *On the second day my friend Clive Bell, who I'd met in Japan, took me to the Environmental Music Festival organized by David Toop at the London Musicians' Collective (LMC). There I saw Steve playing the piano with his feet, standing upside down. He also played many toys frantically, but sincerely. With my jet-lagged head, I thought it was utterly incredible. Steve had imprinted on me the essence of England on that night. It matched the image of the country I had formed since my*

childhood. That place where the real and the unreal cross and mix, the distinction between adults and children disappears, creativity overrules reason and originality repels conformity – the world of *The Borrowers, Mary Poppins, Winnie The Pooh, Alice In Wonderland, Dr Doolittle* and *Narnia*. I could never leave that world behind, even after I had grown up and been to university in Japan, where I had always felt a misfit and slightly ashamed of being myself. Steve Beresford's England cured my complex, though he was not quite Mary Poppins or Winnie The Pooh.

After I joined the LMC, I met Steve often. Though I could not understand what he was saying half the time as he talked so fast, our encounters were always fascinating. His brain seemed to work even faster than his talk and he often dismissed things as "boring." It was rather intimidating and I hoped not to be too boring for him – I was glad to be Japanese, which was still quite unusual in London at that time. Since then, we have collaborated on many projects – we made two Frank Chickens albums, and I made two solo albums with Steve's Piano Orchestra for the French label nato. To my ears, he created beautiful magic in those projects, just like those children's books I loved.

* * *

Alan Hacker improvises amazingly, on clarinets plus soprano sax, on *Dancing the Line*.
And he always said he was a terrible improviser! I got to know Alan through Tony Coe – they had a clarinet/ soprano saxophone duo that segued from the theme to Alfred Hitchcock Presents, into free improvisation, then a piece by Harrison Birtwistle for two flutes, transcribed for saxophones. They were both extraordinary classical clarinetists. Alan was in The Fires of London – Peter Maxwell Davies' ensemble that performed *Eight Songs for a Mad King*. He died about ten years ago.[3]

Did you know Kazuko Hohki before?
These things intertwine. Kazuko Hohki was one-third of The Frank Chickens, who originally sang karaoke. David Toop suggested we could write some new tunes with them – we did one and a half albums. This was a time when Japanese people were – as Kazuko said – unusual. There was still a certain "Ooh! What is this funny food?," and Japanese pop music wasn't very well known. The Yellow Magic Orchestra were just coming up – and karaoke, the culture around monsters and Godzilla, and girl groups.

Kazuko Hohki Sings Brigitte Bardot was with a small Anglo-French group. Brigitte Bardot did some great songs. She did some catchy ones by Serge

Gainsbourg, and some good songs by Gérard Bourgeois – a lot of her hit records were cheesy and charming. Kazuko looked nothing like Bardot and didn't sound like her, which we liked. So it was an Anglo-Japanese tribute to Bardot's recording history, which was a lot of fun.

* * *

JEAN ROCHARD created nato records in 1980. He began writing about music in 1976 for various publications, which he still does. He created the Chantenay music festival (1978–88) and in 1995 was a founder of Les Allumés du Jazz, a collective of independent record labels. He sees music as an essential language, and this remains his principal motivation.

> *Meeting Steve Beresford was one of the decisive encounters of life's little adventure. He represented a generation challenging the codes of free improvisation, and allowed me, and many others, to get familiar with many genres of music, some of which I continued to love almost covertly. It gave me the feeling that it was alright to like many different things at the same time – that loving Evan Parker was not opposed to loving Dionne Warwick, or the Kinks. Free Music became an element of a gigantic and very lively fresco, in which songs, funk, rap, soul, calypso and many other styles took their place in an endless exploration – a highly liberating idea, and an experience of freedom in music. With Steve, music had all kinds of connections to other parts of the world, all kinds of expression. My search as a "producer" – the word has its strangeness – has been strengthened by those developments.*
>
> *We often chatted about movies, and corresponded a lot by postcard. Ideas were fast and plain. Singing – and what a singer! – was just as natural for him as experimenting with whatever elements were around. Being in the studio with him, there was always the joy of invention, of exploring all situations, of transforming anything. There was no standard model, but each situation became a challenge – a kind of challenge without gravity, but with a lot of depth and a strong poetic aspect. We had a lot of fun. Steve has a real sense of what musical language and its translations are, as if he had the dictionary ready at all necessary moments. With him, exploration and inventiveness were not opposed to grace and charm. One of his solo albums, just before we met, was called "The Bath Of Surprise." With Steve Beresford, surprise is always what it is about.*

* * *

How did you get to know John Zorn?
The first time I met him was on my first trip to New York, with David Toop and Nigel Coombes – I used the money I'd been paid for playing on the last Portsmouth Sinfonia record, *20 Classic Rock Classics*.

I stuck around after Nigel and David went back to London, and appeared on a record with Eugene Chadbourne called *The English Channel* (1978). It had Zorn, and lots of the New York guys from that period. So, I knew Eugene already, I think.

I played with Zorn, Chadbourne and Toshinori Kondo at a club run by Giorgio Gomelsky called Zu Space in downtown New York. It didn't have a back wall, I noticed one day – I pulled the curtains back and you just saw outside.

Fred Frith was there – I knew Fred already.

I imagine you'd have a sense of humour similar to Eugene Chadbourne's?
Yeah, a bit.

But John Zorn?
He's got a sense of humour. He's very funny.

He's also very sensitive.
I'm told. I've never knowingly pissed him off.

Maybe it's just writers he has a thing about.
Ah, yes – writers.

The first time I worked with him, I thought he was a bit of a prima donna but after that, I never had any trouble at all.

You were involved with Zorn's game pieces early on – *Cobra* and *Xu Fung*. What's the principle behind them?
Cobra is the ultimate game piece – you have a prompter who sits in front of a semi-circle of musicians, who can prompt changes in the music. But changes are decided by the musicians as they are playing. It's extremely funny. You can see Zorn's face, he was conducting us – the audience can't see this. You might try and gain his attention, but he might turn you down.

I did *Cobra* in Switzerland, in Zorn's band with Bill Frisell, George Lewis and Joey Baron. It was recorded, I think, but not issued. We played a few days. I think that was where that great Zorn/Lewis/Frisell trio was born.

I love Bill Frisell. I've known him for many years, we were in groups together, and I think he's a really great musician. His style has a slowness which I like, and it gives him time to twiddle knobs on pedals. The joke was when he was in Naked City he never played fast; even when they were playing thrash [metal] he would be playing half-speed. He doesn't play fast. Everything he plays is him.

He uses more pedals than Derek [Bailey] did – he's more interesting than most of his generation of jazz guitarists because he's constantly changing the sound of guitar. Dynamics are really important. He has a really organic approach.

Zorn is a great patron of the music.

He is a *huge* patron. He thinks he's a genius but then, he thinks lots of people are – it's not like he's undiscriminating, but he loves other people's music. There's stuff he loves that I don't like at all, like spiritual minimalism . . .

Arvo Part and Gorecki?

That kind of stuff. I can't stand it. Zorn is very well versed in the history of the music. He plays really good alto and is incredibly versatile and really, really good to musicians. I've never had a problem with him. He's just delightful to work with.

Like you, he doesn't like jazz snobs.

I didn't know that. Though I used to be one myself . . .

At a gig in the late 1980s at Leeds Trades Club, he wore a T-shirt that said "Jazz Snob Eat Shit."

But what does he mean by "jazz snob"?

Wynton Marsalis, I think.

Oh, yeah.[4]

* * *

In an interview with Richard Scott in 1988, you said you weren't doing much free improvisation.

That's right – it was very strange.

I very rarely turn a gig down – things go one way or the other, and it's nothing to do with what I'm trying to achieve.

There's a time lag – it takes a while for people to hear what you've been doing.

That's a possibility.

I never make any conscious decisions. Radu Malfatti or Cornelius Cardew put up walls and said "Everything I did before this was wrong." Cardew disowned *The Great Learning* and the Confucius pieces – which I think are fantastic – when he became a Maoist.

He thought he had to do populist music.

Or what he thought was populist music – most people wouldn't think of it as that. And Radu became a high priest of minimalism. He denounced the pieces he wrote for the Brotherhood of Breath, which I thought were great.

He was in the Brotherhood of Breath?[5]
Exactly. Nick Evans was also a trombonist with Brotherhood of Breath – he gave up playing, and did maths tuition or something. I really liked his playing. I'm a huge trombone fan. I'm thinking of buying a small plastic trombone.
There are plastic trombones?
Yes. I think they're fantastic.
Charlie Parker and Ornette Coleman played plastic alto saxophones.
The Grafton was a good saxophone.

If you go to the basement of Honest Jons, they have one hanging up. The problem was, if you broke it, there was no way of repairing it, although I would have thought by now there would be the technology to put it back together.

You mentioned the Brotherhood of Breath. In the 1990s you produced tribute recordings by the Dedication Orchestra on Ogun: *Spirits Rejoice* (1992) and *Ixesha (Time)* (1994).
Evan [Parker] was instrumental in putting it together, with Louis [Moholo] and Hazel Miller. It was about twenty-five people – that's quite a lot, I think the Count Basie band was about sixteen. The Orchestra was a tribute to Chris McGregor, Dudu Pukwana, Mongezi Feza, Harry Miller and Johnny Dyani, and it was very nice to revisit their compositions. I think that was the first time I worked in Gateway Studio in Kingston-on-Thames – obviously we needed a large studio to record in.

Dudu and Chris wrote a lot more tunes than the others, but each of them wrote at least one amazing tune. They were in very different styles – a bebop twelve-bar [blues], a township one, a luscious ballad. There was a single album, and then a double album, with a variety of arrangers – Mike Westbrook, Django Bates – who'd been associated with those composers.

I was the producer of the records, and conductor when they needed one – I did a couple of arrangements, including Chris McGregor's "Travelling Somewhere," which was a feature for Lol [Coxhill]. Evan wanted a vocal aspect, which most orchestras don't have – because there's a great tradition of singing in South Africa. So the Orchestra included vocalists – Maggie Nicols, Julie Tippetts, Phil Minton and David Serame. And we supported Ladysmith Black Mambazo, at the Vancouver Jazz Festival.

South African traditions use quite simple harmonies, like STAX in soul music – harmonically simple, but the language is so powerful. Louis [Moholo] can play very straightforward but exciting dance rhythms.

You love that music, but you don't play it – though there's nothing so unusual about that.
I did sit in for Keith Tippett in Vancouver – he couldn't make it.
You mastered that style?
I don't think I mastered it at all! Keith sounds more like avantgarde Count Basie in that context – I really like that, it's very sparkling piano-playing.

* * *

South African drummer and improviser LOUIS MOHOLO-MOHOLO was born in Cape Town in 1940. Following the 1962 Johannesburg Jazz Festival, where he won first prize for drums, Moholo became drummer for The Blue Notes. He has since been a member of Brotherhood of Breath, and led his own bands Spirits Rejoice and Viva La Black, which toured South Africa at the end of the apartheid era in the 1990s, releasing the album *The Freedom Tour*. Moholo has toured extensively across Europe, America and South Africa, and collaborated with Cecil Taylor, Kenny Wheeler, Derek Bailey and Evan Parker.

I heard Louis in Five Blokes recently.[6]
That's a great band – they're really exciting.
Sometimes they're Four Blokes.
Sometimes Shabaka [Hutchings] is there, sometimes he's not – there's always Jason Yarde, Alexander Hawkins and John Edwards.
They change the title accordingly.
Well, you would do, wouldn't you?
You wouldn't!
Louis Moholo constantly reinvents himself. The group that I put together a few years back, featuring Guillaume Viltard and Louis, was originally going to be a trio without a drummer. Then I realised that Louis was in town, and that it would be mad not to have him. So it became a conventional John Coltrane quartet-type line-up. But we had a lot of fun with it. The first gig was at the Vortex.

I realised that I needed to see Louis [when performing] – sometimes John Edwards was standing in front of Louis, and I would ask him if he could move back a bit. Sometimes I don't look at anybody, but it was important in that band to see the drummer.

Shabaka Hutchings said that every time he tried to do something, it was as if Louis took him by the hand and led him away from it – he was always ushering him away from clichés. I think that's true – he's incredibly good at keeping you in a regenerative state of mind.

I took Louis to a club in Portobello Road one evening, and they were playing George Shearing [as muzak]. He got quite impassioned and told them they should be playing free music! For him, free music is totally intertwined with the end of apartheid. Everything he's playing is to do with that struggle, with taking apartheid apart.

He's the last of the South African exiles to Britain – who all died from illnesses arising in some way from their life under apartheid.
He was the guy who survived.
He's in amazing shape.
Every time I hear him, he's better than the last time. He's a huge inspiration.[7]

* * *

Your album with Otomo Yoshihide, *Museum of Towing and Recovery*, was released in 1995 – that's a great title.
It came out on Hot Air, a see-through vinyl ten-inch record.
What did Otomo play?
He played turntables and electronics, I was on keyboards and electronics. He plays guitar too. Hot Air liked the music immediately. I must have sent them fifteen different album titles, and the one they liked was *Museum of Towing and Recovery*. It's the name of a museum in Chattanooga, Tennessee. The full name is Museum and Hall of Fame of Towing and Recovery.[8] The whole museum is about recovery trucks – I went there, it was great.

You know those big photographs that look like oil paintings? The Hall of Fame is a series of middle-aged white men in similar suits, who've won awards for their endeavours in the field of towing and recovery. People with tow trucks, recovery trucks. They have a Ford Model T tow truck, it's really cool. They discovered I was English and they said, "You must look at the Hall of Fame because there are several English people in the Hall of Fame of Towing and Recovery!" I was thrilled to find a picture of a man from Manchester who'd won the annual award for Towing and Recovery. He looked exactly like all the other men. It's probably the number of vehicles, but heroic acts would be great. That would probably be a special medal or something, saving a baby or doing it in a violent thunderstorm.

I was there because of the Shaking Ray Levis, a group from Chattanooga who worked with Derek Bailey quite a lot – I don't know where the name comes from.[9] I worked with them and went to Chattanooga three or four times. I really liked it.

At that time I'd been taking Otomo to theatrical material shops in Berwick Street. They did hideous purple-sequinned material for light entertainment artists, and at least one of them had its own record label, specialising in electric organ records. It was the post-Reginald Dixon era, and these were MOR cheesy organ records from the 1970s – blokes with enormous flared trousers and bouffant hairstyles, playing medleys of songs from the shows.[10] Otomo really liked them – they ended up in Cheapo Cheapo Records, also in Berwick Street, for twenty-five pence each, so he bought a pile.

I think I took my Farfisa VIP500 organ to that session. That was my severance pay from The Slits. It's still under my bed – it doesn't seem to work anymore. When they split up, I thought, "I'm going to keep the organ," because I quite liked it. But being a piece of 1970s technology it's ridiculously heavy, so I rarely took it anywhere. On the album, sometimes it's cheesy organ records that Otomo's playing, and sometimes it's me playing the cheesy organ. Reginald Dixon definitely had input on that record.

Neal Hefti used cheesy organ on his Batman theme-music – it's on YouTube.[11] I didn't know the bits with Farfisa solo. Excellent!

My Dad's favourite record was *The Atomic Mr Basie*, all written by Neal Hefti – I know the Eddie "Lockjaw" Davis solo on "Whirlybird" by heart.

RIP Adam West [who played Batman, and died in 2017]. He was very good in *The Big Bang Theory*.

* * *

Born in 1954, saxophonist JOHN BUTCHER began playing in jazz bands whilst studying physics at the University of Surrey. After completing a PhD at London University, he focused on music. His first album was *Fonetiks* (1984), a duo with pianist Chris Burn. In 1992, he joined the final version of the Spontaneous Music Ensemble, with John Stevens and Roger Smith. His work involves improvisation, his own compositions, multi-tracked pieces, and explorations with feedback. As a solo performer, he engages with the uniqueness of place; Resonant Spaces involved site-specific performances from a tour of non-concert locations in Scotland and the Orkney Islands. His recent compositions include "Good

Liquor . . ." for the London Sinfonietta. Recent collaborators include Gino Robair, John Edwards, Polwechsel, Rhodri Davies, Okkyung Lee, Keiji Haino, Mark Sanders, Eddie Prévost and Matthew Shipp.

Since the 1980s, you've worked a lot with saxophonist John Butcher. I think of him as a "sonic researcher," perhaps because of his scientific background.
He constantly changes the perspective. He can be playing like Peter Brötzmann, or a cooler thing. Sometimes he comes across a bit like a scientist, and at other times, like a post-r 'n' b free jazz saxophone player. I really like that about him.

He's using feedback a bit more now – he did it early on, and he's brought it back. There's a microphone on a stand onstage that goes down the bell of the tenor, and by changing the position on saxophone, he can change the pitch of the feedback – or stop it by moving the bell away from the microphone. It's a tipping point thing. Obviously you can't have totally untrammelled feedback, but you can use it in different ways.

"Research" is like the word "experimental" – Cage didn't like that term, as in his comment "I do my experiments at home, and you don't hear them."
Alvin Lucier's *Vespers* has people wandering around the hall with electronic handheld echo-locating devices – the clicks get faster, the closer you are to an object. That feels like an experiment, though you're not gathering data, you're creating a piece of music out of it. Equally, a feedback thing would be dependent on the features of the room, which could change if it's full of people.

A scientist can have a hunch, or a good idea, what the outcome of the experiment will be. "Research" is a correlative notion to "experiment" or "experimental."
The Michael Nyman model – from his classic book *Experimental Music* – is that you set something in motion, and you don't know where it's going to end.[12] That's why he rigidly excludes any form of free improvisation – though he touches on AMM. You might set up something quite carefully, but then it will run through its own pattern.

Isn't that more like indeterminacy?
I think the idea of seeing where something goes, once you've set it in motion, is Nyman's model more than Cage's – although obviously Cage figures in Nyman's book. I think it's a great book – I was just disappointed that none of the people I was working with at the time were mentioned.

I first heard John Butcher at the 100 Club in Oxford Street, of all places. I think he was playing with an early Chris Burn band. He immediately impressed me – I thought he was a fantastic saxophone player.

He's a free improviser who's furthest from jazz – though he sometimes sounds like a free jazz player.
I think he likes Lee Konitz, and Paul Desmond.
It's hard for a saxophonist to resist a jazz sound.
I think John did resist it. I remember John Stevens being very excited when he first heard him – he said, "He's got a more classical sound on tenor."
A classical sound is usually fairly horrible.
Yes, but John's sound is related to that – it's certainly not Coleman Hawkins or Ben Webster or Coltrane. John has a more "legit" sound – he doesn't sound like John Harle, but he doesn't have a jazz grain. It's very weird, that classical sound – of course, it was designed to blend in with the orchestra.
Some people say that Konitz has a classical sound – but it's not true, it really is a jazz sound.
It's like a kind of racism – that Aretha Franklin is a black singer, but Dionne Warwick isn't because she's got a lighter voice and she doesn't do as much improvising. There are lots of traditions in African-American music.
The jazz sound is never vibrato-less.
Vibrato is actually to do with changing pitch – tremolo is to do with changing the dynamics. For instance, on Ben Webster's ballad-playing, some of his notes end in air.
You can certainly hear Coltrane in Evan [Parker].
Some instruments have a heritage of what's predominantly been played on them – piano and violin have a classical heritage, for instance.
Absolutely.

John Butcher writes [email 2018]:

At first, I mostly heard freely-improvised music semi-accidentally, as a side effect of going to jazz gigs in the 70s. Some was amazing, especially if Derek Bailey was involved, but it could be confusing too. Steve probably puzzled me the most. Was his contribution music, or "just" playing games with music? Fortunately, for me, Steve was one of the least abstruse writers in "Musics" magazine. I put it down to reading him there, that I began to slowly adjust my thoughts on what a musical performance, and a musical life, could be. By the time we first played a concert together – in 1992 at These Records in South London – I no longer made distinctions quite like that, and I'd imagine Steve had changed a bit too.

I've worked with Steve as an improvising partner, the boss, MD, conductor and composer. He loves, and has a deep and practical knowledge of, so many areas of music and sound-making, it's mind-boggling. Somehow, this all feeds in positively to his own music. He's a true original, on and off the bandstand.

He responds to our discussion on "research":

Part of my attempt to expand the saxophone's colour-palette was to discover ways of playing that avoided the usual ingredients of jazz – those ideas of flow, rhythm, and wind-instrument phrasing. I used to try to imagine I was doing real-time "musique concrète" tape splicing, or layering electronic sounds and filtering them – but all acoustically.

But over time I've found it fruitful to reintroduce more of the typical saxophone role into my encounters . . . I made a decision to just use the sax – and I think it always sounds like a sax – even if I'm just using air sounds or feedback or violent tonguing.

Regarding "research" – I think this is best when the seeds of it come from the actual playing situations, and I guess this is something in common with jazz (in its pre over-schooled days) whatever the results may sound like.

Other musicians that Beresford first worked with in the 1980s and 1990s include Paul Hession and Hannah Marshall.

Drummer PAUL HESSION was born in Leeds in 1956 and took up drumming when he was fifteen. Largely self-taught, he began playing jazz in the mid-1970s, and free improvisation in 1980. He has played and recorded with Derek Bailey, Paul Rutherford, Marshall Allen, Peter Kowald, Joe McPhee, Evan Parker, Squarepusher and Jeb Bishop. While relishing the interaction of collective music-making, he also responds to the challenge of solo performance. He was awarded a PhD from Leeds University in 2018, his thesis titled *Augmenting Percussion with Electronics in Improvised Music Performance*. He writes:

In August 1998, I invited Steve to come to Leeds for two nights to lead The IML (Improvised Music Leeds) Ensemble, with a rehearsal on the first night followed by a performance the following night at The Adelphi pub. The brief was to devise a piece(s) for the group which could use graphic or conventional notation, with verbal or written instructions, conduction or any other method that the musician chose. Steve was keen, and by phone, quizzed me about the ensemble's instrumentation and experience.

At that time, the group consisted of alto/soprano sax, alto sax/clarinet, cor anglais/ oboe, four tenor saxophones, trumpet, French horn, electric guitar, keyboard and drums. Steve devised a piece called "Check Your Change," presented as a combination of graphic symbols and written instructions on six large sheets of 18-stave notepaper with minimal conventional scoring. The score was clear and easy to negotiate – I'm sure that Steve had considered this, as there was only one 2½ hour rehearsal.

During the performance at The Adelphi, he alternated between directing the piece and playing his small instruments set-up on a table top. There was an emphasis on controlling the sounds and playing with great delicacy, as well as allusions to different musical styles – instructing the guitarist to play "octaves like Wes Montgomery" or the drummer to play a "medium shuffle" and the horns to "play your most or least favourite slow tune"! Steve's sense of humour and his catholic musical taste were clear, and the music was well received by players and audience. Although Steve claims not to have run improvised music workshops, his direction of the IML Ensemble was keen and skilful.

*   *   *

I love Hannah Marshall's cello-playing. I really like her trio with Veryan Weston and Satoko Fukuda. I'd love to work with her more. But not many people offer me gigs where they say, "Who do you want to play with?"
The people who are rung up and asked, "Who would you like to play with?" – that would be Evan Parker and not many others?
You might well be right.
I guess there's few people on the scene that you don't know.
Most musicians between the ages of forty and seventy, on the UK free improvisation scene, I know.
Most improvisers are not interested only in their own music, because they play with other people.
I don't know anyone who only performs solo.

HANNAH MARSHALL is a London-born improvising cellist who also makes theatre with The Ding Foundation that she co-runs with Amelia Pimlott. She collaborates with artists in dance, visual art and film, as sound designer, musician, composer, and other roles that she has to make up. She has worked with Veryan Weston, Trevor Watts, John Butcher, Roger Turner, Ingrid Laubrock, Tony Buck, Evan Parker, Sylvia Hallett, Shabaka Hutchings, Maggie Nicols, Christian Marclay and Steve Beresford. She writes:

> Steve seems to be involved in the totality of music-making, including but not exclusive to place, people, community, seriousness and silliness. There are few gigs

that I go to where Steve isn't there, and to my great pleasure he is often in the audience to support me. I really appreciate his caring for a community of creative musicians. He seems to be present, through the peaks and pitfalls of keeping experimental music alive. So Steve is as much a listener, a talker, a digester, an audience companion as he is a music-maker. I have learnt a huge amount from watching him perform. I often have the sense that he is battling away at some intensely complex game of Space Invaders that is captivating and limitlessly rebellious. I think of Steve as a real improviser – turning on a dime, he seems to enjoy testing the waters with something that, played with less conviction, would seem wilfully inappropriate. I am delighted to receive feedback from him, especially when he doesn't like something. He speaks with honest subjectivity, and we enter into a pleasant disagreement – keeping things in play both musically, and communally.

Notes

1. Tonie Marshall (1951-2020) was a French film actress, screen-writer and director, best known as director of *Venus Beauty Institute* (1999).
2. A British DIY post-punk/art pop supergroup, active from 1979 to 1982, and created by US expat Andrew "Giblet" Brenner in London.
3. Alan Hacker (1938–2012): www.theguardian.com/music/2012/may/03/alan-hacker
4. Wynton Marsalis is discussed in Chapter 13, "The Improv Scene."
5. South African pianist and bandleader Chris McGregor formed the Blue Notes in the early 1960s, with Mongezi Feza, Dudu Pukwana, Nick Moyake, Johnny Dyani and Louis Moholo. Suffering government harassment, they fled their homeland in 1964, settling in London in 1966 and making a great impact on London's jazz scene. The Brotherhood of Breath was a successor band, comprising the Blue Notes plus British players, and released three albums during their peak years between 1971 and 1974.
6. http://www.londonjazznews.com/2016/03/festival-report-bergamo-jazz-festival.html.
7. See *The Wire* 400, June 2017, *Invisible Jukebox* by Louis Moholo, tested by Mike Barnes.
8. https://www.atlasobscura.com/places/international-towing-and-recovery-museum.
9. The Shaking Ray Levis are a Chattanooga, Tennessee-based collaboration of free improvisers, conceived by Dennis Palmer and Bob Stagner; Palmer died in 2013.
10. Theatre organist Reginald Dixon (1904–85) left school at fourteen to become a church, and then cinema, organist in Sheffield. He worked for forty years at the Tower Ballroom in Blackpool, where on Wurlitzer organ he developed the

characteristic Blackpool sound for dancers. He made over three hundred records, and at the peak of his popularity the audience for his weekly half-hour radio programmes averaged six million. His signature tune was "I Do Like to Be Beside the Seaside." There is rare video footage of him at www.youtube.com/watch?v=K-U7yl7tvtU.

11 Hefti, Riddle and the Caped Crusader: https://www.youtube.com/watch?v=kK4H-LkrQjQ
12 Nyman (2011).

11

Film Music + Christian Marclay + Video Artists + Visual Art

Beresford has diverse experience with the medium of film. He has written several film soundtracks, and taught film music at Westminster University. He worked with John Zorn on *Cue Sheets,* and with Christian Marclay on *Screenplay,* a thirty-minute video comprising Hollywood film clips. He has also worked with video artist Blanca Regina. This chapter covers the value and problems of writing music for film, including the difficulties of working for directors with little apparent understanding of the contribution that music makes. We look at writing for commercials, and the changing environment that curtailed Beresford's career in the medium. We then move on to the aesthetics of film music, including the concepts of score and underscore. Experimental music has had enduring affinities with the visual arts and art colleges, and we conclude with a discussion of that connection.

The first movie soundtrack I did, in 1987, was Liria Begeja's *Avril Brisé,* set in Albania, based on a novel by Ismail Kadare, Albania's most famous novelist. The film was French-produced, very low-budget – it had an actor in it who looked exactly like Richard Gere. I loved doing it.

I used Max Eastley. We had a scene in an abandoned Albanian village, and there were black slates everywhere – Max plays slates, it's semi-white noise, but they do have pitches. Then at very short notice I added Alan Hacker, on soprano sax and clarinet.

I'd been sent EP's of Albanian music by the director, which I really liked – it was incredibly bleak. So is the movie.

The three features I've done have been very different.

The second was *Pentimento* in 1989, directed by Tonie Marshall, and the third was *Bollywood Queen,* directed by Jeremy Wooding – that was a musical, and obviously you can't shoot a musical until you've got the music. I co-wrote the music with [singer] Najma Akhtar – we'd already done a short film on a similar theme, called *Sari and Trainers*, set in Brick Lane [in London's East End].[1]

Bollywood Queen was a homage to the Bollywood genre, also set in Brick Lane. I wrote string parts and sent them to Mumbai. They came back with authentic Bollywood strings, with glissandi, portamenti and ornamentations. Everything else we recorded in London, including a more Vaughan Williams sort of string ensemble. Director Jeremy Wooding was very nice to work with, because he said things that were really useful. It was his idea to use a DJ, because he wanted a contemporary edge – a great idea. So we used a very good improvising DJ – Patrick Carpenter, who I knew as DJ Food.[2] I'd seen him play with Steve Noble and others. Then Jeremy said, "The DJ sounds like he's on his own a bit too much. There's a gap between him and the live music, why not use a few more samples?" So we made samples of some of the phrases from the Bollywood strings and spun them in like a DJ. Samples helped because they were recognisably from the score.

What Jeremy suggested made sense, and it was useful to have that feedback. A lot of directors are really hard to work with because they have no idea why the music isn't working.

In film music, you're writing music for things you haven't seen?
No. Occasionally the music's written beforehand – I think Michael Nyman did that for Peter Greenaway, but I'm not an expert on their work.

If I had the choice, I would never work with anything but a final cut. But filmmakers like to fiddle with things – you write the music for a scene that you think is finished, and then they'll move everything by a couple of seconds, which is not big for them but is really big for a composer. I *hate* that.

Writing for film is mostly time-consuming in terms of things that the director has changed at the last moment.

With a musical, obviously you have to write the music in outline first. You must have a pretty well final vocal, you need to have a rhythmic structure, though you might not have put in all the parts.

You also worked with film-maker Helen Petts.
She was directing a programme about weddings in a TV series with [writer/presenter] Paul Morley called *The Thing Is*. I brought in Alex Balanescu on violin, and it turned out Helen was interested in free improvisation. You don't expect that from a TV director. Then it turned out she lived up the road from me – she still does – and we became friends. She subsequently worked with free

improvisers on a series of films. Sylvia Hallett, Adam Bohman, Roger Turner and Phil Minton worked on one on Kurt Schwitters. Those musicians and montage go together well. She makes beautiful films where the music is very important. There's a lovely one on Lol Coxhill.

The violin pieces I wrote for her were definitely schmaltz.

I also did the music for her film *Space & Freedom*, improvising on prepared piano [in 2018]. It's about the artist Li Yuan-chia, who had an art gallery, and was very interested in experimental music, and John Cage. [Recording engineer] Dave Hunt and Helen came over to my house, and she just said things like, "Play something slow for five minutes." We got a series of cues that she fitted into the film.

* * *

Artist film-maker HELEN PETTS was born in 1956 in Yorkshire. As a teenager she met Tony Oxley at Ronnie Scott's, saw Lol Coxhill play in Amsterdam and attended Feminist Improvisation Group (FIG) concerts. She worked in mainstream film and TV as researcher and director. But after studying Fine Art at Goldsmith's College in her forties, she turned to more experimental film-making. She set up an early YouTube channel *helentonic*, an archive of creatively filmed free improvisation. Her recent film installations have been at Manchester Art Gallery, Hatton Gallery, Newcastle, Royal Festival Hall, London, and Trøndelag Centre, Trondheim. She writes:

> I have been sitting in cafes in Portobello Road talking about music with Steve Beresford for the last thirty years. He is my neighbour, and we both had dads who were 1950s dance-band musicians; we were both involved in left-wing politics in the 1970s, and go to the same gigs. I first met him in 1990 when I was a TV director and needed a composer for a Channel 4 arts documentary about weddings, seen through the satirical eye of Paul Morley. I wanted music that could add an extra layer of humour to the film, and Steve was the perfect choice. I knew of his improvisation work through the London Musicians' Collective. He was a massive fan of Doris Day, and composed some slightly too romantic violin pieces, played by Alex Balanescu, and solo piano played by himself. Since then Steve has introduced me to some amazing musicians – Lol Coxhill, Phil Minton, Roger Turner, Adam Bohman, Sylvia Hallett – that led me to making films with them. This has totally changed the way I work, and was an important element in my shift to more experimental films. The humour, the element of chance and playfulness, the need to work in the moment with sometimes small, very low technology equipment,

have now become my way of working as well. I use sounds and silence in much more intense detail. In 2018 I invited Steve to improvise on prepared piano for my film "Space & Freedom." His music is delicate, haunting, hesitant, fractured and playful – and absolutely right, as it interacts with my field recordings. That is collaboration at its best.

* * *

I don't do so much writing for film now because most people just use library music – that whole area of writing for media has gone, for all sorts of reasons. It's much more difficult to get a job, and the budgets are zilch. There's all this pitching, where they ask three or four different composers to write a piece of music for nothing, and you give it to them, then they choose, and say, "OK, you've got the job." I absolutely hate that, because having auditions means they don't have faith in what you're going to do. If there's no faith in what I'm going to do, I can't really write the music.

I need people to have faith, then I know what the fuck I'm doing. If I work with John Edwards and Mark Sanders, they know I can do it. That's not an issue. It's not like anybody's checking me out to see if I can do it before they say yes to it. For instance, I did a gig with Pat Thomas last night, and he's enormously encouraging all the time.

What about jealous rivals?
I suppose there might be a couple of gigs I've done, that people would like to have had. And obviously people would like to have won the Paul Hamlyn Award.[3] But I've never encountered a jealous rival.

Anyway, I tend to turn those film jobs down – I don't do stuff for nothing. In a lot of situations, you should do stuff for nothing. Of course I play music for nothing all the time, and obviously if it was a little student film, that would be a different thing, but anything that's for a TV show, they should have a music budget, and they should make a decision about the composer and stick to it. It's not that difficult. You don't sack an actor halfway through the shoot, do you, unless they're really bad?

Many directors have no idea about music.
That's a huge problem – it's really bizarre. There are people who've got fantastic knowledge of dialogue, what cameras do, costumes – and who really do not know the first thing about music. I've been in a studio where the director said, "I don't like the toy piano in this." But there wasn't any toy piano – they meant

the accordion or something. This is somebody who works with musicians all the time, and they don't know the difference between the sound of a toy piano and an accordion.

It's completely bizarre, but it happens all the time. Directors know music's really important, that it can create moods where you haven't got a mood in the film – it can suggest things that aren't suggested in the film, and it can do it in a mysterious way. But rather than finding out how that mysterious stuff works, they leave it as a mystery, and that means it's really hard for composers to work with them. Not that I have, but I know composers who've said things like "Well, there are four people in this scene, so I wrote it in four beats to the bar."

You must have heard some idiotic descriptions.
Very idiotic.

They're taking the piss out of the director.
Yes! But directors love this kind of talk. They think it's conceptual. The violin has four strings! How great is that? Four people, four beats in the bar: how fantastic is that? Somehow that makes them feel secure, they've got something to hang on to – rather than asking "Does this music work in the scene?" Directors find it very hard to talk about music – particularly about genre. They often have a very lowbrow interest – they like music that sounds like Kenny G or Eric Clapton. Clapton's the most boring guitarist . . .

Isn't he a skilled technical player?
No, he's not.

He's an imposter?
Yes.

It almost feels like every year directors are going to some kind of class and they're told, "This year, you will like Michael Nyman."

Michael Nyman and Peter Greenaway started off making films for the Central Office of Information – films about how to plant your crops. So their own early films, which I think are very funny, are parodies of Central Office of Information films. They're quite short, not features, and they're genuinely funny – and the music works really well. Then they made *The Falls* [1980], a mock documentary about victims of a Violent Unknown Event, whose surnames begin with the letters "F-a-l-l." It's completely hilarious.

The sheer pointless repetition of Michael's music in *The Falls* is in itself funny.

Greenaway thinks of himself as a painter in images.
Steve McQueen came out of visual art, and he's a really great film-maker.

What went wrong with their film-making?
I don't think Peter Greenaway ever really understood cinema.
The Nyman–Greenaway collaboration is one of the rare cases where the music is as important as the images. It's a real partnership. And on a certain level, they're beautifully made films.
Definitely. The things about *The Falls* that it lacked, made it an interesting film.

Years later, when Michael [Nyman] was much better known, I got called in to the Central Office of Information, next to Lambeth North station [in London]. I'd done a couple of jobs for them, and I was brought in to talk about another one. They said, "Frankly, we would have asked Michael Nyman, but he's much too expensive now, so we've asked you." That's great! That gives me a lot of confidence in the project. The woman who spoke to me said, "I'm not going to give you any clue as to how the music should sound, because I've no idea about this. It's the same as all my movies, I never know how to use colour. For instance, you'll notice I'm only wearing black and white." Her explanation was that she knew when it was right or wrong, but she didn't know why. That kind of stuff comes up all the time. At least she was honest about it.

There are exceptions.
I've never worked with Scorsese or Kubrick. There's a documentary about Bernard Herrmann where Scorsese talks with him about the score to *Taxi Driver*, which I think is a fantastic score. It's absolutely central to the movie. You could take the movie away and you would still feel the same thing.

Scorsese used lots of bought-in music for *Mean Streets* – the Ronettes, the Rolling Stones, music with a greasy surface. He's very knowledgeable. He did that series about the blues. Directors I work with a lot do know something about music.

You wrote soundtracks for commercials – I imagine that might be fairly lucrative.
It was certainly more lucrative than playing the upstairs room in a pub. But I think people got the impression that somehow I was getting paid a million pounds per advert.

I did a Victoria Tea advert for my brother-in-law, Andrew Gillman, for Japan. The schtick was that "Victoria Tea is England's favourite tea" – which was not the case, we've never heard of it. We did three adverts, all based on teddy bears. One bear was crossing the Abbey Road zebra crossing, another was having a suit made in Savile Row . . . They wanted something quintessentially English, so I gave them a large number of sketches. Elgar, Vaughan Williams, The Beatles

– what is quintessentially English? We ended up with a kind of jazz piece that didn't seem to me to be quintessentially English at all.

You did commercials for the Norwegian Vital insurance company, Sure deodorant, and Ovaltine Power.
I don't remember Sure deodorant. The Ovaltine advert said "Ovaltine gives you power."

I thought it was supposed to send you to sleep.
Yeah, I know. There were lots of power-chords in it – it was very short, a ten-second piece of music.

My brother-in-law directed *The Day Today*, Chris Morris's parody of a news show. I think it's astounding. It had Steve Coogan, Rebecca Front – but they weren't famous in those days. I had a small part – I played a Mattel Optigan organ, for a supposedly bought-in American news item about a couple on death row. It's been decided that as they get married, they will be electrocuted, so they make a double electric chair.

I was asked by the director to play "Stand By Your Man," and "Mr Blue Sky" by Electric Light Orchestra. They got me a Mattel Optigan quite accidentally – it came from a place called Beat Around The Bush, a music shop in Shepherds Bush. This is an early playback organ, a toy organ, with a 12-inch slot. You get these transparent discs, like LPs but floppy, to slide in – a drum-machine loop, a cat miaowing, the sound of breaking glass. . . . I knew about the Optigan, and I was thrilled to get to play one.[4]

Did you decide to stop doing commercials, or did you just stop getting called?
I stopped getting called.

Also, it became a standard thing to expect you to do a demo, for no money. I said, "No, I don't work for nothing."

Commercial work can be very soul-destroying – I'm not saying anything new here. The endless to-ing and fro-ing with the director and the client – and then another person from the client's company comes in, and they finesse it to death. I've done adverts where the whole point of the advert was obliterated by the endless numbers of changes I've had to do.

* * *

The *Cue Sheets* project with John Zorn was based on soundtracks. How did you get Zorn interested in that project?
I didn't get him interested. He was interested.

Did he contact you?
Oh, yes. He'll tell you if he's interested, and if he's not interested, there's nothing you can do about it. I like that, that's great, it saves a lot of time.
These were all soundtracks or theme music to British TV programmes.
Not all television. Some of them were little indie films and things.
They were originally done with the idea that they'd be released together?
No, they were different projects, completely unrelated.
Do they have a unity?
I think so. Some of them were hack jobs that we tried to make as interesting as possible. Sometimes you do music that's very simple and isn't really worth listening to on a CD, but which works in the context of a movie.
I love "Screaming Reels."
They gave me a lot of scope there. It was interesting, the director really didn't mind what I did, it was one of the few times when they've been very non-prescriptive.

The series was about fishing. The reel screams when the fish bites it. There was a proper budget, and once we'd established the general genre, I could run with it, which is nice. I think that's how directors should work with actors, generally speaking. You tell the actor, "It's about this, you have to stand there, go!" I think you get a much better result than if you try to control everything. An actor acts. That's what they do. Musicians create music. Once you've set the parameters, it's probably best to leave the musician to get on with it.
You felt the music was being treated more equally?
That depends on the technical role of the music. For fairly obvious reasons, opening titles music has a more important role than music under dialogue.

* * *

American/Swiss avantgarde DJ and video artist CHRISTIAN MARCLAY was born in California in 1955 and brought up in Switzerland. He explores the relation between sound and image, and hybrids of music and visual art.[5] Much of Marclay's work involves working with turntables and records. In an early series entitled *Recycled Records*, he assembled broken pieces of vinyl records that could then be played. *Video Quartet* from 2002 comprised over seven hundred film clips on four synchronised screens, all with a focus on music and sound. Beresford was involved in *Screen Play* from 2007, in which Marclay composed a silent collage of found film footage partially layered with computer graphics to provide a framework in which live music can develop. "Moving images and graphics give musicians visual cues suggesting emotion, energy, rhythm, pitch, volume, and duration. I believe in the power of images to evoke sound," he comments. The film was interpreted by three small groups of musicians – including Steve Beresford, John Butcher, Roger Turner and Blevin Blectum.

You've had a long association with Christian Marclay.
I think I first met him on one of The Slits' tours of America. We got on very well. I knew him at that time as an avantgarde DJ. Nine or ten years ago he moved to London, and of course since then he's worked much more with British musicians. He's Swiss-American – his wife Lydia Yee is chief curator at Whitechapel Gallery.

I worked with him on *Screen Play*, a twenty-minute montage of clips from movies – black and white clips with colour overlays, coloured shades superimposed on the footage. You use the film as a score, usually with three small improvising ensembles. I've seen lots of different performances. Some people use realistic sound effects – for instance, if there's water on the film, you use the sound of water.

I always like using it as an improvisation, but using it as a score, rather than trying to underscore it. But sometimes you have to use it like that.

I don't really understand that.
An underscore is the music that's accompanying action on the screen. There's a book about it by Claudia Gorbman – *Unheard Melodies: Narrative Film Music*. We're only talking about traditional movie music here, not the way that Godard uses music, for instance – which is very interesting and different. On a conventional movie, most of the music is meant to be unheard.

People are not supposed to attend to it.
Say someone is sitting reading a newspaper, and the composer might be told – "At this moment, they see an article that says their brother has been arrested." So their emotion changes, but the actor doesn't show it – a lot of good screen acting is doing absolutely nothing. The music will be the only clue – it will go into a minor key, or there'll be tremolandi, or two bass clarinets playing.

The underscore is essentially a vehicle of manipulation.
Film is manipulative. I don't mind being manipulated.[6]

Another example – we cut to a grass-covered hill, and hear the bagpipes, so we know it's in Scotland. Or someone is thinking about their beloved, and we hear a vibrato-filled leitmotif.

There are many roles for underscore. One of the things is that we're trying to sellotape the movie together. Underscore gives it a unity in various ways –

by a set ensemble, or by a particular harmonic language, or by material that recurs. Say there's a cut from a duck in a pond, to a raging inferno. The music in conventional films is a kind of glue, to give it more continuity.
The aesthetics of film music is a really neglected area – which reflects the ignorance of directors that we've discussed. It's such a vital aspect of film, and so poorly understood.
I think you're right.

* * *

Christian Marclay's *Screenplay* is an approximately thirty-minute video comprising film clips, occasionally superimposed with animations of lines, dots, and colour-fields. (It seems to be spelled as either *Screenplay* or *Screen Play*.) *Screenplay* was created by Marclay as a "visual score" to be interpreted by a small group of musicians. Marclay's visual scores aim to expand the possibilities of graphic notation, and improvisation is essential to them. Musicians respond to any visual aspect that could function as notation. Literally, an image of a train could suggest the sound of a train; a city street could suggest frenetic sounds; the musician could mimic on the instrument the movement seen in the film; or they could do all or none of these.[7]

* * *

The principle of going through a cut with the music is a very important one – particularly when we come to *Screenplay*. It's not a conventional film, it's a score – so if there's a sudden change in the film, maybe the music should have a sudden change. There'll be a sequence of pictures of the sea, and then you will suddenly have a ballerina. Do you stop at the cut between them, which – as it's a live performance – is very difficult, to change directly on the cut, as opposed to after the cut? John Butcher and I ran the video, and tried to do things on the cuts, rehearsing changes – that's not something an underscore would do. But we just got more confused. So we decided, "We're going to improvise, because we know we can improvise."
It's an interesting concept, that you have to treat what you're doing not as film music, but as following a score.
In a way, that's what we're doing. But we're not doing it mechanically – "here's a change so the music should change." And it's also technically very difficult. Some people prepare it very carefully, with lots of detailed Foley.[8] If you're saying this

is a score – except it's images not music notation – then absolutely you would change the music when there's a cut [in the images]. You have some music for the sea, and then some different music for the ballerina.

The issue is, *film music* doesn't work like that – it does not see the images as a score, it sees them as a sequence of events that need something underneath it, the underscore. Generally, the underscore glues those scenes together – the sea, the ballerina – by not stopping or radically changing on that cut. Something might change – drums might drop out, the tempo or the key might change – but not radically.

Carl Stalling's Warner Brothers cartoons changed incredibly fast and very abruptly. A hillbilly violin is interrupted by an enormous explosion, and a bassoon playing a sad tune – exactly in sync with what's going on onscreen. It's called "Mickey-Mousing." They never do that on *The Simpsons*, it's much more underscored.

Is the rapid change method an older one?
Yes.

With *Screenplay*, we always end up between those two extremes. But what we have to offer is that we improvise, not that we remember very complicated scores – that's Ian Pace's gig.

There's a grey area between the underscore and the score.
Of course. Gorbman does say that. She says that there are all these rules that are habitually broken.⁹

Everyone recognises *The Third Man*'s "Harry Lime Theme." Is that the score or underscore?
There's a point where the music is so strong, it becomes a score. *The Third Man* is an amazing film. They had no idea what to use for the music, until absolutely the last minute. And somebody said "What about this guy, Anton Karas?" Nobody thought too much of it, and of course it's one of the most recognisable movie scores ever.

It's a combination of zither and guitar. There's film of Karas playing it. You can't bend strings on a zither, which he does all the time. He's really adept at this – he worked very hard at it.

Sometimes the Morricone scores for spaghetti Westerns do this – you know, "du-ey, u-ey yah!" It's the most obvious leitmotif. So there's a point where the music is so strong, it becomes a score. You can't get away from it. It's very often to do with instrumental timbre, more than anything.

Bernard Herrmann was one of the few Hollywood composers who did his own orchestration – most of them farmed it out. You know the stabbing scene in *Psycho*. Most people were looking for a nineteenth-century Wagner or Richard

Strauss big string sound. Herrmann didn't remove all the vibrato, but it was a colder sound. Michael Nyman has inherited it. And also that use of the repeat – John Williams' score for *Jaws* feels like a Herrmann score.

Bernard Herrmann always wrote in 2/4, because composers got paid by the bar.

I used to teach *Lift to the Scaffold*, Miles Davis's score for the Louis Malle film. It's a fantastic film – ultimately the plot's a bit ridiculous, but it's so well done. It's a love triangle – one of the ironies of the movie is that the lovers never meet. Miles has a very good band, with Barney Wilen and Kenny Clarke. The chords are quite vague – it's the beginning of Miles's interest in modal jazz, and it's interesting how he bleaches the harmonies out. There's minimal Foley – you're in the middle of Paris, but you don't hear much in terms of footsteps or traffic.

We learn there's going to be a murder only when the lover goes to a drawer and takes out a gun. If this was Herrmann, it would have dramatic music – he'd probably have three contrabass clarinets and arco basses. But in *Lift to the Scaffold*, there's no music in that scene at all – it starts only when the guy with the gun moves towards the victim. And it's a Harmon-muted trumpet, which in those days wasn't associated with adverts for expensive perfumes.

Schoenberg complained about the redundancy of expressionistic film music. If you see that the character is taking out a gun, why the three contrabass clarinets?

It depends what the movie is. Sometimes you do need that. I think Herrmann is such a tasteful composer.

* * *

Theatre, Dance, Art

I never go to the theatre – all these people on stage pretending to be people they are not.

You're a fan of Brecht, though.

The cast recording of *The Threepenny Opera* is one of my favourite recordings ever. But I like Kurt Weill's songs with other writers, such as "Speak Low" which had lyrics by Ogden Nash – he worked with lots of different lyricists after he moved to America.

You love related forms like movies, so you have a particular problem about it being live.

Yes.

I like dance when it's Merce Cunningham, who I saw with Cage in the 1970s.

Actually I've enjoyed working on dance films. But I wouldn't want to work with most dance groups, live. I was in Steve Blake's ensemble for the Cholmondeleys and the Featherstonehaughs.[10] I enjoyed being a sideman there – Steve Blake is a great musician, and great to hang out with.

As Blanca Regina mentioned, Unpredictable did two exhibitions at Oto's project space.

I did just archive stuff, photographs and things like that. I've never done visual art – except for one piece, for Poloumi Desai's show at Usurp Gallery in West Harrow [The exhibition, titled "Naissance," was held in 2010]. She said, "You know when you put things on tables, why don't you do something like that?" So I just put small objects on a Thai folding children's table – that's the closest I've got to any form of visual art.

This exhibition [at Oto] was art done by musicians?

Yes. Terry Day does lots of visual art. Evan Parker gave me two tiny little Duchampian pieces – one's a bit more like Joseph Cornell, actually. Max Eastley makes beautiful sound-sculptures. David Toop brought photographs of people playing. It was a mixed show, about improvised music.

It's not uncommon for musicians to do visual art. Cage did.

He's really good!

And Schoenberg painted, mostly self-portraits.

Schoenberg was a *terrible* painter. They're awful!

There's one of the back of his head.

It must be better than the ones of the front of his head.

But of course he hung out with Kandinsky, and they were very interested in the relationship between music and visual art. I think Kandinsky composed, but I don't know what his compositions were like.

Kandinsky had synaesthesia.

I went to the Rauschenberg exhibition at the Tate the other day – amazing. I loved all the connections with Cage that I kept seeing. The plexi-glass creation ["Shades," 1964] is a very Cagean idea – Cage used overlapping transparencies to create scores.

I love the variety – like Max Ernst's frottage. Virtually everything I loved. At secondary school there were lessons about art, none of which I could relate to, until we got to Abstract Expressionism. Kandinsky, Klee and Miro were the three figures I liked immediately – I just felt I got it.

Notes

1. Najma Akhtar is a British-born singer, songwriter, composer and actor, and a pioneer of fusing Western and Eastern musical styles, including jazz and ghazal (Urdu ballad) and sufi (devotional poetry) repertoires. Her debut album *Qareeb* (Closeness) was followed by several others including the latest, *Five Rivers*. She writes: "I have learnt a lot from Steve as he has introduced me to the world of improvised music, seeking out new ways of expression. His knowledge of jazz and other genres, including very strange avantgarde music, never ceases to amaze me. He has an eclectic directory and memory of musicians, writers and producers."
2. DJ Food is also a collective, originally formed by members of Coldcut.
3. Beresford was awarded one of the Paul Hamlyn Awards for 2012, and received £50,000 over the following three years.
4. The Optigan – the word is a portmanteau of "optical" and "organ" – was released in 1971 by Optigan Corporation, a subsidiary of toy manufacturer Mattel.
5. See www.tate.org.uk/art/artists/christian-marclay-6852, http://whitecube.com/artists/christian_marclay/
6. Manipulation in art is discussed at the end of Chapter 15.
7. See https://whitney.org/Education/EducationBlog/MarinaRosenfeldSpeaksAbout PerformingScreenplay.
8. Foley is everyday sound effects added to film, video and other media in post-production, to enhance audio quality.
9. Coatsworth (2019) argues that Gorbman is wrong to assume that because film music is not listened to closely, it is "unheard." He argues that she does not address cinematically compelling spans of cinema without music, so it is not clear that music has the privileged status that she claims.
10. The Cholmondeleys are a London-based, all-female contemporary dance company, formed by Lea Anderson and others in 1984; in 1988 she established an all-male company, The Featherstonehaughs.

12

Graphic Notation + John Cage + Classical Music

Conventional Western scores use staff notation, but many of Beresford's collaborations have involved unusual concepts of the score, and left-field methods of notation, including *graphic notation*. Many of these are more open, rather than closely specified. For example, most contemporary Western musicians regard a system of notation that leaves pitch open – as medieval notation did – as alien. But John Cage upset their assumptions. However, openness is always relative. Cage was very specific in certain parameters, and not others; for instance, his *Number* pieces specify duration, but not pitch or instrumentation, very closely. Anthony Pryer's *New Grove* entry defines graphic notation as

> A system developed in the 1950s by which visual shapes or patterns are used instead of, or together with, conventional musical notation. One category attempts to communicate particular compositional intentions: Feldman's *Projection* (1950–51) and Stockhausen's *Prozession* (1967). Another presents visual, often aesthetically pleasing, symbols, to inspire the free play of the performer's imagination, such as Earle Brown's *December 1952* (1952), and Cardew's *Treatise* (1967).

Graphic notation in the first sense uses shapes and images to define parameters not easy to capture in conventional staff notation.

Graphic scores perhaps undermine the distinction between interpretation of a composed work, and improvisation. Thus Corey Mwamba comments about one recording session:

> I asked the saxophonists whether they each felt they were "improvising" or "reading." One musician said they were clearly improvising, even though they were paying close attention to the score. Another countered that they were in fact reading: "everything was coming from the score."[1]

And Roland Dahinden comments on his score *Talking With Charlie*, a mix of conventional and graphic notation dedicated to Charlie Parker, "In the graphics the players find a balance of interpreting and improvising, together with my conducting."[2] He agrees that "the graphics undermine the distinction between interpretation and improvisation." The interpretation is subjective – not like a code to be worked out.

This discussion brings us to Cage's occasional influence on Beresford's aesthetic. JOHN CAGE (1912–92) was a hugely influential avantgarde and experimental composer, most famous for his "silent piece" *4'33"* – four minutes and thirty-three seconds of apparently silent performance. In the 1940s, Cage became interested in East Asian philosophy, which influenced his aesthetic of non-expression. His highly distinctive approach to composition centred around indeterminacy and chance. In the 1950s, Cage worked with Earle Brown, Morton Feldman and Christian Wolff, exploring indeterminacy through such works as *Music Of Changes* (1951), composed using the *I Ching*, a classical Chinese divination text. In 1959, Cage recorded *Indeterminacy* with David Tudor, who improvised on piano and recording equipment in one room, while Cage read a series of minute-long passages in another, neither able to hear the other. From 2010, Beresford toured *Indeterminacy* with comedian Stewart Lee, and performance/sound artist and free improviser Tania Chen.

Several of your projects with Christian Marclay featured graphic scores.
We did a Barbican gig featuring *Graffiti Composition*, with John Butcher, Orphy Robinson, Alex Ward and others. This composition was created by Christian posting up music manuscript paper on the walls of various places in Berlin, then going back and photographing what people had done with them – which was sometimes writing conventional music notation, or weird notation, tearing them, painting on them. Photographs of this became the score.
Is this graphic notation?
That's a good question, because Christian is always blurring the distinction between conventional and graphic notation. It's important to remember that he doesn't read music himself.

Bad music notation is a sort of graphic notation.

A lot of Christian's music is based around designs that use music notation, by people who don't read music – decoration for sweet wrappers, album covers and so on. There's a piece called *Ephemera* that comes in large folios, about twenty-six of them – rostrum camera shots of a table covered in things that have music notation, chocolate wrappers, record sleeves. These serve as your notation.³

What makes something graphic rather than conventional music notation? That it's meant to inspire you in some imaginative but subjective way?
Well, every year one of my students has the idea of looking at a Kandinsky [painting] and playing it as a score – that's an understandable first reaction to the idea of graphic notation. Classically, perhaps the best-known piece of graphic notation is *Treatise* by Cornelius Cardew – a whole book of black and white, very neat images. The published version is quite hard-edged – the original was sketch-books, I find that much more exciting.

It always has two staves at the bottom, but there's nothing on them. Famously, Cardew didn't want to give anyone an idea about how to interpret it. Whatever rules you might construct – such as "when the line rises, so does the pitch" – Cardew does something that makes it clear that you can't use the score like that.

I guess in graphic notation, any rule is subjective.
What does "graphic" mean?
The *OED* says, "relating to visual art, especially involving drawing, engraving, or lettering" – from the Greek *graphikos*, "writing, drawing."
In Bach's day, as you know, there were many things left out of notation – tempo, dynamics, instrumentation. These were not part of what Bach wrote down, because there was an understood way of playing his music.

It's only [relatively] recently that people have felt everything ought to be in the score. With Bach, it's clear from reports that what they were doing amounted to improvisation, and that a lot of the stuff isn't in the score. It's also clear from the fact that you've got figured bass – just as a jazz keyboard-player would look at the chord symbols.

If the score says simply, "Play a loud note followed by a quiet one," that in a sense *is* absolutely definite. Peter Kivy argued that in medieval music, where people didn't specify very much, actually the score is very specific in its own terms.⁴
Even up to Romantic music, how much decoration people put in, we don't know. We can sort of draw conclusions. That's how we know that Bach was playing with a swing feel – *notes inégales*.
So he was a jazzer.
That's the theory – from the way they designed the violins.

He didn't need to "Go To Town" – he'd gone to town already.
My dad had a record of "Bach Goes to Town," played on some early electronic instrument. Alec Templeton [its composer] was a Welsh guy who went to America. Benny Goodman played it – quite nice.
So – musicians knew that a sarabande was a certain tempo.
If you read Ben Piekut's book *Experimentalism Otherwise* – and also David Grubbs' *Records Ruin the Landscape* – you'll find that this applies to figures like Cage too.[5] As with Bach, the people working with Cage understood what he wanted – and it's clear that they improvised within that style. He didn't call it that, for all sorts of reasons. He always thought improvisation was indulgent self-expression, which, for theoretical reasons, he didn't want.

[David] Tudor knew what Cage liked and didn't like. For instance, he knew that Cage wouldn't want a repeat echo on a sound – that's not him. And introducing a whole record of Elvis Presley into a performance would not be to Cage's liking.

Cage did make aesthetic choices, despite what he said. That doesn't invalidate his music – which I love.

Maybe there's a short period [in the twentieth century], particularly with Stravinsky and Bartók, of very strict notation – Bartók's pieces have timings, they are all very carefully notated. But then you get to Brian Ferneyhough, where there's a different stave for every string of the cello, and you'll get hemi-demi-semiquavers, played ridiculously fast, each one with a different dynamic marking.
Is graphic notation a kind of reaction to that kind of extreme specification?
I don't know. I don't think it is. I think graphic notation appeared a long time ago.
What is notation? A set of instructions that enable performers to reproduce music too complicated to memorise. You might think that in medieval notation, they didn't specify the pitches because they didn't care about them – but it was because the players knew what the pitches were. That's a deflationary account of the score.
I think that simplifies the history too much. I'd guess there's a give and take between the score and musical performance. I think they piggy-backed on each other – that's my guess. There's a dialectic between producing music and notating.

A friend of mine went to classes with Don Cherry. Don had a rule of not writing anything down. He would sing a tune, and you would learn it. But my friend said it was very annoying, because he would sing the tune differently each time. Whether that was a form of psychology, or a failure of Don's memory, I don't know. He was very good at playing amazingly complicated bebop lines, with Sonny Rollins and Ornette. I would have thought that reading music would have helped him.

Most music around the world doesn't have notation. Don Cherry took much of his inspiration from music that doesn't.

When does interpretation become improvisation?

That's a good question. That's a whole book! Obviously cadenzas in concertos were traditionally improvised, usually with some reference to the material.

It's a matter of degree of freedom. The performer must always have some freedom, to express their personality.

I'd like to say that. But if you're playing on the last desk of the second violins . . .

I mean with small groups.

Yes. One of the reasons I like the Ligeti Quartet is that each member of the group has got such a strong personality. With smaller groups, that freedom is possible.

A less prescriptive Cage score might say, "Play a long note, then pause for ten seconds." A rather minimal instruction – you're helping to realise the score, not just interpret it.

That's a grey area, I agree. What do we mean by "long" – three weeks, or ten seconds? What do we mean by a "note"? These are not usually pure sine tones – there are overtones. On piano, could we sneak in a D over a G, if we played the D really quietly?

What's the boundary between a Cage-type score, and a graphic score? Though he did produce graphic scores.

Cage did an enormous variety of different scores. The graphic scores became something like paintings.

With a graphic score, maybe the performer makes an entirely individual response at the time – there's no rule. For instance, a star in a graphic score doesn't have a specific meaning.

Classical musicians love rehearsing – they have to rehearse. I imagine that Nancy Ruffer or Mark Knoop might say "I've got a star, what are we going to do for that?," and they might specify something.

Very often, composers kid themselves about how much looseness they are going to allow. A composer might say, "I want you to be yourselves and have fun with this" – which usually means they are going to micro-manage everything I play, because actually they have very specific ideas.

Christian Marclay is a great improvising musician, on turntables. He's spent years working with musicians who were not going to take any shit, like John Zorn.

Zorn is the epitome of someone who's not going to take any shit.
Absolutely. So it's very nice to work with Christian, because he understands what the parameters are.

Thinking about his use of notation that has gone wrong...
He doesn't know it's gone wrong – he doesn't read music.

You can find lots of products with designs based on music notation, all of which is complete nonsense, notation-wise – clearly the designer can't read music.

Christian Marclay was basing pieces on misunderstood conventional notation. *Ephemera* has that, because it uses an art director's idea of music notation.

Bad music notation becomes a sort of graphic notation – like, it says 4/4 and it has three beats in the bar.
It's like my favourite website Engrish, which every day has an amusing use of English, from Japan or China.

Shuffle is a piece I did in Finsbury Town Hall, with Sylvia Hallett, Byron Wallen and BJ Cole, among others. I wanted people with a strong sense of melody. It's based on those large, novelty playing cards – each one has a photograph, by Christian, from his collection of photos of music notation. We had a good time with that.

In 2011 we did *Pianorama*, an interactive performance for Ron Arad's "Curtain Call" installation at the Round House – various artists made films that were projected onto a huge suspended circular curtain of silicon rods.

Christian's was a 360 degrees endless piano keyboard. You saw my hands – quite a lot of them – playing short phrases. The installation wasn't interactive, but one night they got a grand piano in, and I played along live with my multi-handed self.[6] This reminded me of one of my favourite movies, about a sadistic piano teacher – *The 5,000 Fingers of Dr. T.* It's early psychedelia.

Everyday is an ensemble piece for Alan Tomlinson, John Butcher, Christian on decks, Mark Sanders and myself. It's about forty-five minutes and it's a montage, a sort of score – it says "play high stuff," or "play low stuff." We've done it a few times in music festivals.

* * *

Marclay's *Investigations* at Huddersfield Contemporary Music Festival (hcmf) 2018

Beresford was involved in the premiere of Christian Marclay's *Investigations* at Huddersfield Town Hall – Marclay was artist-in-residence at hcmf. The composition is at the more conceptual end of Marclay's output, and continues his exploration of the relation of sound and image through found objects and video. It illustrates the Swiss-American artist/composer's ethos of chance, interpretation and cooperation, using graphic scores with non-traditional notation. As well as Beresford, the twenty pianists involved at Huddersfield included Philip Thomas, Sarah Nicolls, Reinier van Houdt and Claudia Molitor.

The score consists of a hundred photos of pianists in the act of performing, with empty staff lines below – the performers transcribed what music they imagined each photo shows, shuffling the sheets before playing. The duration varies – this performance lasted about forty-five minutes. Many interpretations required two or more pianists to execute – as well as playing, we saw them sitting with their back to the keyboard, lying on the floor, going to get help, or standing on the stool. Marclay values performer participation, hence his half-ironic comment, "I get [musicians] involved in the process. I'm not one of those fascist composers who says, 'Play this!'" As Beresford said in a public interview later in the festival, "Piano players don't hang around together, because usually there's only one in any ensemble – the whole experience was lovely."

* * *

PHILIP THOMAS specialises in performing experimental notated and improvised music, as a soloist and with leading experimental music group Apartment House. His recent performances and recordings include the complete solo piano music of Christian Wolff and Morton Feldman, and music by John Cage, Christopher Fox, Cassandra Miller, Michael Pisaro and Linda Catlin Smith. He has performed recently with pianists Mark Knoop, Ian Pace and John Tilbury, and with the Merce Cunningham Dance Company. He is Professor of Performance at Huddersfield University, and co-editor of *Changing the System: the Music of Christian Wolff* (2010).

> *Steve Beresford talks. (A course which would be to everyone's benefit.)*
> *Tinkering, the importance of play (Christian Wolff)*

Elder statesman of the experimental.
V *– where others might stick two fingers up to the conventions of the concert hall, allegiances towards or antagonistic are of no concern here.*
Ego-free conduction. A gentleman, responding to all players' contributions with delight and curiosity, a reciprocal relationship. Tommy Cooper-like, everyone's in the know. No mystery here, just playing music.
B*ack to playing with toys*
E*nthusiastic, youthful, always engaged*
R*ushing off to another gig someplace else. An almost guaranteed presence at London concerts. Maybe there's more than one Steve Beresford?*
E*ncouraging, always.*
S*lapstick (but not as in Fluxus)*
F*oregrounding investigation, the practice of playing*
O*rganist, a solitary figure, back to audience, matter-of-fact, delighting in each new register combination*
R*ange of references to* ~~other~~ *musics and musicians encyclopaedic. (Anecdotes in abundance.)*
D*enying pretence of art, always curious, excluding exclusion.*

* * *

I think I've been more influenced by Cage in the last five years than before that – partly because it's just so difficult to avoid, but also because I work with people like Tania Chen.

Did Tania come from a classical background?

Yes. I think she started coming to improvisation gigs.

In 2002/2003 you released *Ointment* (Rossbin RS018), a duo with her.

There's very little piano-playing on this – it's mainly small instruments. I think the label went bust – Tania reissued it.

Tania and I did *Indeterminacy* with Stewart Lee, and produced a CD. *Indeterminacy: 90 One-Minute Lectures* was a double album which Moe Asch put out on Folkways. Cage recorded it in 1959 – he's in one room, David Tudor is in another, doing stuff with a Revox and piano; they can't hear each other. Cage reads these stories, all of which are one minute long – about Merce Cunningham, Jasper Johns, Japanese monks, things like that. Sometimes David Tudor's playing is sufficiently loud to drown out Cage – it's not an accompaniment, it's something that's happening at the same time.

Cage liked making rules, though usually fun rules, like this one: all stories must last one minute. Some of them have lots of words, so you have to talk really fast; some are quite short, so you have to talk really slow. Actually they're not all *exactly* one minute long. At certain points, David Tudor plays something from the *Concert for Piano and Orchestra*, or uses bits of *Fontana Mix*, I think. Sometimes, when he's louder than Cage, you'll miss the punchline. The stories are structured like jokes, they're quite funny.

I used to take CDs around to Tania's – because she didn't know much about pop music. Then I discovered she'd never heard Cage's *Indeterminacy* – given that she played lots of Cage, I thought that was funny. She said, "This is a fantastic record, why don't we do this piece?" I suggested that she and I did the David Tudor bit, and acted like we were not listening to the reader – but who would that be? I immediately thought of Stewart Lee, because he doesn't sound anything like John Cage.

I knew Stewart, and knew that he loves improvised and experimental music – he also loves The Fall, and country music, he's an obsessive record collector. Obviously he's a bit of an expert at talking in public because he's a stand-up comedian – one of the best I've seen. We've done it about half a dozen times now.

We have a table full of noisemaking things, and a grand piano. Stewart has a little table to the side. I was thinking "Oh shit, I'm going to have to transcribe every story." But just about the time we were going to do it, the publishers put out *Do Your Own John Cage "Indeterminacy,"* with a set of ninety cards, and even a kind of countdown, as to how fast you had to say them. Also we didn't know what rules David Tudor was using – but the score says you can do anything you like, or nothing. So we thought "OK, we'll just improvise."

When we do *Indeterminacy* sometimes we get lots of laughs, sometimes we don't get any. Partly that's because Tania and I sometimes make noises, which, as they say in comedy, step on Stewart's lines; sometimes people don't hear the last line of the story anyway.

When we did *Indeterminacy* on the South Bank, we had Harry Hill performing John Cage's *Waterwalk*. Cage performed it on TV – it was one of the great videos of all time! It was a game show, like "What's My Line?"[7] The presenter says to him, "Mr Cage, this is a nice audience, but they may laugh at what you do. Is that OK?" And Cage says, "I prefer laughter to tears," which is a great reply.

There's a score, and Harry did it maybe twenty times the day before the gig. This was Stewart Lee's idea – obviously I didn't know Harry Hill.

TANIA CAROLINE CHEN performs internationally on piano, keyboards, digital, vintage electronics, found objects and video, and creates multi-dimensional sound pieces for video and live performance. Her albums include *Ointment* and *Bad Dreams in the Night*, and Cornelius Cardew's Piano Sonatas. She is best known for her interpretations of Cage, having recorded his *Music of Changes*, as well as touring *Indeterminacy*. She has worked with Henry Kaiser, William Winant and Wadada Leo Smith, and recently recorded Feldman's *Triadic Memories* and *For Bunita Marcus*. She writes:

Things I know about Steve:
Steve and I like talking a lot on the way to shows, on tours and on long train journeys.

We have very different approaches to the piano. We both improvise. We share pianos a lot of the time, such as when we have played John Cage's "Indeterminacy" together with Stewart Lee. We are very good about sharing pianos, and also jokes and good chords. Steve has taught me a lot about humour and that's why we love playing "Indeterminacy," this combined with Cage's profound sobriety.

We play together as a stylophone duo with great sobriety.

I knitted Steve a scarf once which he has worn maybe once.

We both like shopping together. We do this more than rehearsing. One of our favourite shops is Tiger (of Copenhagen). Now I live in New York we compare the merchandise in both cities. Recently we both bought the same plastic DJ turntable. Mine didn't work as well as Steve's. He told me to buy three. Only two of mine worked. He convinced me it wasn't because of the American batteries.

We love eating together. Mostly Japanese food as well as Southern Indian.

Steve has taught me another thing: WHY MAKE THINGS MORE COMPLICATED THAN THEY SHOULD BE.

Also CHEAP GREAT THINGS ARE PERHAPS EVEN GREATER THAN EXPENSIVE THINGS. But we both enjoy a top-class grand piano.

Steve very patiently explained and drew inputs and outputs on a napkin when I first started to play gadgets that needed wires running electricity into them.

Whenever we meet we often quote that George Dawes song from "Shooting Stars": "In 1942, I invented the shoe, and in 1943 I invented the tree" (1944 was the year of the floor).

We made my first ever album together – OINTMENT – and it has never been bettered yet by any other ointment, even in a high-end pharmacy. I spent a lot of time snoozing on his sofa between takes. All proceeds went to an orphanage in a small village in South America.

We still don't quite remember how we met. I think it was over a cheese platter at the Conway Hall while I was in the last year at Goldsmiths.

I have learnt a lot from Steve about Derek Bailey and what life was like in London's early free improvising and experimental music scene – it sounds incredible.

Steve has always been incredibly encouraging, and will always remain one of my closest and dearest music friends whom I respect hugely.

* * *

Cage liked popular culture.
He loved being on TV shows, evidently.
But why did popular culture like him?
He was a very charming man, very articulate – he's immediately an interesting man. I think the *Waterwalk* interview is very entertaining.
Did you meet Cage?
I never met him, though I was in the same room when he gave a lecture at York. He was wearing a denim jacket cut like a suit-jacket – I thought that was *very* cool. I was super-impressed by him. The view at university was that he was a philosopher, but that his music sucks. I never believed that. I thought his music was very interesting.

I heard Cage at ICES [International Carnival of Experimental Sound] in 1972 at the London Roundhouse – a festival of new music organised by Harvey Matusow, who was married to Annea Lockwood. She made instruments out of glass, and put contact mics on grand pianos and burnt them.[8]

Matusow was – as they say – a "larger-than-life" figure, that is, a hugely egotistical pain in the arse.

I still have the ticket somewhere, it was a piece of plastic that looked like a piece of ice. They did Cage's *HPSCHD* on the first night – and Charlotte Moorman did a piece with so-called ice cello.[9] This was an enormous piece of ice they'd frozen over the road at Marine Ices – still one of my favourite ice-cream shops by the way. She played it with a glass rod, so it made no sound whatsoever – of course, she was naked, as well. It was a really horrible piece – can't remember whose it was.

ICES also did a lot of the early, quite aggressive, rhythmic minimalists like Jon Gibson.

Your music's not ideological, but there's a celebration of ordinariness, an anti-elitism.
That's a definition of surrealism – making the ordinary extraordinary.

There's a collection of small photographs by Brassaï, called *Sculptures Involontaires*.[10] A rolled-up bus ticket, some toothpaste that's dried on the end of a dispenser . . . very run of the mill things, they're fantastic, I wanted to use one for an album-cover. Those are very inspiring to me. I love the idea of the ordinary becoming extraordinary.

Yours isn't directly political art like Ken Loach's films, or Nono's performances in factories, or Cornelius Cardew's Marxist music.

No. I don't celebrate insane mass-murderers like Mao Zedong, as I think Cornelius did.

Did you know him?

A little bit. He was very sweet – he was very nice to me. Except at Musician's Union meetings where I sat with the Trotskyists. Then when I sat with the Maoists, the Trotskyists hated me. They always voted against each other's proposals. They wouldn't speak to each other. It was very Monty Python *Life of Brian*, really.

You don't like people who take themselves too seriously – you like to puncture pomposity.

Well, I love Scelsi's music, and he took himself very seriously. I don't get much of a laugh out of it, and maybe he was a bit pompous at times – sitting in his mansion with his ridiculous 1950s electronic instruments, creating this extremely arcane music, it was very exciting.

This is probably furthest away from the idea of worker's music. He was a great aristocrat, wasn't he?

His wedding reception was held at Buckingham Palace. In contrast to Scelsi's "aristocratic music," Christian Wolff's is intended as a model of social organisation.

I think Christian's done a pretty good job, but some of the pieces give me a headache to look at. Like "For One, Two or Three People." I love David Tudor's version of that, it's fantastic. I did look at this piece, but I thought "It's going to close me down." It's got directions something like "If someone plays three E flats you've got to play a B, but if they play a C you've got to play an F sharp." But why?

Cage based compositions on the *I Ching* – that's arbitrary!

On *Indeterminacy*, I'm playing an improvisation to go with Cage's words – in the style, and in homage, to David Tudor.

So much is left to the performer.

Cage's music isn't always like that – sometimes it's absolutely definite what you've got to play. There are a lot of different techniques. Sometimes the notation is conventional – or it still tells you a lot about what you're supposed to do.

Cage uses arbitrariness in all sorts of different ways, according to the piece. On *Indeterminacy*, the score says that the musicians can do anything they want – which obviously includes free improvisation.

From interviews I read, David Tudor and others who worked with Cage clearly knew that he liked this thing, and didn't like that thing. So quite often they were improvising, but steering away from stuff that Cage didn't like.

Are you ever in a situation where you think, "I'd better not do that, it doesn't fit with the ethos"? Or is it that it wouldn't occur to you?
It's more like it wouldn't occur to me.

When I played with Nigel Coombes, I think I played more obvious quotes. When I tried it with Satoko [Fukuda] it didn't work at all. I realised, "No, that's not part of this world." You don't consciously create a soundworld with a particular musician – it develops. My duo with Satoko has developed into something quite identifiable, without either of us saying "Let's play music that's like this." The same with Mandhira [de Saram].

Some composers have certainly despaired of performers. Cage did, at one point. I think that's where his quotes about being against improvisation are from, when he was trying to get conventional classical musicians to play music that they thought was rubbish. Some of the composers of that era – not just the modernists, but Cage with *Freeman Etudes* and *Etudes Australes* – wanted musicians to play what was almost unplayable.

Maybe the problem was that people understood how you can twist and turn nineteenth-century music with *rubato* – there's lots of ways you can interpret that music that didn't seem to be applicable to, say, Cage's music. People didn't feel comfortable playing his music because they didn't know what the parameters of interpretation were. And also some of them just thought he was an idiot. I don't know any improvisers who'd say that all orchestral musicians are robots these days – maybe they said it in 1973.

But thinking about really complicated music that's almost unplayable, like Brian Ferneyhough's – I heard him talk and I thought he was very interesting, very unpretentious and very lucid.

That struck me too – it seems surprising, given the complexity of his music.
It does. Composers have certain assumptions – that the person playing this piece of piano music, even if it's Ian Pace, is going to spend quite a few months of their life learning it. When I wrote string arrangements for Alex Balanescu, and he said "This bit's really difficult," I'd say, "OK, I'll change it." I have no compunction about that. But clearly that's not how classical composers function.

Part of the aim of New Complexity composers like Ferneyhough is to write things that are too difficult to play.
Or on the cusp of being unplayable.
That generates a kind of indeterminacy – you can't be sure what will result.
I think some of Ferneyhough sounds great – I've seen *Time And Motion Study* for cello and electronics, and I've absolutely loved it. How much the cellist fails to play what is written, I don't know.

When I went to secondary school, they started playing classical music, always Romantic orchestral music – the "1812 Overture", Mussorgsky's *Pictures at an Exhibition*, maybe a Rachmaninov piano concerto, a bit of Mendelssohn – and I didn't relate to that at all. The classical music I first related to was Bach's *Preludes and Fugues*, and then Vaughan Williams' "Tallis Fantasia," which I still think is a fantastic piece of music. I suppose it's Romantic music, but it's got a modal approach, which is very un-nineteenth century in a way, isn't it?

I don't choose to listen to a lot of Beethoven. I did go and see Ilan Volkov conduct the *Eroica* Symphony the other day. I don't mind it, but I wouldn't go away and say, "I've got to go and find the best record of the *Eroica*" – I don't have that impulse. Nigel Coombes does – as I said, he listens to that music all the time. I don't listen to much nineteenth-century Romantic music. Schoenberg's *Transfigured Night* is the best piece of Romantic music I've ever heard, it's the end of his Romanticism. I find it incredibly moving, maybe because I was brought up with Romantic music.

I bet for any improviser, if you name them, I can tell you some unexpected taste they have – for instance, John Russell loves Swing guitar players and is almost obsessed with that era of guitar playing. I think anybody you name, I could say, "Well, actually, I think you'll find that they love Pat Boone," or something.

You're a friend of composer Chris Newman, who now lives in Berlin.[11]
He had a band called Janet Smith which was small and subversive.

He writes symphonies – Symphony No. 10 is for violin and double bass.

Actually Symphony No. 12 he wrote for the London Improvisers' Orchestra, but it was logistically impossible, so he rewrote it for a solo soprano.

So it's not a symphony – which literally means "sounding together."
He keeps telling me, "What you did with the Flying Lizards in the 1970s was great," and I keep saying I had nothing to do with it, except miming.

He's a surrealist or Dadaist.
Maybe.

He wrote a piece for Tania Chen to play with COMA, like a piano concerto, which I thought was absolutely brilliant.

He's a composer, not an improviser. He likes talking about improvisation; he thinks he'd like to try it someday.

I was listening to Julius Eastman's Zurich Concert – it's like he's improvising on Berg's Piano Sonata. It's as if he's trying to resurrect a moribund form, which classical composers used to be masters of.

We know that Bach and Mozart were very good at improvising – I'm not sure that all composers were.

* * *

I've been playing with Mandhira de Saram a lot. She's from a classical background – she's the niece of Rohan de Saram, who was a member of the Arditti Quartet, and also played with AMM. She's first violin with the Ligeti Quartet. I met her through the pianist Liam Noble. I got a call from Mandhira who said, "Liam Noble says you're interesting, can we meet?" I went to a gig by her quartet, in Shoreditch. I thought it was amazing – I go to most of their gigs.

She did a solo set for us, for Strange Umbrellas.[12]

Violinist MANDHIRA DE SARAM, born in London of Sri Lankan parents, performs internationally as a soloist, chamber musician and improviser. She is a founder and leader of the Ligeti Quartet, and plays regularly as an improviser with Steve Beresford, Benoît Delbecq and TableMusic. She has collaborated with Wadada Leo Smith, Shabaka Hutchings, Pat Thomas and Alex Ward. She performs classical and contemporary compositions, experimental music and free improvisation, and works with sound artists and musicians across genres. Her violin teachers included Igor Petrushevsky, Howard Davis and Levon Chilingirian, and she currently plays a 1735 Sanctus Seraphin violin kindly loaned to her by Derek Clements-Croome. She comments [email, 2018]:

> *Over deep-fried soft-shell crab and hot sake at our favourite restaurant [Asakusa], I am, as ever, blown away by the breadth and depth of Steve's knowledge, and his knack for finding interesting musical objects! He is excited about his recent acquisition of a plastic alto trombone, and we discuss slide trumpets. I venture, rather sadly, that a plastic tuba might be too much to expect – I had recently started learning the tuba but couldn't afford to buy one. This leads to some hilarious stories about the Portsmouth Sinfonia . . . We laugh, talk to excess about very silly things, like the stunning technique of the Pistol Shrimp, and then matters more serious –*

opera singers with vibrato of around a fourth either side of each pitch. As usual, I feel as if I am absorbing a few years' worth of interesting facts and anecdotes over a modest dinner conversation. We discuss the album I've just recorded with pianist Benoît Delbecq. Pondering titles, Steve recommends Ian Rawes' "Honk, Conk and Squacket" – now my go-to dictionary for unusual descriptions of sound.[13]

In his playing, Steve balances a wicked sense of humour with a fine sense of interaction, reaction and even a face-off with his fellow performers. For me, a large part of making music is searching for an answer to some undefined question, concept, or even sensation. When I improvise with Steve or watch him play, I know I will be challenged constantly with new sounds and utterances. I don't think he sets out to say anything profound – in fact, he might dare you to find such truths in music. But I come out wondering if perhaps he does unwittingly present something which at least closely resembles such a truth. I am so thankful to have met Steve all those years ago. On my travels, I now take a quick peek inside pianos that I come across, just in case there's a little electronic bug lurking there, which he might have left behind. They're harder to find in the shops now, and who doesn't like the sound of a robotic insect inside a piano?

Notes

1. Mwamba (2020), p. 216.
2. Roland Dahinden, *Talking With Charlie* (Hatology, 2018).
3. David Toop comments: "In another life, Marclay might have been a professor of linguistics. He is fascinated by the language of signs, constantly returning to ideographic languages, semiotics, codes, translations and transliterations," *The Wire* 332, p. 43.
4. Kivy (2002).
5. Grubbs (2014).
6. "Painting in Slang" by David Toop, *The Wire* 332, Oct 2011, a feature on Christian Marclay, discusses the performance: https://reader.exacteditions.com/issues/9409/page/6.
7. Composed in 1959, and premiered on "Lascia o Raddoppia," televised in Milan, 5 Feb 1959. Subsequently performed on "I've Got a Secret," the popular American game show, 24 Feb 1960.
8. Matusow's ICES book – review in *The Wire* 401, July 2017.
9. *HPSCHD* is pronounced "Harpsichord."
10. https://www.pinterest.co.uk/pin/13159023883835600/

11 Chris Newman (born in 1958) is an English composer, singer, writer and visual artist. He studied with Kagel from 1979 and since then has lived in Germany. His work is hard to categorise, but shows affinities with composers and artists as varied as Christian Wolff, Joseph Beuys and Bruce Nauman. His ensemble Chris Newman and Janet Smith, which he describes as a rock group, shows his rejection of the distinction between popular and art music. He uses familiar Classical and Romantic materials, quirkily defamiliarised.
12 The "umbrella organisation" set up by Beresford and Blanca Regina – see Chapter 14.
13 Rawes (2016). The book provides titles for tracks on *Old Paradise Airs* (Iluso) by Beresford and John Butcher (2020).

13

The Improv Scene + The Audience

Our discussion of the social and economic context of free improvisation, begins with gender issues – its early gender imbalance, which is no longer as skewed as it was. We look at the existence of enduring groups, less common in free improv than in jazz. We discuss the availability of funding and the role of the Arts Council, and touring – and how players need to create their own gigs. We conclude with the nature of the audience, patronage and promoters.

You must feel that free improv was very male.
Of course it was – no question!

But Evan [Parker] was working with Irene Schweizer and Maggie Nicols early on in his career. Derek worked with Christine Jeffrey – she vanished from the scene, but I thought she was a fantastic singer. She was on *The Music Improvisation Company* on ECM [1970, with Derek Bailey, Evan Parker, Hugh Davies and Jamie Muir]. Obviously, Irene Schweizer is a total genius.

In New York, there seemed to be more women involved from the beginning. There was trumpeter Lesley Dalaba and the violinist Polly Bradfield.

If you look at *Musics* magazine, there were pieces about feminism – we were very conscious of that.

Did you come across chauvinistic attitudes in free improv, in the early days?
Not onstage. But yes.

Jazz also seems to have a problem. It has a particularly male audience – improv maybe less so.
Ironically, classical music has a lot more women involved in it than free improvisation or jazz – I'm talking about performers. Classical music has always had a larger percentage of women – it's more conservative, but perhaps it's not more macho than jazz or improv. There's huge amounts of bias in orchestras – there are very few women conductors, for instance.

Saxophonists and drummers used to be almost exclusively male.
Now we have amazing players like Rachel Musson and Julie Kjaer – Laura Jurd is a great [jazz] trumpet player. Not so many drummers, it's true.

That's partly because the free improvisation scene has got much bigger – in London at the beginning it was about twelve people.

The Feminist Improvising Group [FIG] got lots of gigs, because it was a box-ticking manoeuvre by promoters. Good for them, I thought they were a fantastic band.

Improvised music is collaborative in its values – but there must be players who can be accused of grandstanding.
Of course. There are people you think, "I wish he'd stop being so much of a show-off – but actually he's done really amazing things."

The male ethos would be high-energy free jazz – Mats Gustafsson and Paal Nilsson-Love – that is remarkably male. I like that music, I think it's great. Mette Rasmussen can do all that stuff – she's everywhere these days. She's a pretty classic energy saxophone-player.

The audience has changed hugely. But it's true, you can still go to gigs where it's almost entirely guys who drink beer and have beards – who are over fifty, and white. But they are really involved and dedicated people. I did a tour of Germany about a year ago [2017], and it did feel like the 1970s in London – they were all blokes. Everyone was very nice – I've nothing against blokes, obviously, but you'd get a much wider spectrum at Café Oto in London.

The other night at Oto, there was a fair proportion of women to see Alterations. It was a really healthy audience. We had a fantastic time.

Do you spend more time listening to live music than recordings?
Probably I do these days. I go to two or three gigs a week.

How would you say the scene has evolved in terms of popularity and numbers?
I think that happens in waves. I play a gig to two blokes and a dog, and the next night there's a couple of hundred people. That happens all the time. But Cafe Oto, and the spin-offs from that, has made a permanent change. There was a time when you could get a big audience for American players, but not for UK ones. I don't think that's true anymore.

There are lots more people who want to listen to the music – and lots more people who want to play it.

* * *

You haven't often been in enduring groups – Alterations was an exception. Is that typical of free improvisers?
I think so. I've worked with many different people. I've had quite a long relationship with John Butcher, but it hasn't resulted in lots of concerts or CDs. We recently put a duo record out, but if we look back at our duo discography, it's strangely thin.[1] There are lots of pieces recorded live as part of compilations, or half an album for Martin Davidson that was about a venue.

Alterations was the group that has gone on the longest – of course, it had a huge hole in the middle. Melody Four was ten years, but again, we didn't play all the time. The Four Pullovers was probably two or three years ultimately.

It's partly the nature of the genre, isn't it?
Oh yes.

Your seventieth birthday celebration at Oto in March 2020 was characteristic. A common format for a free improv event is a number of fairly short sets.
Actually, it's not so typical. I've not been to that many gigs recently that have consisted of four acts. For instance, when Fred Frith and Mike Cooper did their birthday residencies, they each had one group per night, which was a quartet. I love doing short sets too. Everybody I spoke to said yeah, we're very happy with short sets, but that's much less likely to happen now. We didn't let people ramble on. Not that you could throw someone off the stage halfway through a gig if they wanted to play twice as long. There's not much you can do about it but actually everybody respected that.

This rarely happens in jazz.
I used to go to Ronnie Scott's for the first night of the London Jazz Festival, and I think there were always four acts. You could call them showcases – the sets were twenty minutes at the most.

But in free improvisation, it's quite common to get a pool of eight or ten, and an evening would consist of various combinations.
Yes – Derek [Bailey] didn't invent that format. I'm not sure if that happens so much now.

In jazz you have a pickup group that does standards, or your own group with material you're presenting – and you want people who know the material. In free improvisation, that's not the way.
There is no material until you start making it, yes.

But is that entirely true? Material can't be created from nothing, and yours seems to have a wide range of sources. For instance, that sounds like a quote, around the 18-minute mark in *Shining Leaf* with Terry Day [Unpredictable].

It's not a quote, it's a generic pastiche – Satie's pieces for children, and/or 1930s novelty piano music about toy soldiers. I think I quote styles, rather than from a specific piece. I just recorded a two-minute piece on video, for John Russell's Mopomoso next week, and I realised that it's like a boring piano exercise that Victorian children used to learn. It wasn't a deliberate quote, it was just how the phrase came out. Or I might hit on a chord that sounds like a Bill Evans chord. Mostly those things pop up absolutely by accident.

I like music that reminds me of things, I have no problem with that.

Of course, there are master quoters – Sonny Rollins, for instance. Clearly he's a genius, and he likes quoting.

I don't do that – but one of the styles I end up quoting in, is Satie's children's pieces. Lol Coxhill played them with a Japanese rock 'n' roll band, I recall.

This is a big issue, which we'll have to leave for another occasion. It arose because we were talking about groups.

Yes. In fact there were enduring groups in free improvisation. Misha Mengelberg and Han Bennink; Evan Parker and Paul Lytton. Sometimes, it's a trio with Barry Guy or somebody else but the Evan and Paul combination has been there for decades. The Schlippenbach Trio with Alex Schlippenbach and Paul Lovens was the classic group that went on forever. I'm not sure Paul Lovens is playing so much now but I love that trio. I saw them at Cafe Oto and thought, it hasn't got stale at all.

But you don't have a partnership quite like that.

No, definitely.

The groups you've mentioned are closer to free jazz. In jazz, if a player like Lee Konitz isn't in a group, you're looking for some explanation – maybe it's because they don't like running a band. In free improvisation, it's not untypical.

I have relationships I go back to. It's not like I won't play with John Butcher for a year now. But I can see that point, the ones I mentioned were mainly free jazz groups.

There's not many people that would agree with Derek Bailey that things often get worse when you get too familiar with people.

That may have been influenced by his history with Evan Parker.

But Derek always adored playing with Han Bennink. That was an enduring relationship, well documented on records. You can track that band from ICP4, which was really early, which absolutely completely turned me around in terms of understanding how people play together and how you play guitar and how you play drums; it's an amazing record. But I've never heard a bad record by those two.

There's no equivalent to Lee Konitz showing up in Nottingham, and being fixed up with a piano-player, bass-player and drummer. That doesn't happen in free improvisation. Somebody did write to me the other day, asking to do a trio with myself and this great saxophone player. I couldn't find anything online, and saxophone stuff she'd sent me for the third member was entirely notated – he was more of a classical saxophone player, which is not something I like. There was no evidence that they were capable of free improvisation. I said let me know where you're playing and I'll come and see you.

Forty years ago I would've said yeah, let's see what happens. But I've been in situations that have been very uncomfortable – when I was a little pressured to play with somebody, and I was nearly always right that this is not going to end well. Possibly because I do fewer gigs, and the gigs I do have a slightly higher profile, I'm much less likely to say yes to an unknown quantity now.

* * *

You've played gigs all over the world. Do you enjoy travelling?
I love trains – they're great. I hate aeroplanes – not aeroplanes per se, but they seem to have made it so it's impossible to have fun while travelling anywhere by aeroplane.

It's hours of boredom, followed by minutes of naked anxiety followed by some fear.
How many gigs do you have a year?
It varies ridiculously. I'd easily have a month when I have no gigs.

This week I'm really busy.

For me, every gig is a major gig.
Jazz has a touring network – with organisations like Jazz Services, as it used to be. Free improvisation doesn't have anything like that.
I never do tours of England now. There are no touring schemes.

The scene is massive in London – the audience varies from almost nobody to packed. With Alterations, both gigs we did at Café Oto were packed.

If I started wondering about audience size too much, I'd never do anything.

Some players have commercial careers.
Kenny Wheeler and Tony Coe did.
It didn't have a bad effect on their jazz playing.
They were the exception. It often does. If I ever got a gig like playing bass guitar in *The Lion King* . . .
Have you had gigs like that?
Only for tiny runs, just a couple of nights – on bass, not piano. And by the second night I'm bored stiff. I did a musical in York that ran for two nights. People are in these things for months. And if you're playing every evening, you can't do other gigs. It takes you out of circulation. If you're not visible, no one will call you up.

An improvising musician has to organise their own gigs.

I was asked at a forum, whether producing a magazine, and running these gigs, get in the way of you being a musician. I said, "No, not at all."

On a practical level, no one else is going to give you a gig.

James Malone is a really talented guitarist who comes out of thrash metal, and is now interested in contemporary classical music and free improvisation. He said, "Can I come round and have a jam with you?" and I said "Yes." It turned out he did this for pretty much everybody – he organised all these jams. And now he's organising a gig in South London. Very quickly he got involved in the whole scene. He's really good, and motivated to do stuff. We always had to do that.

What do you think about arts funding for improvisation – and the misapprehensions of the Arts Council?
I think the misapprehensions have become less. Just in terms of the administrative way of thinking, there's been a big change in how people see free improvisation. It's been around for so long, people can't ignore it anymore. Sound and Music take it very seriously now.[2] They categorise free improvisation as a form of composition, and I don't have any problem with that at all. Not just because there's a possibility that free improvisers will get taken seriously and paid properly, which is obviously something I like. But also on the level that this is a form of composition – it's just real-time composition, you can't go back and change it.[3]

John Kieffer at one point ran Sound and Music, and has had lots of other jobs. He came up working in a little bookshop in Brighton, doing a mail order service for free improvisation and world music LPs. He knew all about the music, way back, and now he's an important arts administrator. That wouldn't have happened fifteen years ago.

Free improvisation is now the subject of archival investigation – which Derek Bailey might have been uneasy about, given his views on academic elitism.
I don't have any problem with archives – it depends who's doing the archiving. **The philosopher Burton Dreben commented that "Garbage is garbage, but the history of garbage is scholarship." He wasn't attacking scholarship.** Even if you think all religion's nonsense, you can still study it.

There's a huge backstory to this music now, even if you date it from 1963 or whenever.

* * *

What role does the audience play at free improv gigs? What are the rules of conduct/engagement?
In his new book, David Toop describes a gig he did with Paul Burwell, where some of the audience clearly thought it was a total joke. They came on the stage and started hitting Paul Burwell's things. I was there, and they were laughing in a joyless, dismissive way.

I remember seeing Alan Tomlinson at the Wapping Project – a master of trombone, and he was playing particularly well, it was a very resonant downstairs space. Also on the bill was the tabla-player Aref Durvesh. He doesn't play a lot of improvised music, but he'd worked with me on a movie score. He came up to me while Alan was playing and asked, "Would he mind if I joined in?" And I thought "What an interesting idea." This was someone coming from outside the improvised community, and he didn't know the conventions. But I thought "If you're joining in because you love the music so much, I'm sure he won't mind."

So he just joined in – and I think Alan took it in the spirit in which it was meant, which was, "I think you're so great, I just want to play with you."

Trombone playing was spectacularly good that night.

* * *

Wynton Marsalis has this thing with free jazz and free improvisation, because he's imposed a Whig history of jazz.
That history includes Ornette Coleman.
Just about. But Cecil Taylor?

Ornette writes amazing tunes. He played at the Sonny Rollins eightieth birthday party, at Sydney Opera House [2011], which I saw on TV. That was astonishing. Roy Haynes looked about fifty, and he was ninety. Ornette just sounded astounding – really still something from outer space, not that it didn't fit, it was just that nobody else would ever play that solo over those changes. He was beautiful, it sounded incredible. It was a fantastic concert.

I heard a story about trumpet player Paul Smoker, who did a rehearsal with Ornette. Ornette said, "OK, Paul, now I'm going to tell you what harmolodics is." Like everyone else I know, Paul Smoker never understood Ornette's explanations, so he thought, "Fantastic! Now I'm going to discover what the fuck harmolodics is!" And Ornette said, "OK, you see that tune I've written there? You play that tune and I'll do anything I like." That's it.

It's basically somebody playing a tune and then somebody else playing anything they want to. He would come up with formulations like "You can play any note over any chord." Bach knew that. This word "harmolodics" – maybe Ornette takes it seriously, but basically it was a fantastic phrase that everybody latched on to.

It's a high-concept, as they say in Hollywood. A high-concept is when you go into a studio and say, "Have I got an idea for you! It's ER meets Night of the Living Dead," or something. It has to be in one sentence.[4] Everybody wants a quick fix, so they can latch on to it.

Wynton is a great player. He makes a huge amount of money, but seems to be pretty generous in his patronage.

Well, I'd like to think he is. But people who make a huge amount of money – they're described as "wealth creators" these days – are usually creating wealth for themselves. Maybe he's generous, but there was a huge kerfuffle around who was getting the gigs.

If it hadn't been for Wynton, there wouldn't be the gigs to be had for many musicians – so I suppose that's the debate over capitalism.

Entrepreneurs like Richard Branson provide jobs...

That's a good example...

... of a wonderful man who gets a remarkably good press.[5]

Yeah... But in fact – not that anything's going to change – if nobody had a huge amount of money, then things would still happen, wouldn't they? If people have a lot of money, that means power is resting in their hands.

Wynton has a huge dynamism and a can-do attitude...

Yes.

The best shouldn't be the enemy of the good.

He's a very good trumpet player.

I mean in terms of his patronage.
At least he's open-minded to *some* forms. I think the most dangerous thing is that awful *History of Jazz* by Ken Burns where he loves Wynton so much – Wynton can talk about Buddy Bolden as though he was there.
But he's charismatic.
I don't find him charismatic actually.
Maybe young African-American players in particular – but not exclusively – find him charismatic. He's a great educator.
You might well be right. I've seen so many people who think they're coming across as being keen on music, when actually they're keen on themselves.
He probably is quite keen on himself. Power should be broken up and shared – that sounds like a good liberal principle, because power corrupts.
Exactly.
To name another example, which probably shouldn't go in the book – Serious Productions.[6]
Very good example.
There shouldn't be that kind of power so that every saxophone piece goes to Andy Sheppard when there are other great saxophonists.
He's a good player.
But is he a great original like Lol [Coxhill]?
He was good in the trio with Carla Bley and Steve Swallow.
He worked with Carla for years, with really great, original musicians. He's a very good saxophone player. But Lol, who was a brilliant saxophone player, never got that kind of support.
He could've done with 10 per cent of those [Serious] gigs.
Absolutely.
You've got very broad tastes.
With some huge holes in it, like Western opera.
But you don't want to know about opera.
No, I don't want to know anything about it.
There must be things you don't know much about, that you want to – Tibetan throat-singing, or gamelan.
Yes. Evan Parker came out with a list of contemporary flamenco singers that I've never heard of. Like David Toop, he's a student of many kinds of music.
Evan doesn't go to gigs like you do.
No – it's mostly records. He made that famous comment, "My roots are in my record player."

But you think it's important to hear things live.
I can't easily decide the relative importance of records and gigs.
I have friends who just listen to records. I don't understand that.
I don't understand that either.

Also, I think some people would rather talk about music than hear it! Sometimes talks about music are better attended than gigs – which is fine, but quite odd.

* * *

Have you had any experiences with promoters…
…which were less than favourable? That would take a whole day.

When I hear people on the scene say – as I did the other day – "I gave them their start," that might be true in show business, but there's no big break in improv.

I was greatly encouraged by Evan and Derek. And among promoters, [saxophonist] Seymour Wright's dad, Geoff Wright, was a great help.
The oddity is that some people, who shall be nameless, think they can make money from a genre that's not lucrative.
That's the puzzle.
I noticed that in Italy, ordinary people go to avantgarde gigs – though the same happened when Durham Jazz Festival put on Soweto Kinch at Miner's Hall.
I think audience preferences are very different, from country to country. When I played with David Toop in Bologna – I love playing in Bologna, it's great food, and a left-wing city – most of the gigs were put on by the Communist Party. I'd love to play in Bologna again. There were large audiences in the open air, listening attentively.

In improv, if either side starts with the view that you're doing the other person a huge favour, you're not going to get very far. Promoters who think they're doing you a favour by putting you on, that's insulting. But equally insulting is the musician who thinks you're doing the promoter a favour by playing for them. If you're a musician, you need to play.
You meet promoters who think they're doing you a favour?
Oh God yes.

Notes

1 *Old Paradise Airs* (Iluso, 2020).
2 The UK national agency for new music.
3 See discussion on improvisation as compositional method, Chapter 8.
4 According to Wikipedia, "high-concept" is a type of artistic work that can be easily pitched with a succinctly stated premise; "low-concept" is more concerned with character development and other subtleties that aren't as easily summarised.
5 Richard Branson (born in 1950) is the founder of Virgin Records, which signed the Sex Pistols, Can and Captain Beefheart as well as more obviously commercial names. He is now one of the UK's best-known business magnates.
6 The UK's dominant promoter of jazz, world and contemporary music.

14

Post-2000

In the last two decades, Beresford has continued to make improvisational collaborations in diverse fields, including with musicians who have a background in contemporary composition and in video art. Recent collaborators include Peter Evans, Shabaka Hutchings, Okkyung Lee, Elaine Mitchener, Satoko Fukuda and Mandhira de Saram.[1] He founded a trio with Roger Turner and Alan Tomlinson. In 2011, he created Strange Umbrellas with video artist Blanca Regina, a platform for free improvised music and visual art; in 2013, they collaborated on The Unpredictable Series, focusing on free improvisation and performance. The period is also notable for the revival of the group Alterations, that initially existed from 1977 to 1986. Two important albums recorded in this period include *Check For Monsters* with Peter Evans and Okkyung Lee, and *Trap Street* with Roger Turner and Alan Tomlinson.

You recorded an acclaimed trio album with Peter Evans and Okkyung Lee in 2009, *Check For Monsters*.
I quickly built up a friendship with Okkyung, and she said "Let's do a tour of the States." She suggested that just in case we didn't get on, we got a third person, who was Peter Evans – those guys were coming up at that time. There's nobody else that plays trumpet like him – I went to see him at the Vortex, and all the trumpet-players' jaws were dropping.

We got a really horrible review in *The Wire*, and I was distraught. I know I shouldn't feel like that – but musicians do take bad reviews to heart. Lol [Coxhill] got absolute rave reviews for *Spectral Soprano*, except one, which he photocopied and gave to everybody.

Peter Evans' playing is about as far from my own trumpet-playing as can be – which is obviously lacking in chops.

You used to play trumpet.
I haven't played it in ages. I did get the euphonium out recently, because David Toop and I, and David Cunningham, resuscitated our project General Strike for David Toop's seventieth birthday celebrations at Café Oto.[2]

* * *

Born in 1946, drummer ROGER TURNER developed a love for jazz while growing up in Canterbury. His first performances in free improvisation were in a duo with saxophonist Chris Biscoe, before he moved to London in 1968. He then collaborated with Steve Beresford, John Russell, Nigel Coombes and Garry Todd, and has worked with Lol Coxhill, Derek Bailey, Paul Rutherford, Eugene Chadbourne and Cecil Taylor, touring extensively in Europe, the USA, Japan and Australia. Turner has also collaborated with visual artists, film-makers and dance projects.

Roger is incredible. Drummers in particular absolutely adore his playing. His free jazz thing is pretty unstoppable.
He comes out of jazz.
He loves jazz, and he's obsessive about jazz drummers. He's a great expert particularly on Swing Era drummers, and loves Big Sid Catlett. He played a lot with Chris Biscoe, a long time ago – that's an interesting combination.
They still work together – I heard them in Newcastle recently [2017].
I had a trio with Roger and Alan Tomlinson that I adored. I thought, "This is very entertaining. Alan and Roger are hilarious, and I make interesting noises – there'll be no problem getting gigs." But there was, sadly. I think we did Freedom of The City, and I really love our record, *Trap Street* (Emanem, 2003). People who made maps didn't want their design stolen, so they put in a fictitious street, usually a cul-de-sac, which was called a trap street.

I sent Roger the mix and he said, "You can't hear the drums at all." That seemed unlikely, but anyway Martin Davidson and I remixed it slightly. We gave the extreme bottom a bit of a boost, and put in a teeny bit of reverb on the mic that Alan Tomlinson used for very small sounds, which came through a small speaker in the room. And we sent it to them, and they said, "Yeah, that's fine."
Some great free drummers are great time drummers, and others are not.
Yes, it's as simple as that.

There's one free drummer who is sometimes half a beat out at the end of a fill. Another tends to turn the beat around – two becomes three or one.
Alan Tomlinson isn't a jazz player.
No. He plays with jazz orchestras and groups, and I think he plays fantastically. His background is probably classical music, or brass bands – I've never asked him.

At one gig, Alan dressed himself as George Chisholm, the comic trombonist – he wore tights and funny shoes.[3] He gave a short lecture about the piece, "Solo For Sliding Trombone" by John Cage. It was charming and very funny, and totally unpretentious. He explained that Cage didn't go to a jazz or classical trombonist, he went to a comedy trombonist in the Spike Jones Orchestra. He asked, "How many different ways can you configure the trombone?" At the end of the score, Cage writes, "You can do all of these things, or none of them."

* * *

Born in Manchester, ALAN TOMLINSON studied trombone at Leeds College of Music. He has been involved in improvised music since the late 1970s, and has worked professionally in most fields of music. He was a member of groups led by Tony Oxley, Peter Brötzmann and John Stevens, and is a long-time member of London Jazz Composers' Orchestra. In addition to his own trio, with guitarist Dave Tucker and drummer Phil Marks, Tomlinson works with contemporary music groups Sounds Positive, and London New Winds. He has toured extensively in Europe – solo, with his own trio, and a Berlin trio with Christoph Winckel and Willi Kellers. He writes:

> *I don't read the music press or think a great deal about improvised music, I just play it from time to time when I get a gig. I've known Steve and played with him since the early 1980s. He is one of the few players who has asked me to do decent gigs over the years – such as the occasional duo gigs, a trio with Roger Turner and the CD "Trap Street," and asking me to work with Christian Marclay, and Stewart Lee. I have always found Steve easy to play with, he is musical and listens. There is (breathing) space whenever we've played together, and he is not afraid to stop mid-set for a bit of silence – unlike some who play for forty-five minutes non-stop, or if one is unlucky for an hour! So, thanks Steve, for asking me from time to time to do some good gigs!*

* * *

In 2007 you worked with Ray Davies.
The manager of the Guillemots, who I knew, briefly became Ray Davies's manager. I was contacted about an Electric Prom that Ray was doing at the Round House – they needed a musical director, and I said yes. It was a big gig. Obviously I like Ray Davies's songwriting – I have a Kinks Greatest Hits, but that's about it. He has got a great voice.

He was using the Crouch End Festival Chorus.

But I never understood what I had to do. I went to all the rehearsals, but everything I tried to do, somebody had already covered it. That was fine, I got paid, it was nice to work with Ray. I got to travel round Muswell Hill in his Ford Cortina.

He was unpretentious.
Really unpretentious, yes – I thought he was very nice.

There were two memorial shows dedicated to Lol Coxhill, and I did one of them at Café Oto, the best bits of which were amazing. I was very pleased that I got Ray Davies, who read an excerpt about Lol from his book, and Tony Coe.

* * *

How has the scene changed since you were a young musician?
On a social level – there was still a tail end of the jazz musicians in competition for the same gigs. Over the years, people realised that free improvisation pays almost nothing at all, so there's no point in getting Thatcherite about it. Competition is not a good thing – competition in music is horrible.

You must feel that the music has more recognition now.
Of course.

People must have a better understanding of what improvisation is.
I think it's filtered down over the years.

Though it's still not well understood.
No. Although to some extent that's our own stupid fault for doing things that are so open-ended. If I say "This is based on a picture...," people love that. If you say, "I'm going to sit down and make things up..."

People love having images.
Yes. When I was growing up, people played me classical music that was descriptive of something, like *Pictures At An Exhibition*, or "Fingal's Cave." But I preferred things that weren't descriptive, like Bach's E flat minor "Prelude" from the 48, or Vaughan Williams' "Fantasia on a Theme by Thomas Tallis."

* * *

You worked with free improvising vocalist Elaine Mitchener – who has a classical background.
When I met her, Elaine [Mitchener] was working for a classical music publisher – she has a strong connection with contemporary classical music, she's a classically trained singer. But her father played dub records all the time, so she had a strong Jamaican music background as well.

I really like working with her. We had a duo for a bit, usually I was on electronics and Elaine on voice. We probably did Iklectik – we did a couple of South London gigs I think.

And she was improvising?
Definitely. Well, as far as I know she was. I don't know what else it would have been. I was improvising, what she was doing you'd have to ask her about really.

[*laughs*] But you didn't do a recording?
We probably did but people record everything these days. We didn't release a recording.[4]

* * *

ELAINE MITCHENER was born in East London of Jamaican heritage. She is a vocalist, movement artist and composer, whose work encompasses improvisation and contemporary/ experimental music theatre. She has worked with George E. Lewis, Moor Mother, David Toop, Christian Marclay, William Parker, Tansy Davies, Dam Van Huynh, Apartment House and the London Sinfonietta. She is founder of the collective electroacoustic trio The Rolling Calf, with saxophonist Jason Yarde and bassist Neil Charles.

> *In the late 1990s and early 2000s, the free improv scene wasn't as open as it is now for people with classical music training, like me. Extemporisation after all is an integral part of classical music – for example, church organists or instrumental cadenzas. But the art of musically extemporising or improvising still isn't seen as an important part of classical music education – although I have noticed a loosening of attitude since the time I was at music college. [After all], musicians are always improvising, based on the situation.*
>
> *Steve and I started working together in the early 2000s. After my music degree, I began exploring free improv and experimental vocal music – that seemed a natural progression from contemporary new music and extended vocal technique/ gospel or jazz improvisation.*
>
> *Dada and Fluxus are obviously a huge influence on Steve, combined with his very English sensibility. Playing with him is like a musical Keystone Cops – constantly*

changing, we enjoy keeping each other on our toes, or throw a spanner in the works to see what happens. He's very supportive, and has an excellent ear. Things keep criss-crossing, and the duo partner is either responding or trying to share an idea at the same time, but it's never overcrowded.

He doesn't have a signature style in the sense that everything he does is informed by this style. That doesn't mean you can't tell that it's him. In a twenty-minute free improvisation he will reference all different types of musical material. It's a very democratic process and completely focussed, even if it doesn't always appear that way. It's not some kind of pastiche. He's not nostalgic, he's very present.

An audience will take away what they want to. If they're coming to be entertained, they will be entertained. If they come and need some mystical experience, they may or may not have that. He takes playing seriously and he's serious about music, but maybe he doesn't do "serious" in the way it's really obvious to everyone.

* * *

In recent years, you've worked a lot with video artist Blanca Regina.
Blanca's the only video artist I've really worked with closely – and the best I've worked with, by a huge margin. She's very sympathetic to the music. Somehow, out of nowhere, she creates things; she also uses electronics.
How does she improvise?
I don't know. She has some stuff and processes it, and creates images. I don't know how electronic musicians work either – I don't really understand how a theremin works – so it's no surprise I don't know what Blanca does. What she does just seems to work musically. I think there is improvising going on, technically.

She can also turn a technical disaster into a complete performance – which is sometimes what you have to do.
How do you respond to what she does?
I don't.
But she responds to you.
Yes. I went to see Leo Smith improvising in front of a screen with a movie on. He said, "All I can see of the image is a tiny little reflection in the bell of the trumpet, and that's what I look for." I thought that was fantastic.

* * *

Spanish-born video artist, teacher and curator BLANCA REGINA is a lecturer at Kent University. Born in Madrid in 1980, she creates audiovisual performances, sound works, installations and film. Her research and practice encompass sound art, spontaneous music, moving image, live events, electronic music and performance. She recently released an album *Spontaneous Music: Duets with Blanca Regina* (Unpredictable Series), produced by Beresford, on which her voice is embedded, and interacts hypnotically, with a plethora of electronic and acoustic sounds. On the duet with Beresford, "Elrington," toys and other mechanical devices complement her raspy vocalising. She comments:

> *My PhD was about audio-visual performance. I was researching the sampling and electronic music scene connecting to visuals and light art, and I mixed and created graphics in real time, following the music. After I finished it in 2010, I got a grant for post-doc research at Chelsea College of Art and Design. In 2011, Kazue Kobata, who was researching free improvisation and had translated a book on Derek Bailey, was invited by Chelsea College for a week – she was interviewing Steve Beresford, and I helped her film the interview. That was when I met him.*
>
> *I hadn't heard of Derek Bailey at that point, and the conversation was amazing. Suddenly free improvisation became a natural path that connected with my previous research and practice. I started making a film about Terry Day, and Steve became co-producer. In 2016, we got funding from the Arts Council for an Alterations Festival, that brought them together after twenty years.*[5] *For the Art of Improvisers show in 2017, we invited musicians to show their artworks – Evan Parker produces fantastic collages – and at Cafe Oto, we presented their art and music.*[6]
>
> *Sometimes my art is Dada, sometimes it's minimal – I'm always changing, always exploring. When I perform with Steve, there is an opportunity to create and reply with total freedom, where listening and playfulness seem to be the only request.*

* * *

I played with Leila [Adu-Gilmore] while she was living in London. She plays piano, and sings – she accompanies herself on piano. She formed a trio with John Edwards and Steve Noble.

I think she's a great free improviser. She now writes a lot of notated music, for orchestras and maybe chamber music.

She is very cosmopolitan.

We meet up when she's in London – I'd like to work with her again.

LEILA ADU-GILMORE is a New Zealand composer of Ghanaian descent who has composed for the Brentano String Quartet, So Percussion and Gamelan

Padhang Moncar. She received her doctorate in composition at Princeton, and taught music to prisoners at Sing Sing Correctional Facility. Adu-Gilmore currently plays improv, and with Lucked In Sound System she is active in New York and Paris. With a voice described as "like hot treacle on broken glass," she has released four albums, and produced a short-film and documentary soundtrack screened on BBC. She comments:

> *A forcefield of spontaneity, quirk and bragadocious playful charm, Steve Beresford entered my musical stratosphere when I moved to London in 2006. Steve became one of a handful of names that I would follow from pub to club to boat and back, to see London Improvisers Orchestra at the Red Rose, John Russell's Mopomoso at the Vortex, and Sibyl Madrigal's Boat-Ting on a boat in the Thames.*
>
> *Some of these improvisers would become my collaborators: Steve Noble, John Edwards, Hannah Marshall and Beresford himself. I was first struck by Steve's singular ability to namedrop and tell a story about everyone on the global experimental scene. He's inspiring, funny and fun.*
>
> *Steve Beresford is an incredible performer. On both piano and electronics, you hang on the edge of your seat. He could sport a tuxedo or a wizard hat and either would be fitting. He takes from British comedians of yesteryear, and classic and Afrofuturist musicians alike. As I sit listening to one of his CDs, my sense is that Steve Beresford cannot be completely trapped into tape, plastic or metal.*

* * *

Legacy

Free improvisation has had a huge influence – look at the books by Ben Piekut and David Grubbs. There are boundless opportunities in performances of Cage, to use improvisation – David Toop discusses that in *Into the Maelstrom*.
Do you think your music will survive in succeeding generations?
Free improvisation will. . . . But no, I couldn't give a fuck! I'm not doing *anything* for posterity. It would be nice if it did survive, but I don't feel that I have to leave anything behind.
Do you think there are improvisers who are thinking of future generations?
Oh God yes.
But it seems inimical to the music.
Why?

Because it's music of the moment.
But all music is music of the moment.
Great artists are those who have the talent, and the ambition. There are so many talented people who – for whatever reason – lack the ambition.
But could you be ambitious without wondering about your legacy? You're assuming those are the same thing – I'm not sure they are.
To be artistically ambitious is to create work that's of interest as an example to be emulated.
Yes.
You may not have to think of artistic ambition, and being concerned with future generations, as connected – but they are connected.
Yes.
You're objecting to someone like Tony Blair who sets up a foundation?
Clearly, hugely egocentric people like American presidents and bosses of newspapers want their name on everything – they want memorials, museums, concert-halls.
And what about recognition now?
That's *very* nice. But you always have to be ready for a fall.

It was very nice to pop down to White Cube, work with incredibly good musicians and get paid properly – and have your record pressed almost immediately. That's amazing! To have the cover designed by Christian Marclay – fantastic! But when that stops, you're back marking papers [at Westminster University]. That's alright, much better than many, many jobs in the world.

* * *

CARA STACEY is a South African pianist, composer and researcher who plays southern African musical bows (umrhubhe, uhadi, makhweyane). She collaborates with percussionist Sarathy Korwar in Pergola and is a member of the Night Light Collective. Her debut album *Things That Grow* features Shabaka Hutchings (2015, Kit Records). Her latest album, *Ceder*, is with Peruvian flutist Camilo Ángeles. Her PhD looked at the makhweyane musical bow from eSwatini. She studied bows and other instruments with Bhemani Magagula and Dizu Plaatjies. She now teaches at North-West University in Potchefstroom, in South Africa's North West province. She comments:

> The first time I heard Steve Beresford play was at a "Miss Havisham Presents..." event in 2012, a few months after I had first moved to London. He performed there,

as did Elaine Mitchener and Shabaka Hutchings. Coming from South Africa, I had heard freely improvised music only a few times before. I have always wondered about the link between free improvisation and freedom. I don't know when South African musicians like Louis Moholo began playing free improvisation – notable records were also hard to come by in SA.

This music only became part of my life once I was based in London, and I heard Steve play many times. My ears have been stretched extensively – to quote Charles Ives – by many great improvisers, and in my own playing I have been gently encouraged from afar by Steve's energy, creativity and irreverent humour.

Back in South Africa again, I find moments of that sound and feeling amongst collaborating makhweyane players in eSwatini, electronic musicians and others. I search through live performances, ethnomusicological archives and record collections looking for the humour and fresh creativity of spontaneous composition in the various southern African and African musics I am surrounded by. With other improvisers on this continent, I am seeking out a new language for the freedom that exists in Steve's huge and diverse body of work.

Notes

1 Other recent projects are discussed in Chapters 11 (Christian Marclay and Blanca Regina) and 12 (*Indeterminacy*).
2 General Strike is discussed in Chapter 10.
3 George Chisholm (1915–97), Scottish trombonist and comedian, was influenced by Jack Teagarden; he worked in the Bert Ambrose Orchestra, played with Coleman Hawkins and Benny Carter and appeared on The Goon Show.
4 The 2015 release *Elaine Mitchener And Steve Beresford Live At White Cube* (VF147 Live 9) has Beresford and the London Sinfonietta on one side, and Elaine Mitchener on the other.
5 http://www.unpredictable.info/project/alterations-festival/
6 https://www.cafeoto.co.uk/events/art-of-improvisers/

15

Comedy and Entertainment

Steve Beresford has many connections with the world of comedy and light entertainment, and comedy is a vital part of his artistic world. However, its role isn't straightforward. We start by discussing his sense of irony, and links with Dadaism, and then consider his work with Scottish humourist, poet and songwriter Ivor Cutler. We discuss the album he helped produce with Vic Reeves, and then turn to his work with comedian Stewart Lee, and his collaborations with the Bohman Brothers. The chapter concludes with a discussion of the aesthetics of entertainment, and the role of artist-entertainers. We consider the role of perfection in entertainment, and the idea of classic pure entertainment.

Does it annoy you that people think of you as a comedian when you're not meaning to be?
I don't mind at all. The only time it's felt awkward was one occasion when the audience seemed to find everything Paul Lytton did funny. Sometimes he is funny, but not generally – maybe they had just had too much of other players who are quite consciously funny. In experimental music, that can be an ambiguous area – are you trying to be funny or not?
How long have you used musical humour?
I don't know, you'd have to ask someone else. I don't know if I'm being funny or not.
You're an ironist, ready to see the absurdity of things.
Yes, I enjoy that very much. That is true.
A deadpan reaction can be taken either way.
Yes, that's sometimes very useful. I think it's very good that you're pointing these things out, I think they're all true.
    I'm glad you haven't said this, but people are always saying that Americans aren't ironic, or don't get irony. I think *The Simpsons* is the most ironic programme I've ever seen, and it's quintessentially American. Sometimes ironically so, of

course. It's no accident that its creator Matt Groening is a friend of Eugene Chadbourne, who is also very ironic.

Are you a subversive?
I love Dada. I prefer Dada to surrealism but that could just be because Dadaists seem to be more interested in typography, which I love. Surrealism is maybe a bit pompous, and misogynistic – Dali was extremely reactionary in his attitudes. The whole idea of painting in a conventional craftsmanlike way, you could say that's a form of subversion in itself.

[Comedian] Peter Kay comes out of the Northern working men's clubs. He played a character called Keith Lard, an anal-retentive fire inspector with absolutely no sense of humour. That was a classic character who was funny but also rather sad, yet treated with real affection. It wasn't a vicious parody of fire inspectors who are a bit sad and lonely and consequently a bit obsessive about pointless details – punctilious, or pedantic. I love pedantry. That's one of the reasons I really like Stewart Lee, because he's ridiculously pedantic, and that's in itself very funny. I would hate to think that I am a fascist pedant. I think I am a humanist pedant – something like that.

People forget it's possible to mock affectionately.
I think Derek [Bailey] thought "Laura" was a really great tune. It *is*, it's fantastic. The movie [of the same name] is interesting, and David Raksin is a great composer. I like Spike Jones's parody of it, it's one of my favourite of his records. Derek would probably go into "Laura" after ten minutes of ear-splitting feedback with Han [Bennink] looking like he's going to explode. Of course, he knew that was a funny moment. But the very romanticism of it, and the fact that Derek's playing it really well, made it funnier. These are elements to be manipulated to some extent.

Miles Davis explained to Keith Jarrett that he stopped playing ballads because "I love playing ballads so much." I think Derek was a bit like that.[1]

* * *

Writer, poet and performer IVOR CUTLER was known for his surreal eccentricity. He was born in Glasgow in 1923 to Jewish immigrants who had escaped from pogroms on Eastern Europe. He joined the RAF in 1941 and trained as a navigator, but was soon dismissed. After the war he became a teacher at A. S. Neill's progressive school, Summerhill. Cutler began to write poetry only at the age of 42, but became widely renowned and admired by John Peel, Billy Connolly, John Lennon and Paul McCartney. He died in 2006.

Beresford and David Toop produced Cutler's album *Privilege* (1983), with Cutler's vocals accompanied by a range of instruments including keyboards, banjo, euphonium and flute. The LP is co-credited to Linda Hirst, who recites a number of poems and provides vocals on some tracks. The final track, "Women of the World," was released as a single and became a minor hit on the UK Indie Chart. It was covered by Jim O'Rourke on *Eureka* (1999) and by YACHT, and re-released in 2009 by Hoorgi House Records.

Ivor Cutler got famous when he was quite elderly.
I don't think he was ever particularly young.

He was Buster Bloodvessel, tour organiser on *Magical Mystery Tour*. Supposedly the Beatles' use of harmonium was influenced by him.

I loved *Life In A Scotch Sitting Room, Vol. 2*
I said to him, "I haven't got Volume 1." And he said, "There is no Volume 1" – that's such an Ivor thing.

I think he began as a jazz pianist.

He had something in common with Lol. Having worked with Lol a lot, I was "prepared" in working for Ivor – they had overlapping aspects.

David Toop and I were asked by Geoff Travis at Rough Trade to produce an Ivor Cutler record. I suggested Denis Bovell's studio, which had a large room with a grand piano – I had worked with Dennis with The Slits. Dave Hunt had wired up the studio. The record was called *Privilege*. We thoroughly enjoyed it, though it was slightly frustrating that we couldn't get Ivor to make his songs any longer. They would be fifty-five seconds, but he wouldn't repeat the chorus.

He was very funny. As a performer, he never corpsed – except for one occasion on the album we did, when he did laugh uncontrollably. I think it was a poem called "Use A Brick." Linda Hirst was his near-neighbour in Tufnell Park. She sang on this record, which was very unusual because mostly Ivor didn't like other people singing his songs – I think it was alright for Robert Wyatt to do them. Later, Jim O'Rourke covered the single "Women Of The World" – he got permission from Ivor, permission that was very rarely granted.

Ivor would pop down to Compendium Bookshop in Camden and sign copies of his tiny poetry books. They always had a display on the front till. That bookshop was fantastic. Virtually everyone who worked there was interesting – Nick Kimberley, Paul Hammond . . .

* * *

VIC REEVES, born James Moir in 1959, is an English comedian and actor, known for his double act with Bob Mortimer, which displayed their surreal humour. *Vic Reeves Big Night Out* began on Channel 4 in 1990, followed by *The Smell of Reeves and Mortimer* on BBC2, and then their most acclaimed show Shooting Stars. They have been a frequent presence on British stage and screen since.

Evan Parker told me, "This Vic Reeves show, it's really excellent." He purchased his first VHS machine so he could record *Vic Reeves Big Night Out*. I mentioned this to [journalist and author] Paul Morley, and he told me he was executive producer of a forthcoming album by Vic – it was released as *I Will Cure You*. He asked if I'd like to produce some tracks on it. I had Evan play on them. We did a sort of James Brown version of "Oh Mr. Songwriter," and some songs that Vic had already sung on the show, but in very different versions. There was some money, so we had Han Bennink, Wolter Wierbos on trombone, Dave Green on bass and BJ Cole on pedal-steel – and Harry Beckett, Tony Coe and Evan Parker. I wanted a contrast between the two soprano players, Tony and Evan – because on soprano, Tony sounds like Johnny Hodges.

One song was based on 1950s British library music, and Vic had written words about the Buzzcocks and other famous punk groups.[2] I thought it was fantastic – I loved the idea of having a song about a genre of music, where the genre it's performed in is completely unrelated.

The record sold very well – Vic was on Top of the Pops, I remember he appeared with serried rows of washing machines.

Reeves and Mortimer were compared with Morecambe and Wise, with some justification.

* * *

STEWART LEE, born in 1968, is an English stand-up comedian, director, and writer. In 1987, he began in stand-up as a student, with Richard Herring, at the Edinburgh Fringe. Much of this early work was poorly received, with one of Lee's shows being labelled "the worst show on the Fringe." In 1992, Lee and Herring wrote their first radio show, *Lionel Nimrod's Inexplicable World*, and in 2001, Lee directed *Jerry Springer: The Opera* for the Battersea Arts Centre, which moved to the West End in 2003. Lee won a BAFTA for his BBC2 series, *Stewart Lee's Comedy Vehicle*, first broadcast in 2009. He has a great interest in free improvisation, and has performed in venues such as Cafe Oto, including a version of John Cage's *Indeterminacy* with Tania Chen and Steve Beresford. He has appeared in Gavin Bryars' radio documentary about John Cage, and has interviewed musicians at Just Not Cricket, a festival of British free improvisation in Berlin in 2011. It appears on the film *Taking The Dog for Walk*, http://ni-vu-ni-connu.net/film/taking-the-dog-for-a-walk-film/

We discussed [in Chapter 12] about how you worked more recently with another comedian, Stewart Lee.
Our CD [*Indeterminacy*] is on its second run – we've probably pressed a thousand by now.
For an album of improvised music, that's an amazing figure.
It's got John Cage's name on it.
There's loads of records by Cage.
But how many of them have got a famous UK comedian on?

Stewart Lee is *very* good at selling things. At the end of a three-hour set, he'll leap off the stage and run through the audience to get to the little booth at the front of the theatre. He's devoted to his audience – he really respects them, and wants to sell them good stuff. He makes really good DVDs.

Indeterminacy probably confuses some Stewart Lee fans, because they don't know that side of him. He won *Celebrity Mastermind*, answering questions on Derek Bailey.[3] He worked for months preparing – he got someone to ring him up in the middle of the night, and ask him questions like "What year was Derek Bailey's second solo album released?" Ben Watson set the questions.

Anyway, he won! The money went towards motor neurone disease, which is what Derek died of.

When Stewart gets into something, he really gets into it. His act is hugely analytical and self-referential. He will carefully analyse how a joke works. Normally, explaining the joke makes it completely unfunny, but this makes it funnier.

Some of the stuff is about "You guys felt uncomfortable about that joke, but went with me on it." He'll analyse the audience's response – but I think if Stewart didn't get a laugh, he'd be very upset. What's great for him about *Indeterminacy* is that he's reading someone else's words – John Cage's – and he'll do the same story and one night he'll get a huge laugh, and the next night, nothing.

His first book, *How I Escaped My Certain Fate*, is extremely funny and has footnotes to footnotes. He wrote footnotes in the original piece and then comes back and writes another footnote, extending or qualifying what he said, because he thinks very deeply and incisively about these things, and that makes him funny. The *Daily Mail* calls him a know-it-all, but he's not like that, actually.

But are his analyses of humour serious?
Well, they're true. I think you can say something that makes people laugh and still be serious. Look at George Carlin; I never liked him that much actually, but clearly he was the lefties' stand-up comedian. Richard Pryor is maybe my favourite stand-up of all time, his act was all about saying terrible truths and people going "Oh my God! Did he really say that?" – talking about his heart attack, about setting fire to himself when he was freebasing. Eric Morecambe did a piece about his heart attack.

Are you a fan of Morecambe and Wise?
I love Morecambe and Wise! Not everything they did but I loved that diversity – they could sing and dance quite nicely. I like their music jokes, they were always really hip, I think. Obviously the sketch with André Previn was a work of utter genius – I love to see the orchestral players trying not to laugh.

There are sincere entertainers who respect their audience, and cynical ones who hold them in contempt. Many of the sincere ones come from the same milieu as the audience – like Les Dawson, maybe. He presumably started in working men's clubs.
He was a disaster for years, Les Dawson. Actually, he got a laugh when he played a wrong note on piano – that's where all that stuff comes from.

He was trying to play properly and they laughed?
Yeah – and he thought maybe I'm onto something here. Also, his grumpiness is very funny.

How many stand-up comedians are improvisers? Not many.
No. Stewart and I have had this conversation many times. I keep opening the subject of relationships between improvisation and stand-up comedy, and he always says that he does stuff that he's worked out, and I don't.

That's not my point. I'm not saying he's a free improvising comedian, though when he does improvise he is hilarious – I've seen him do it, it's brilliant. I'm saying there are certain things we have in common, such as timing which is very important – non-metrical timing, psychological timing. When do you hit the punch lines? Do you have punch lines? How do you say this joke so it works better?

But he tries it out at home and you don't.
Well, personally I don't, as we discussed earlier.

People assume that comedians are spontaneous. I assumed that when André Previn says, "I'll get my baton. . . . It's in Chicago," and Eric Morecambe punches the air in delight, it was an ad lib. But what delighted him was the timing – the line was [script-writer] Eddie Braben's.

Stewart Lee tells me this all the time. But I've seen him deal with a heckler – he's brilliant. And he does hone his shows – he does them dozens of times.

I read that Bob Hope, if he was going to meet someone important, would ask his gag writers for some jokes.

I think Bob Hope is superb. Some of those *Road To* . . . movies were really great – I've stolen some lines for titles from them. Stand-up comedians always look like they're improvising and, of course, they have material – some of them have virtually every "ooh" and "aah" written down. Frankie Howerd was said to be infuriating to write for because if you left the "ooh no, missus!" out then he'd say where's all my "ooh no, missus" stuff? Then if you put it in, he'd say "I can do all that!"

He came out of variety.

Here it was The Windmill, and in New York it was Minsky's, the famous striptease joint where people like Phil Silvers would go on before the naked ladies. That was the hardest gig, because nobody wanted to see you, they were there to see naked ladies. So you had to be really funny and of course it was fantastic training. They had to make horny men laugh.

Why didn't they just have more naked ladies?

That's a good question. Maybe there weren't enough. Maybe nobody could think outside the box of light entertainment, which was always a juggling act, a comedian, a romantic singer . . .

We don't have variety anymore – except when the Queen goes to the London Palladium.

You know, John Stevens was on that – Donovan did the Royal Variety Performance, with John Stevens on drums. I think that's hilarious.

* * *

The Bohman Brothers

London-based Jonathan and Adam Bohman – the Bohman Brothers – have been recording and playing since 1974. They use found objects, text and an array of sound sources, and in the spirit of Fluxus, create musique concrète, sound poetry and often grotesque soundscapes. For several years they ran one of the handful of London's experimental music clubs at The Bonnington Centre in Vauxhall, south London, and regularly appear on London's art radio station Resonance 104.4FM. Their recent projects include a feature length film with Richard Thomas and James Holcombe. Beresford and I discuss the Bohman Brothers before their gig at London's Iklectik.

I played with Adam Bohman in the London Improvisers' Orchestra.
The Bohman Brothers are brothers?
Yes, they're not like the Walker Brothers.

Adam plays a tableful of objects using contact mics, such as bowed toast racks – pieces of wood, strings roughly made into some kind of banjo instrument, glass bowls, record-racks and light bulbs. Like Terry Day, for years he's also made pictures. Adam usually makes montages, using stuff from colour supplements, Chinese restaurant menus, maps, and inter-office memos. He uses biro a lot too.

The Bohmans were a bit of a fixture when Resonance Radio started – it felt like every week there was a bunch of kids just out of school, with, say, a toy football game that they'd converted into a sound-producing object. Every time I went in, there was another group of people with unlikely sound-producing objects. It felt like the whole world was turning into the Bohman Brothers. Of course, they have precedents – Hugh Davies is an obvious influence.

They're sound artists?
I would call them musicians – they started before anyone used the term "sound artist." I think they have Swedish origins. Their father was a child prodigy concert pianist, so they grew up with classical music – but you wouldn't think so.

Adam Bohman can imitate any sound you make, uncannily accurately. If you make a noise, he'll do something almost identical – using a piece of wood and a pencil, it'll sound just like what you did electronically.

He keeps very detailed notes, in longhand in an exercise book, about different tabletop set-ups that he's developed over the years.
He uses noise as well as musical tones.
I don't think he thinks there's a real distinction.
When someone hears a noise, they tend to ask "What's causing it?" That's less true of musical tone.
There's definitely an issue about people wanting to know where the sound is coming from. I began to realise that, after about twenty years of people making

and performing electronic music sitting in front of laptops, and all you can see is the top of their head.[4]

With a conventional instrument, people know where the sound's coming from.
I think it might be part of human nature, the need to know.

Maybe it's a product of evolution – the noise might indicate a predator – whereas musical tones create their own world.
I went to a gig yesterday, by a group with Mandhira de Saram playing violin, John Edwards playing double bass, with Jennifer Allum on fiddle and Douglas Benford on squeezebox, and bits and pieces. There were moments when it was very hard to believe there are only four instruments – it felt like an orchestral density. You knew how it was formed, because it got there in a logical way. But there's a certain mystery as well with conventional instruments – you can wonder "What the hell are they doing to create that?"

Are the Bohman Brothers entertaining?
Sometimes I think "Is this funny or not? Do they think it's funny? I don't know." Adam is conscious that some of the things he does are funny, but I'm not sure at which point he isn't. Grey areas are very productive. Do you know that you're not playing in time with the drummer, if the drummer is indeed playing in time? Those misunderstandings, which might be quite deliberate non-sync moments, make the music interesting.

Adam's very interested in using texts, either as a score, or as source material. Sometimes simultaneously, the Bohman Brothers read from Chinese restaurant menus, and inter-office memos. Adam does a show about language with an Italian woman called Patrizia Paolini. English is her second or third language, and Adam has quite a pronounced stutter sometimes – like Alvin Lucier. You know Lucier's *I'm Sitting In A Room*, where he stutters?

The Bohmans don't try to involve the audience, do they?
I sincerely hope not, I *hate* audience involvement!

Alan Tomlinson is another musical comedian. I think you said his act comes from music hall and variety. Emptying the spit, reversing the bell, pretending to sweep the carpet with it – it's a routine.
I adore Alan's performances. Complaining that he has schticks is like complaining that Monk always plays piano by pressing down the keys with his fingers. Alan has "bits" – routines or shticks – but he's improvising. He's a big fan of Spike Jones and George Chisholm.

Returning to our earlier discussion – are you an entertainer?
I'd like to think that I am entertaining.

People in light entertainment have very specific skills which I don't have. It was one of Derek Bailey's major decisions to leave light entertainment, but he was very good at it.[5]

There's also stuff that is seen as being entertaining, but which turns out not to entertain us at all – such as *Jim'll Fix It*.

And it entertains you even less now.
Yes.[6]

Do you think improvising musicians don't pay enough attention to being entertaining?
I've certainly gone into jazz clubs recently and immediately wanted to walk out, I felt completely alienated. It's probably just me being sensitive. In improvised music, an idiosyncratic approach to performing can be extremely amusing. I found the Spontaneous Music Ensemble with Roger Smith and Nigel Coombes uproariously funny, but clearly they weren't meaning to be. They did the most extraordinary things musically, but also physically.

There was a moment at the Jackson's Lane Community Centre [in North London], when I was sitting in the audience between Evan Parker and Victor Schonfield. It was SME – the trio of John Stevens, Nigel Coombes and Roger Smith – playing in the bar. At one point, everybody had their eyes closed except me, and presumably Roger Smith – who got up, walked to the back wall, and banged his Spanish guitar against it, rubbing it very violently up and down. He then returned to his seat with several broken strings.

John Stevens opened his eyes – he didn't know what had happened – and said, "Ah, Roger's broken a couple of strings, I think we'll have to stop." It was hugely entertaining, and also utterly terrifying – like watching *Aliens* or something.

That group was absolutely naked in its idiosyncrasy – you really didn't know what they were going to do. I share an SME obsession with David Toop – he's written quite a lot about that trio, I think in *Haunted Weather*. They were absolutely amazing.

John Stevens was renowned for his super-smart suits, and the fact that he *totally* fancied himself. He was very conscious of his appearance. He went through a long-haired, big-bearded period, but when I knew him he wore natty suits.

His setting-up of drums was a sort of choreography. Spinning the stand, and looking to the back of the club – it was all to do with John's concept of what a jazz drummer looks like. He modelled himself on Phil Seamen.

Phil Seamen was the first great British jazz drummer.
I didn't ever see him live. I probably could have just caught him, before he died. Phil was worshipped by both John Stevens and Ginger Baker.

But if you talk to Paul Lytton, he will say he preferred Johnny Butts.[7] Paul felt that other UK jazz drummers were too metrical.

We're talking about having an image, which a serious artist is not supposed to have – though look at Miles Davis or Duke Ellington.
[John Stevens'] dad was a tap-dancer, and John was coming out of light entertainment as well. His heroes included the Ornette Coleman Quartet – those pictures of them in black suits, on the Atlantic album-covers, show they clearly thought about their image. I still get shivers when I see that [Atlantic] label.

But my point is, although John Stevens was a renowned poseur, he was also 100 per cent serious about music. And that music was absolutely uncontainable – and unmarketable as well! The things Nigel and Roger did on stage were not conducive to an experience of light entertainment – but they were very entertaining.

Being a poseur was his least interesting vice.
Yes. It never got in the way of the music.

"Light entertainment" is "mere entertainment" – it has no artistic content. "Pure entertainment" is a less negative term.
As I said earlier, there are two ways of looking at this. There are people who come out of light entertainment – but also, people who are entertaining almost by default. The SME were entertaining by default. John Stevens' first record was *We Love You Beatles* – it's not that pop music was unknown to him. He was going to form an improvisation group with Marc Bolan.[8]

Was Marc Bolan an improviser?
We'll never know! He was a good basic rock guitarist, I would say.

* * *

Harrison Birtwistle replied to complaints about his music's inaccessibility with the wonderful comment, "I can't be responsible for the audience: I'm not running a restaurant."
If you're Harrison Birtwistle you've done things before, and members of the audience know what those things are like. Some of that audience would definitely be people who had heard Birtwistle before – so in that sense he is responsible for the audience being there. He didn't make them come, but presumably something he did at some point made them interested enough to come to that concert.

He's saying, "I'm not at the service of the customer." That's true up to a point. But if *nobody* came, the Arts Council wouldn't give him a subsidy. I can imagine Basil Fawlty saying "I'm not responsible for the customers."

With a restaurant or hotel, you *are* there for the customers – you're not running it as a form of self-expression. But obviously if someone is creative and excited about their hotel, it will probably be better.

There's a live double-LP called *Nonaah* [from 1977] where Roscoe Mitchell comes on as a replacement for Anthony Braxton – there's been an announcement that Braxton can't make it. He plays a phrase [sings it] about a hundred times – well, a lot of times.

And the audience are booing – or at least showing their disapproval.

> *TOP TIP No. 6: If you're playing something the audience don't like, you don't have to stop doing it.*

I heard Maceo Parker recently [March 2018]. His set list must be fairly constant – it's the aesthetics of perfection, honed and crafted, of a consummate entertainer. But it looks spontaneous. There's a lot of drilling in popular entertainment.

I'm not sure James Brown was interested in perfection – he was interested in making things happen that were exciting. His set was certainly extremely tight. But it's full of contradictions, as James Brown was. His music was incredibly tightly controlled, and at the same time the wildest thing you've ever seen. It's totally wild music. And the wildness is not just James screaming his head off – it's the music's obsessive repetitiveness.

The whole of [bass-guitarist] Bootsy Collins' band – who was later with Parliament/ Funkadelic – became James Brown's band. They didn't rehearse – they knew all the tunes. They came onstage and James said, "Sex Machine," and they went into that.

They must have rehearsed it at one point.

Not with James before the first gig. There was that "seat of your pants" feel.

There's a fantastic track called "Since You've Been Gone," on the album *Motherlode*. It features Bootsy, not long after he joined James Brown, and Bobby Byrd doing second vocals. I couldn't work out the bassline – then I realised, "He's making this up, it's not a riff." He's improvising all through that very long D minor 7th section – then they go into a bridge where he plays something set. That's very unusual – funk bass-players tend to play riffs, and slight variations on them. The drummer is playing in the same place all the time, which makes it even more exciting.

"Riffs" in the proper sense.[9]

Yes. And Bootsy was riffing in the wrong sense – he's improvising.

I used to write down Chic basslines, and Bootsy Collins basslines. It helps me to understand some things, to notate them.

Sly Stone followed out of James Brown, with a totally different ethos. Integrated groups with white musicians, and female musicians – the horn-lines are extremely tight. Alto and trumpet in tight unison, for instance – the music was innovative and creative, but not made under the conditions that James Brown was making it.

When I heard Maceo Parker, trombonist Dennis Rollins was improvising. But some aspects were very fixed – like (I assume) the playlist.

Part of James Brown's choreography was that when he turned round and pointed at somebody, that meant they were fined five dollars [for making a mistake]. Mainly it was to do with the drummer not making an accent when James fell to his knees. He had kneepads, because if you fell on your knees repeatedly, you'd break your kneecaps.

Later he had the heart attack routine.

He had a long career. He was a Republican who supported Richard Nixon, and he was incredibly misogynist. But he was totally African-American, a revolutionary. He was very militant about that. When the cities were erupting, he was asked to play Boston to calm the people – he did and it worked.

Recently there were some programmes about minimalist music, which I don't think even mentioned James Brown. Come on, that's minimalist music! There's a fantastic track called "Same Beat" – what a great title! It's a band vocal – they just say, "Same beat," it's almost a parody of the idea of repetition. There's a free jazz solo by St. Clair Pinckney – he looked like a bank manager, with mutton-chop whiskers and a grey suit, and played like Albert Ayler.

So "Same Beat" uses repetition/minimalism, free jazz, and taped *musique concrète* squeaky door sounds. It uses a recording of a speech by [black politician] Jesse Jackson, where he recites the poem, "I may be unemployed/unskilled/uneducated/But I am somebody."[10] These were the things The Pop Group used later: noise, free jazz, politics, wildness.[11]

James Brown is an artist-entertainer.

Oh yes.

Great art doesn't manipulate, but entertainment or propaganda – such as Michael Moore's films – does. Obviously *The Big Sleep* is cleverly exploiting certain conventions.
Certainly film music is built around conventions, and those can be used in many ways. I don't think we're totally gripped by a story, to the point where we're not conscious of edits, pans, types of music – but we're also absorbed by the story.
With art, unlike entertainment, the audience is left space to form a view. In one episode of [TV crime series] *Foyle's Law*, when the murderer is finally revealed, he turns into a monster with a maniacal expression, to ram home that he's evil. It treats the audience like idiots.
But then on some level, people find clichés quite amusing. Most good horror films have a level of irony and humour about them – even *Night Of The Living Dead*, which is pretty doomy.
I don't think there's irony in that episode of *Foyle's Law*.
My point is that anything that's become a cliché can be parodied.
Don't you think that's one difference between art and entertainment – with art, there's room for the audience to reflect? Obviously there's great art that entertains.
Yes, art should have ambiguity about it, and entertainment tends not to.

But when we get to a very high level of pure entertainment, like Morecambe and Wise, or Tony Hancock, or Laurel and Hardy – those things do take on other levels that are very ambiguous.
I think Laurel and Hardy passes the test of time – it's a classic – but it's the test of time as entertainment, not art.
There's no doubt it's a classic.
It doesn't have any meaning – it's meant to divert.
As they watched their films, people would build up an understanding of their relationship. For instance, the fact that they shared a bed – but they're clearly not gay.
That's where Morecambe and Wise got the idea. But what did it mean?
I've no idea. But it's definitely funny.
Is it worth probing what the relationship, as depicted, involves?
Yes. Father Ted and Dougal share what's quite a small bedroom, and it's a big house they live in. I'm sure they could find a room each to sleep in.
If someone asks, "Is *Father Ted* pure entertainment?," I'm not sure what I'd say.
There are levels of ambiguity even in popular culture. One of the ambiguities in *Father Ted* is that it's written by people who grew up as Irish Catholics, but who find quite a lot wrong in Irish Catholicism.

There's a lot of sharp satire – of the bishop, for instance.
Even though we love Father Jack, we're pretty sure he's a paedophile. Clearly he's a monster. At one point we're shown a home for old priests, which is full of people like Father Jack.

It certainly works as pure entertainment, but there's more to it. So maybe it's not purely entertainment. There isn't that edginess in *Laurel and Hardy*.
They are quite violent – people get hit on the head with things, and Ollie manages to smash Stan in the face. But it's not the centre of it, I agree.

I'm sure it's more than pure entertainment – but it works very well as that.

Are there things that are good pure entertainment, but don't have that edginess?
Good question. I don't think Benny Hill is good entertainment – I don't find it funny in the slightest.

Some people think Benny Hill is a great comic genius.
I don't get that.

I thought of Laurel and Hardy as being high-quality pure entertainment. But they're the zenith of comedy craft that could make a transition to art. Do you think the only pure entertainment is low-grade?
I'm not saying that. But I can't find anything that fits your description.

Do you think there's such a thing as classic easy-listening music? Like Eddie Heywood's "Canadian Sunset," for instance.
There is definitely classic easy listening.

Notes

1 Cole (2006), p. 367.
2 Library music – also known as production or stock music – is music recorded in various styles by work-for-hire musicians. It is owned by music-library labels, and leased to TV, radio, film and other commercial enterprises.
3 A BBC quiz show; this was in 2010.
4 Laptops are discussed in Chapter 17.
5 Bailey's light entertainment career is discussed in Chapter 4.
6 After the revelations that Jimmy Savile was a serial sex offender.
7 Phil Seamen (1926–72); Johnny Butts (1941–66). Tubby Hayes wrote a tribute called "Dear Johnny B," on his classic album *Mexican Green* (1967).

8 Marc Bolan (1947–77), English singer-songwriter, musician, guitarist and poet, best-known as lead singer of the glam rock band T. Rex.
9 As discussed in Chapter 8.
10 "I Am – Somebody" is a poem written in 1943 by Atlanta civil rights activist, Reverend William Holmes Borders.
11 A Bristol-based group, friends of The Slits.

16
Popular Music, Popular Culture

As with the world of comedy and light entertainment, Steve Beresford also has extensive musical connections with popular music and culture. He played with post-punk band The Slits, appeared on Top of the Pops with The Flying Lizards, and recorded a dub album with Prince Far-I and Adrian Sherwood. He has also been a kind of pop vocalist himself, on albums like *Signals For Tea* or *Eleven Songs For Doris Day*, where, as discussed in Chapter 10, his singing has more of a pop sensibility. As these conversations show, he is incredibly knowledgeable about many areas of popular music.

I was thinking of connections between popular culture and improvised music – such as AMM playing opposite Pink Floyd. Yoko Ono, John Lennon, John Tchicai and John Stevens did a gig in Cambridge that came out as *Unfinished Music No. 2: Life With The Lions*.
John Lennon appeared briefly on Peter Cook and Dudley Moore's TV series *Not Only But Also*, playing a doorman [in 1966].
That was an absolutely formative comedy, I thought it was brilliant.
Peter Cook and Dudley Moore tried to buy the tapes, but the BBC insisted on wiping them.
Me and my friends watched the series avidly. We recreated some of the sketches on tape-recorders – somebody's dad was in the RAF and had an RAF tape-recorder. We did songs that were clearly inspired by The Who and The Kinks. Also we loved *Dr Who*.
When I read about "dolphin-friendly tuna" on a tin of tuna, it reminds me of Peter Cook's comment, "It could confuse a stupid person."
One of my favourite lines!
After *Musics* folded, we started *Collusion* magazine [in 1981]. We wanted to address other genres, to challenge the conventions of what people regarded as

popular music.[1] David Toop and I interviewed Sonny Roberts, who ran Orbitone Records in Harlesden [North-West London]. Orbitone sold very unexpected records – such as Ace Cannon, you know him? A Country & Western tenor-saxophone player.

I didn't know there was such a thing.
There really isn't, except for Ace Cannon. I think he was on Hi Records – the incredible Memphis soul label that Al Green was on. West Indian people loved Ace Cannon – and that really boring Country singer, Jim Reeves. I've never been moved, even for a second, by anything Jim Reeves did. But he was huge in the Jamaican community.

That's completely weird.
He's also big in Africa.

Orbitone Records would sell all these records, but they never got into any charts. They also sold soppy romantic Jamaican albums that sounded like American doowop. Ballads in 12/8, simpler harmonically than the Great American Songbook – I think they called it Spouge – guys in flared trousers standing in front of a flower bed, singing "Truly, my love."[2]

They weren't in any charts.
No one went to that shop to see how many records he sold, because right from the beginning, the charts were rigged. There were chart return shops – there was one near Dalston Junction, and they always had these exciting-looking singles, everything was reasonably priced. This was all to do with pushing a particular title. A lot of marginalised groups, such as the middle-aged West Indian market, their tastes were never reflected in chart returns.

Is there any arcane aspect of popular culture you don't know about? You seem to know about everything from The Shaggs via Roadrunner to The Addams Family.
Lurch [from *The Addams Family*] is my role model – a genius!

But there are many aspects of popular culture about which I know less than nothing – starting with sport.

We won't go there, then. Can I ask what you think of popular taste?
That's a very general question!

Does it bother you that your music is appreciated by a tiny elite?
I think the word "tiny" is appropriate, I'm not sure the word "elite" is.

How about "specialist"? Who are your audience?
I don't know, anymore. At Cafe Oto [in Dalston] tonight, it seems to be people between the ages of twenty and thirty, who live in the area. Certainly Oto

has vastly broadened the appeal of its music, which ranges from free jazz and improv, electronic music, dance, world music, folk and rock and contemporary composition. I don't know how they do that, but they have. That audience tends not to go to other venues, by the way.

Would you say your music has an intrinsically narrow appeal?
No.

You could put a group together that was just as attractive as ABBA – the women in ABBA were attractive, the men weren't attractive at all, really, were they? Anyway, imagine a band as attractive as ABBA, with really good pop songs, very well drilled, great stage show – but basically if you did it in a pub in Kentish Town, it wouldn't mean anything. Popular music is not just about the content of the music, it's about a bunch of other things as well – being in the right place and having the connections to communicate the music, that's 90 per cent of the effort, not writing the songs. It's about constantly pushing the music. It's very tiring.

Jazz occupies a peculiar position – it's artistic and intellectual, but every performance shows its links with show business.
I think it's very hard not to. Having worked in academia, and with classical musicians, both those worlds are full of people who would deny that their music has anything to do with show business. Clearly, jazz is very much another branch of show business. So is academia – and classical music, really.

There's a Christian Marclay montage of a Deutsche Grammophon record, Herbert von Karajan with his perfectly coiffed grey hair, standing in front of a wind machine. Marclay puts long legs with high heels on it, from some 1970s disco record.

A Deutsche Grammophon cover is just another schtick – "looking towards the future" in a serious way, as composers were meant to do. I think the classical music world are concerned with image, it's just that they're desperate not to be thought to.

Of course, classical music attracts money because it's prestigious. Generally it doesn't make much money for the players, unless you're Nigel Kennedy – but there aren't that many Nigel Kennedys.

Classical music is certainly a branch of show business. You sell some genres of music on not being commercial, but that's how you sell it. All my students believe in some kind of authentic band that just plays for itself, and is not interested in selling itself. But of course that's actually part of selling the band. Authenticity is a huge thing in certain branches of popular music.

That's close to Adorno's view that its apparent lack of commodification gives high art its commodity status. There's nothing wrong with doing things to please the audience, but there is something wrong with doing things . . .
That you loathe, yes. I can think of somebody doing something right now that he's really trying hard to convince himself he doesn't loathe. At some point he's going to realise that he does. You can kid yourself in these things. We kid ourselves all the time about loads of things, so it's not that unusual, but I think people do gather up their self-delusional chops and use them particularly for situations which are quite attractive financially. Who can blame them?

Do you ever have that issue?
Very rarely.

You've had some contact with pop culture. Could you ever have sold out? Jim Hall was asked "How come you never sold out?," and he replied, "No one ever asked me."
That's very true! Evan Parker was, and is, really into Dusty Springfield, and at one time he sat down to write a song for her – I never heard it. If I'd thought there was any chance I could get a song sung by her, I would have written a song like that. But those things are closed off.

Or you might just not have that musical skill.
Well, I never tried. I've certainly written utterly conventional stuff. That's the thing about popular music – access is very restricted. Look at "Nature Boy," that's an amazing story. [Its composer] Eden Ahbez was like a hippy – he had long hair and robes – and this was 1947, not the 1960s. Nat "King" Cole said "I have to sing that."[3]

A popular hit shows some particular skill. We can't all produce one. Schoenberg never had that skill.[4]
It has to be simple, and yet get in your head.

* * *

THE FLYING LIZARDS were a UK experimental new wave band, formed in 1976 and led by record producer David Cunningham. They comprised a loose collective of avantgarde and free improvising musicians that at one point included David Toop and Steve Beresford as instrumentalists. They are best known for their cover of Barrett Strong's "Money," in which Deborah Evans-Stickland delivers her lead vocals in a robotic monotone; it reached the UK and US record charts in 1979. The group disbanded in 1984.

You've been on the fringes of popular culture.
Yes, definitely. In 1979 The Flying Lizards were on Top of the Pops a few times – not to my memory with Jimmy Savile, which everyone asks these days. Derek Bailey was in the band in Leeds that accompanied Savile, and he utterly loathed him – I think Savile was loathed by virtually everybody. So I had some contact with the pop world.

I think that was the *Top Of The Pops* where Cliff Richard sang "We Don't Talk Anymore," which I think was his best record – it's a really good song. Neither David Toop nor myself were on the record of "Money" – I think Julian Marshall was the keyboard player. I think we were on *Top Of The Pops* twice. Also we played in Munich, which was the first time I met The Slits, who were on the same show.

Comparing Dusty Springfield's version of "The Look of Love" and Diana Krall's – both are excellent, but Krall's is somehow more creative. I guess that as a pop singer, Springfield tended to do it virtually the same each time – or is that my inner jazz snob speaking?
I don't love Diane Krall, but I think she's OK. You'd expect her versions to be looser than Dusty's. I like Dusty doing that song a lot, but she was also one of the trio of UK singers – along with Sandie Shaw and Cilla Black – who jumped on Dionne Warwick's Wand singles, did them over with less hip UK session players and got enormous hits.[5]

Dionne had a gospel background but had a more "legit" voice than, say, Inez Andrews or Shirley Caesar. Critics would say that a rough vocal tone signified how close to black music you were. Of course, that's nonsense – light-toned singers like Curtis Mayfield had a deep connection to that history. Sam Cooke's late live album, *Live at the Harlem Square Club, 1963*, shows him in a different mood to his pop singles.

Just before he got thrown into jail [for tax evasion], Ron Isley did a great album with Bacharach of the old tunes where he ad libs much more than Dionne – he has a looser interpretation.[6]

* * *

THE SLITS were formed in 1976 by fourteen-year-old Ariane (Arianna) Daniela Forster (1962–2010), known by her stage name Ari Up in 1976, with drummer Palmolive. (Arianna was the step-daughter of John Lydon.) Within a short time, guitarist Viv Albertine joined. VIV ALBERTINE, born in 1954 in Sydney, Australia, was brought up in North London. She helped form the Flowers of

Romance with Sid Vicious, and then joined The Slits as the band's guitarist in 1976. Their debut *Cut* (1979), produced by Denis Bovell and released on Island, was a key album of the post-punk era. She has written two volumes of raw, uncompromising autobiography including *Clothes, Clothes, Clothes. Music, Music, Music. Boys, Boys, Boys* (2014).

You worked with The Slits in the early 1980s. What do you feel about their music?
I think *Cut* is a fantastic record – I love it. It wasn't a punk record – it was what punk could have become. John Lydon had PiL, that was development, but I think most punk musicians didn't go anywhere musically. The Slits did.

Viv Albertine has written a novel. Have you read her memoir? She said some very nice things about me in it. Rough Trade said they sold thousands [of the memoir]. It's got a few "hide behind the sofa moments."

I saw her at the Stoke Newington literary festival – she's funny, clever, unpretentious. She gets interviewed a lot because she's a really good talker.

You met Viv Albertine because she started coming to Derek Bailey gigs.
She came to lots of Company gigs – with her boyfriend Gareth Sager [of The Pop Group and later Rip, Rig & Panic]. I thought Viv was very beautiful and managed to get to talk to her. Gareth was doing the noisy bits in The Slits but they were looking for someone else.

What was your role with them?
Basically I was replacing Gareth Sager. I don't know why they wanted me to replace him. He played keyboards and a few other things – saxophone, I think.

My impression was that they wanted me to make random noises, but I wanted to get a bit more involved. On "I Heard It Through the Grapevine," I played the chords.

I played a bit of guitar. They got me this really horrible Yamaha electric piano with a stick-on wooden veneer and one noise that was vaguely acceptable. I wanted a Fender Rhodes. We also had a Farfisa VIP 500, which I loved and still have – a dual-manual electric organ, wonderfully cheesy. Farfisas are the essence of cheese. I also played guitar, flugelhorn and euphonium.

The Slits started out as a punk band, but this was post-punk. The first time I saw them, I think it was at a club called The Vortex – obviously not the jazz club – and I thought they were the funniest thing I'd ever seen.

Unintentionally?
Who knows? They had these tutus, and big Doc Martens, and the hair all mad. Paloma [known as Palmolive], the original drummer, was with them. She had all these speech rhythms, but clearly had no idea what metrical rhythm was about.

It's a bit like The Shaggs. It turned out they knew all about The Shaggs, but they didn't tell me! What made The Slits interesting as a punk group was that they hadn't worked out some of the basic rules of punk, for instance that you're all in the same metre – and you're playing four in the bar, and you start at the same time. But they were fantastic – and one of the reasons was that they were absolutely hilarious. They would always go "1 2 3 4," without realising that that was meant to be the tempo – for them, it was just like "Ready Steady Go." And they seemed extremely belligerent, at nothing in particular.

When I was with The Slits, the media focus was always on women musicians. The Slits said, "No, we'd like to talk about the music, actually. Why is it such a big deal that we're women? Wouldn't you like to talk about the music?" People were always asking how it is to be a woman musician in a macho world, blah blah blah – they'd been asked that question a zillion times.

* * *

TESSA POLLITT played bass with The Slits between 1976 and 1981, and again when Ari Up, the band's singer, re-formed them with some new members from 2006 to 2010 – sadly, Ari died in 2010. Her albums with them include *Cut* (Island, 1979), *Return Of The Giant Slits* (CBS, 1981) and *Trapped Animal* (Narnack, 2010). She is now a DJ who plays under the name Bassie, with SoftWax and M.C. Doc. Murdoch, with a roots, dub and reggae sound. She writes:

> *The Slits evolved from punk to experiment with genres including reggae, dub, jazz and world music, with influences from nursery rhymes, and natural sounds – Ari was renowned for her signature bird-sounds. It is difficult to put The Slits sound into any category, it is simply a Slitsy Sound and quite unique.*
>
> *Steve always added a sprinkling of magic when he played with The Slits, both live and on recordings – he appreciated our mixture of humour and seriousness. Steve was always fun to be with – he put up with The Slits' antics and madness, and never a dull moment was had. He added something special to the sound, on a wide array of instruments – toys, trumpet, euphonium, percussion. Steve could master any instrument, it seems.*
>
> *Steve is featured on the recent Slits documentary "Here To Be Heard." I did the sleeve design for two albums Steve released with Tristan Honsinger, "Double Indemnity" [1980] and "Imitation of Life" [1981].*
>
> *I often bump into Steve at Honest Jons record shop on Portobello Road, when I am searching for records for DJ-ing. I am constantly amazed at his knowledge of*

a wide selection of music. For instance, I asked him about Jimmy Scott's version of "Motherless Child," and he made a CD of Scott's songs, and sheet music. I also told him my first 7" single when I was a child was "Tubby The Tuba" and I very much missed hearing it – in no time he'd made me a copy. I have nothing but respect for Steve's fount of knowledge, and musical inventiveness.

* * *

It was never a band that was "strictly no men." Budgie was a fantastic choice – he was a really good drummer. *Cut* was their first record, and it was produced by Dennis Bovell – he's a really good bass-player, and could play drums, and guitar. He was a brilliant producer for the band, because they were already moving away from punk. They reset a lot of the songs they did, with much more interesting basslines and parts. This was their artistically most successful record – not commercially, they didn't sell many. I think Viv Albertine's first book sold more than any single Slits record.

* * *

DENNIS BOVELL aka Blackbeard was a power behind the flourishing of reggae in late 1970s Britain. With Linton Kwesi Johnson, Misty in Roots, the Pop Group, Rip Rig & Panic, Black Uhuru and The Slits, he created a multicultural scene for reggae and post-punk. *I Wah Dub* (More Cut, 1980) is a twenty-seven-minute, almost entirely instrumental album expressing Bovell's Lee Perry and King Tubby obsessions. He plays guitar on all but one track, bass and keyboards. A deep, basic, nocturnal mix, Thom Jurek calls it "a [masterpiece] of dark, twisting, utterly melodic dread reggae."

* * *

We did two American tours, one of them in 1981.
The second one, Neneh Cherry was on. She was Arianna's best friend at that time.
Were these some of the biggest audiences you've played for?
I imagine so. We did the Communist Party event in Ally Pally [Alexandra Palace in London] – with an East German opera company doing Mozart, and a rock 'n' roll stage. Maybe The Raincoats were on it as well.

Touring with The Slits in the late 1970s and early 1980s, we visited Philadelphia – where Sun Ra lived [from 1968 till his death in 1993]. We looked him up in the phone book, and his address was there, under "Ra, Sun."

I suggested we phone up, but The Slits said we should just go there. So we drove, past lots of wooden houses. He wasn't at home – he was playing a Halloween gig, his neighbour said.

Next day I got up really early to go to the Museum and see the Duchamps – but they were all on tour except for the Large Glass.

Some great soul records came out of Philadelphia, and doowop classics.

This is part of your involvement with pop culture.

The Slits were never massively popular, but I suppose so.

* * *

Reggae deejay and producer PRINCE FAR-I (1944–83) was born Michael James Williams in Spanish Town, Jamaica. With his deep bass voice and talking-over style, he described himself as a "chanter" rather than a "toaster"; he became a popular reggae musician, calling himself "The Voice of Thunder." Between 1978 and 1981 he released the highly regarded Cry Tuff Dub Encounter series, which he produced and released on his Cry Tuff label, featuring the Roots Radics under the pseudonym The Arabs – Chapter 3, with Toop and Beresford, appeared in 1980. He spent an increasing amount of time in England, becoming mentor to dub producer Adrian Sherwood. In 1983 he was fatally shot in a robbery at his home in Kingston, Jamaica.

Adrian Sherwood called and said why don't you do a session, playing things over the top of dub tracks – I contacted David Toop, and it became *Cry Tuff Dub Encounter Chapter 3*. David brought his flute, but mainly it was unconventional instruments. I was a session musician on that date – under the auspices of Adrian Sherwood and his label, we just got things thrown at us, which we loved. There weren't many directions, we just played stuff over the top, and those became elements in the dub – that's what dub music's about. I'm very pleased to have been on that record. We don't play on every track.

Prince Far-I was at the recording session in Clerkenwell – I think he was producing it, he gave us a few instructions. I don't think he performed that day. Adrian Sherwood was there as well, I'm not sure who was doing what, I wasn't in the control room.

Prince Far-I had an extremely strong patois and a famously deep voice, so I couldn't understand all of what he was saying. He toasted as well as producing records. My favourite [of his recordings] was "Bedward The Flying Preacher."

Bedward announces in church that he's going to jump off the roof of the mission and fly. He does this and plunges to his death. Far-I had quite a sense of humour in his dry way – it's a great record.

I think they'd lined up all these tracks on multi-track already. On *Cry Tuff*, certainly there was bass and drums, maybe keyboards, when we added our parts. They played us the backing-tracks – the producer would just say "Play something," and we played.

The backing-tracks were recorded in Jamaica. The rhythm section was the Roots Radics. They were not quite as famous as Sly Dunbar and Robbie Shakespeare, perhaps the best-known rhythm section in reggae. The rhythm section went into the studio in Jamaica, and quite likely they'd start playing something with a riff and drum-lick. That rhythm would be built into a song. If the rhythm was looking like a good one, it would get used for dozens of different records – they put in different melodies, toasted over it, put different sounds over the top of that structure.

Dave Hunt was the engineer – this was at Berry Street studios [in Barbican, London EC1].

Was he mainly recording reggae?
I think so.[7] Then Max Eastley, David Toop and I started using Dave for experimental music, which he has a great affinity for. He's got fantastic ears and he loves a challenge. When free improvisers get in the studio, they want to set up the stuff and just play for an hour or two hours, and be confident that the engineer will capture that sound without too much fuss – and he's so good at that, people love working with him.

I did quite a lot of things that had connections with pop music. Alex Balanescu was in a couple of rock 'n' roll bands at that time.[8] There's much more crossover now – then, it was much more unusual.

* * *

In his teens, ADRIAN SHERWOOD (born in 1958) was inspired by reggae to teach himself sound engineering. His career reflects dub's inter-racial UK trajectory, transfused by reggae, punk, acid house and experimental hiphop. He's collaborated with Prince Far-I, Lee Scratch Perry, Ari Up, PiL, Mark Stewart, Depeche Mode, Primal Scream and Asian Dub Foundation. He has recently commissioned remixes from, and toured with, dubstep producers Mala (Digital Mystikz) and Kode 9. To celebrate thirty years of On-U Sound, his most well-known label, Sherwood is reissuing a series of key releases.

I first met Steve in 1979, during The Slits tour. [Author's note: <u>Beresford joined The Slits shortly after the tour</u>]. Creation Rebel and Prince Hammer were supporting The Slits and Don Cherry, who had a band called Happy House that was Lou Reed's backing band. I became good friends with Ari [Ari Up of The Slits] – I introduced her to loads of reggae stuff. After that tour, we were squatting together with [Don's step-daughter] Neneh Cherry, who was only fifteen.

I had Steve play on those gigs with Doug Wimbish and Keith LeBlanc, the first time they came over. I recorded him quite a few times – he played on the New Age Steppers' [eponymous] first album (1980). Steve was always playing with these little funny instruments, I liked him. He was a nice bloke, a bit quirky – but I admired what he did, he had a basket of funny noises! I also met David Toop at the same period – the first Cry Tuff dub album came out on my label Hit Run in 1977 or 78, when I was 19.

Far-I gave me a load of tapes, and I overdubbed Crucial Tony [Phillips], Clifton "Bigga" Morrison, and some of our other mates. I put on some percussion, and a little Rolf Harris stylophone – things to make up Cry Tuff Dub Encounter Chapter 1. It needed a bit of fun adding to it, so we did those overdubs. Chapter 2 we gave to Virgin, and they said "Come and overdub like you did the first one." By the time it got to Chapter 3, Keith Stone at Daddy Kool said he'd release it. So we hired Berry Street [studio], and I invited Toop and Steve to overdub some funny noises, really.

[At the session] Far-I was there, just letting things roll. We wanted to see what these people would come up with – we just let David and Steve have an hour or so, overdubbing a few tunes, adding some colours.

What do you do to make your instrumentals interesting? You find an instrumentalist who's got a sound of their own.

David and Steve were definitely avantgarde and very interesting musicians. I'd happily get Steve on another session, overdubbing – he's a brilliant improviser. I met Lol Coxhill and that crew of friends he had – Steve is a teacher, he's very much his own man. He's got his own little oddities – it was a lot of fun working with him.

With dub, it's like minimalised jazz – you've got four players, and maybe one's playing on his own, and someone jumps in and out. Steve and David occupy an odd part of the world, but they're both master musicians – the fact that they were curious about the dub area is quite logical, because there's more space in dub.

I was overdubbing some rhythms, before we dubbed what we were adding. Reggae works where you make a version of a rhythm – you might have ten different vocalists on a rhythm [on different versions] – which is unique to Jamaican music. You can make thirty or forty versions of one rhythm – people demand more adaptations of the rhythm. So we were stripping down, using little bits of rhythm that you bring back, in washes of delay and reverb. The effect it has on the listener in the end is that they can hear things that aren't really there, like suggestions of melodies. You get something really beautiful – it's all colours to me, sound, anyway.

* * *

Were you a fan of punk?
No.

Sophie [Richmond] from Malcolm McLaren's office was the first to play me a Sex Pistols record. I said, "It just sounds like the Rolling Stones, what's good about this?"

I quite liked The Jam – and "New Rose" by The Damned, I could see that was a good record. Then I heard The Ramones – I thought they were hilarious. I liked the bands that weren't deliberately funny.

Punk was all about what you don't do in music – you don't sing about love, you don't play anything slow, you don't have complicated chords, you don't have guitar solos, you don't have a tune . . .

I remember [jazz pianist] Kirk Lightsey wrote a sleeve note satirising white popular music, from the polka to punk. Is it absurd – or racist – to say that I prefer African-American popular music?
Before they did Chic, Bernard Edwards and Nile Rodgers were trying to form a punk band. All the record companies said, "You can't have a black punk band." Of course, you could – Bad Brains were a black punk band, they were pretty good.

There isn't much black rock music – Hendrix, James Ulmer's Black Rock Coalition, Prince . . .
Come on – half the Rolling Stones' so-called compositions were just Robert Johnson songs.

Isn't that cultural appropriation? I'd call metal a white form.
You're being very essentialist here. There's a lot more black musicians involved in what people think of as white music. Tom Wilson was an African-American record producer who produced The Velvet Underground, Bob Dylan and Frank Zappa – and he did a very good job.

I used to be a jazz snob who didn't like rock, partly because of the effect it had on jazz.
Gigi Campi had been the manager of the Kenny Clarke–Francy Boland Big Band – Tony Coe was a member, it was a very good band. Tony and Lol and I did a

gig in Cologne, and we went to see Gigi, who had a restaurant near to where we were playing. Gigi kept saying, "The fucking Beatles have ruined jazz." A lot of people used to say that. But I'm not sure it's true – even without The Beatles, would people have gone out and bought John Coltrane records?

* * *

Do you like World Music?
Well, I like music that's in the world.
That's like the joke about folk music – "It's all folk music, I ain't never heard no horse sing," as Big Bill Broonzy said.
Or Louis Armstrong.
Do you listen to Indian music, or gamelan?
I like qawwali, that style of Indian singing that Pandit Pran Nath and Nusrat Fateh Ali Khan do. I listen to Bollywood music quite a lot, and I ended up doing a pastiche of a score for a Bollywood movie.
Is there any music that you don't like – apart from the most commodified trash, that is?
I hate power ballads. But I quite like some commodified pop music.
Like what?
Those kind of uptempo girl groups, American ones – Blondie.
But when it's ultra-commodified . . .
There's the stuff that sounds like it's really on total auto, they're just churning it out – which tends to include power ballads. Celine Dion, or pastiches of her – that kind of thing.

But that's a really boring old git comment, we'll have to take it out!
We were discussing the two kinds of artists – those who are eclectic, and those who have a narrow focus.
There's people who say, "I don't have time to listen to all these kinds of music."
Which just means "I don't consider this worthy of my time."
Of course. They mean "Why would I be listening to Bollywood, if I could listen to Bach Cello Suites?"

I'm definitely in your first category of musicians. It was helped along by days spent with Evan Parker, listening to Tibetan chants, African music, Noh, Coltrane and Stockhausen. And with John Stevens and David Toop – those people I would hang out with, who had huge record collections.

But I think I always had broad tastes.

Of course, it depends how you see it. Pop music has such narrow gradations between styles – it could be more to do with their trousers than anything else, that's what the music's about. On *The Wire* [magazine] samplers, apart from a couple of improv tracks, nearly everything is a medium-tempo eight feel, with the snare drum on two and four, and the bass drum on one and three. Nobody would say that's stylistically restrictive. They're right in a way. You could make that drum pattern work for millions of things, as Al Jackson did with Booker T. and the M.G.'s, and Otis Redding – one of the very simplest drummers ever, and when he was good he was amazing.

But those beats get constantly recycled. That's why the Robin Thicke case is so ridiculous; I can think of a million songs that are just like Marvin Gaye's song, because the parameters are so narrow.[9] It's like saying "You just put that article out, and you used the word 'and' and 'the'. I've used those words already, I'm going to sue you." The Marx Brothers did *A Night in Casablanca* a few years after *Casablanca*, and Warner Brothers said they'd sue. And Groucho said that Warner Brothers used the word "Brothers," and *he* was going to sue.[10]

You're right about the eight feel on *Wire* samplers. I hadn't thought much about the evolution of straight time from swing. The evolution of swing, from two-beat to four-beat, gets discussed a lot – but not the evolution of straight time that's essential to rock. If you listen to Elvis, there's a swing feel early on, then it disappears.[11]

"Twist and Shout," by the Isley Brothers [1962] – which was a massive hit – was one of the first rock 'n' roll or r 'n' b records with an "eight" feel. It was produced by Bert Berns, who'd previously worked with salsa musicians. The history books say that it was one of the most influential recordings, in terms of popular music becoming an eight feel.

The Isley Brothers were extraordinary – they had so many hits, in so many genres. They went through a period in Motown, they did covers of white pop songs, and ballads – and they were one of the bands that Hendrix played with. They had so many connections.

Nowadays, almost everything is an eight feel. Shuffles are few and far between. You also get triplet sixteenths. There had been eight feels in black music. Bongo Joe, who played a big oil can – he's on an Arhoolie record – plays straight eights.[12]

[Western] classical music tends to divide the bar into two's and four's.

Improvising over an eight feel is different to improvising over a swing feel.

Lee Konitz said it wasn't so fruitful.
I think that's true for most jazz musicians. You don't hear Konitz playing a lot of eight feels.
 You're right, it's a massive change in popular music.
The only explanation I've heard is that Latin music is an influence.
People who worked with Latin musicians – such as Bert Berns – were also working with African-American musicians.
Matt Brennan mentions the issue in his recent book *Kick It* – a history of drum-kit.[13] **That's another thing I hadn't thought about – its creation in the last century, beginning with the bass-pedal, and the hi-hat, and other elements.**
The development of drum-kit is an interesting thing in itself.

* * *

What would your Desert Island discs consist of?
It would mostly be jazz.
 I certainly get much less out of contemporary pop music than I used to. There don't seem to be any pop records with an autonomous bass-line. At one point, pretty much every pop record had an interesting bass-line – it could be Chic, it could be the Beatles. Melodic patterns, unexpected inversions of the chord . . .
What passes for melody doesn't seem to have melodic allure at all, today – a falsetto singer with robotic auto-tune.
Yes, I find that incredibly tedious. There's always this androgynous voice with auto-tune – they're high-voiced anyway.

Notes

1 In 1981, Toop, Beresford, Cusack and writer Sue Steward founded the magazine *Collusion*. It ran for five issues, with articles on rap, salsa, Nigerian praise songs, bebop vocals, Japanese Enka music, women DJs, radio in New Guinea, Bengali music in London and much else.
2 Steve adds: "Maybe they used the word for anything that mixed styles. Or maybe I misunderstood."
3 Eden Ahbez – who preferred the lower case eden ahbez – reputedly got the song to Cole by slipping a crumpled manuscript to his valet. Cole began performing "Nature Boy" to live audiences, but needed the composer's permission for a

recording. Ahbez was discovered living under the Hollywood Sign, and became the focus of a media frenzy when Cole's version became a hit in summer 1948. A classic recording is Miles Davis's 1955 recording, with Teddy Charles on vibes, Britt Woodman on trombone, Charles Mingus on bass, and Elvin Jones on drums.

4 Schoenberg did write 8 *Brettllieder* ("Cabaret songs"), in 1901.
5 The Wand singles featured songs by Bacharach and David, written for Dionne Warwick.
6 *Here I Am: Isley Meets Bacharach,* by Ronald Isley and Burt Bacharach (Dreamworks, 2003).
7 David Toop comments [email to author, 2020]: "Dave Hunt did do a lot of reggae, but he also engineered groups like Pigbag – it was a studio that attracted a lot of unusual sessions, partly because the costs were reasonable."
8 Alexander Balanescu, born in 1954, was a Romanian violinist and the founder of the Balanescu Quartet, leader of the Michael Nyman Band and a member of the Gavin Bryars Ensemble.
9 The long-running lawsuit involved copyright infringement surrounding Robin Thicke and Pharrell Williams' song "Blurred Lines" and Marvin Gaye's 1977 hit "Got to Give It Up." The Gaye family won their case, and the appeal – a judge entered a nearly $5 million judgement in their favour: www.nytimes.com/2018/03/21/business/media/blurred-lines-marvin-gaye-copyright.html
10 This story seems to be apocryphal, but as George Orwell would say, "Essentially true."
11 This neglected topic is discussed by Stewart (2000). Little Richard pounds a straight feel on his 1956 Slippin' and Slidin', while drummer Earl Palmer still plays a swing shuffle. Palmer commented: "Jazz is all anybody played until we started making those [R&B] records. The backbeat came about because the public wasn't buying jazz, so we put something in that was simpler" (quoted in Brennan (2020), pp. 187–8). Most of Elvis Presley's 1950s hits had a feel between straight and swing.
12 *Bongo Joe* by George Coleman (Arhoolie, 1969) – Coleman ("Bongo Joe," 1923–99) was a street musician who in Houston in the 1940s fabricated a drum-kit from oil drums.
13 Brennan (2020).

17

Electronics, Sound, and Recording

Steve Beresford often deploys electronic media in his performances; he also has extensive experience as a producer. In this final chapter we discuss these connections, beginning with his use of electronics. We discuss the invention of noisemakers such as the Cracklebox by Michel Waisvisz. We move on to consider the role of the producer in a recording session. The chapter concludes by looking at the contrast between LPs and CDs, and the role of recordings in free improvised music.

I don't use a laptop – I don't want to use something that's crucial but might break down. The more technology you have, the more possibilities of it going wrong. Every time I go to a presentation, someone is using PowerPoint and saying, "Why is this not working?"

The problem is, it's got everything in it, so if it goes wrong, everything goes wrong. Whereas if you've got a bunch of things – a sampler, a keyboard, a wah-wah pedal – and something goes wrong in that chain, you can just take the thing out and you've still got the rest of it.

And the possibilities are too huge in how you use it?
Probably that as well. But you never get that feeling when you hear someone playing them – it always sounds like the possibilities are very narrow.
"Keyboard" is ambiguous. On piano, the touch makes an effect, but not on a laptop – yet performers often suggest it does, by their gestures.
Absolutely.

I don't think people are doing a very good job of coming to terms with new technology. It's getting to look like "boys with their train sets," which it does periodically. I've been to a couple of gigs recently which has been like trainspotting music. There's a fetish about "I'm using the latest software." I've been to lectures where people discuss their musical development purely in terms of the technology they have that year.

It was interesting to see how subtle Pat Thomas's music is in comparison. He has a processed mini-theremin, and it was just such a relief not to listen to this "off the shelf" electronics, which I'm supposed to enjoy on a technical level.

There's a fetishisation of old-fashioned technology as well.

But there are people who love – and are trying to preserve – analogue technology. Like Thomas Lehn's analogue synths.

I don't think Thomas fetishizes that. He gets something new out of it. But just as Ben Webster is instantly recognisable on tenor saxophone, it would be nice if people were instantly recognisable on electronics.

* * *

PAT THOMAS, improviser on piano and electronics, is a long-time collaborator of Beresford's. He studied classical piano from age eight, and began playing jazz at sixteen. His unique style embraces improvisation, jazz and new music. He has played with Derek Bailey in Company Week 1990/91, and in the trio AND with Steve Noble; he was a member of Tony Oxley's Quartet and Celebration Orchestra, and worked in a duo with Lol Coxhill. In 2014 he received a Paul Hamlyn Award for Artists. He is a member of Ahmed, a quartet inspired by the music of Ahmed Abdul-Malik; Black Top is his duo with multi-instrumentalist Orphy Robinson.

> *I've known Steve all my career! I probably met him about 1983–4, when I was 23. I was playing in Mayhem Quartet, with Neil Palmer on turntables, Mike Cooper and Tim Hill. It was one of the first groups to use a turntable – we did a gig at the LMC.*
>
> *Steve's a great mentor for a lot of people in improvised music. Working with him, he's a totally open player and as an improviser, you've really got to be on your toes because he's so quick. He's got such a great knowledge of sound, whether it's electronics or piano.*
>
> *Steve doesn't have a "signature style." His style changes constantly according to the situation. But I do know it's Steve – I know there's only one person who can do those things. With electronics, it looks like he's got all this junk, but Steve knows exactly what everything can do. He's got stuff that's there just in case something else packs up. He's very serious about what he does, and knows exactly what he wants.*
>
> *The Melody Four was great, but it confused people. When you play one style, then something else, people are shocked – which is a bit crazy. If John Tilbury plays Bach and then Cage, people don't think "Wow! I didn't know he could do that."*

In the 80s, John Zorn's thing of mixing and matching genres became a New York style. Steve and Alterations were doing that – I'm sure Zorn would've been aware. Really it's about sound and keeping the thing fresh. And if that means playing a chord where it shouldn't be played, that's the aesthetic they're working with.

Alterations were a fantastic group because they developed this approach where everybody could have this independence, and then at the drop of a hat they'd all play the same thing at the same time, which is incredible. They were a big influence on me – I heard them on Jazz in Britain [BBC Radio 3]. There were folk influences, and I could tell these guys listened to a lot of James Brown and all sorts of things.

That was new for free improvisation. The first generation [of free improvisers] were creating this new language. They would be in a similar position to Schoenberg – once he'd created his twelve-tone system, he didn't want any semblance of the old style. Alterations were aware that something familiar, like playing a chord, could sound shocking again. Even though I was interested in jazz, I would never have played Duke Ellington compositions, because I was trying to develop my own language. Once you're confident in it, then you can be broader.

* * *

The Cracklebox is a noise-making electronic device. Michel Waisvisz and Geert Hamelberg designed and built the first Crackle circuit in the late 1960s – a wooden frame with some print boards mounted rear-side up, to be touched by the fingers. The circuits were "malformed" oscillators, very unstable and highly sensitive for finger connections. In 1973 Waisvisz joined STEIM, and together with Peter Beyls, Nico Bes and Johan den Biggelaar worked on more touchable electronic instruments; by the mid-1970s they had created the Crackle Synth and the Cracklebox.

Michel Waisvisz was a Dutch electronics guy – he was director of STEIM for a bit. He's most famous for the Cracklebox, which came about through him putting his hand in the back of mains radios – which is mad, you could kill yourself doing that. He devised something that fitted into a bit of plastic drainpipe – a series of squares of solder – that made crackly noises. It's a lot of fun.

The joke about the Cracklebox is that nobody knew how to get anything specific out of it. They got all these famous musicians to play it – Steve Lacy, Derek Bailey – but they sounded the same. Maybe you could say it's a musical instrument, with its own rules – you didn't know what it would do, when you started playing it.

You knew the soundworld, but what exactly it was going to play was not predictable. The noise was crackles, and maybe a high-pitched squeal.

How did you use it yourself?
I think I used it with Alterations – Pete Cusack may have used one, too. The model I had, had been given to me by Derek Bailey – it was a prototype, with a comparatively big speaker but not much volume.

* * *

You're a prolific recording artist, aren't you?
Nothing compared to say, Evan Parker. Evan records all the time.

Are your preparations for a studio recording session different from those for a live performance – even if the performance is going to be recorded?
I can't remember the last time I recorded free improvisation in a studio – that's interesting. I think the last thing I did was with Dave Tucker and Steven Flynn, in Dave Hunt's basement.[1]

Dave will set up incredibly quickly and get a fantastic sound. So really, it's like doing a gig, only not in front of anyone.

He's a recording engineer, not a producer.
Well, usually the producer is someone in the group, or maybe the whole group. You don't necessarily have a producer for an improvised music record. Producer can mean "recording engineer." It can be many things. Evan wrote a very good letter to *Avant* magazine years ago, which I kept copies of, explaining what a producer does on an improvised music record. He made a fantastic list.

"Brings in the carry-outs," you mean?
That certainly could be one thing, or possibly hides the carry-out until they've done it, then they can have a beer. That's what I'd do, personally – but also a lot of things. Just knowing when it's good to have a coffee break, or when it's good to say, "You know what, it's not working, can we try this?"

Like in film?
It means a completely different thing in film.

The producer used to be the artistic mind behind the film, then the director became that.
Those words change their meaning all the time, but now the executive producer is the person to put the money up.

I remember a very bad session, with an engineer who shall be nameless. He was obsessed with separation. It comes from pop – if you didn't like trombone, you could take it out and put another trombone in. But you're not going to do that with improvised music!

So you don't need separation. Obviously you need to equalise things a bit.[2] But really what you need to do is to make a recording that is basically pretty good to start off with – you just get a good sound on the group.

The group has a way of setting up which is comfortable for them – so they can hear each other, and hear themselves. Most improvisers are very good at that. So don't fuck with that – arrange your microphones around that situation. Perhaps there will be a bit of spill from drums onto piano track, but it actually doesn't matter because you're not going to mess with those things that much. Don't worry so much about the possibility of radically equalising, because you're not going to do that.

You have the layout of the room which will appear in the stereo picture, and you just get a good-sounding recording, as if you were just going straight to stereo.

It's very simple actually. But of course many engineers have got these things that they do, which actually get between you and the music. Dave Hunt knows that he doesn't need to do that. He trusts us and we trust him.

I think it's like wildlife recording. You can't ask the lion to go after another giraffe. You can't say, "Could you do that again please, Mr Lion – could you do that a bit louder, your growling. And more blood this time."

I think improvised music should be like that.

Have you seen that concert footage with Charles Mingus and Eric Dolphy – I think Jaki Byard's in it?[3] The way they set up on stage – they're very close to each other. Obviously the piano-player has to be a bit more distant, but they get as close as possible.

I've been in so many situations where people want to spread the ensemble across the stage, because it looks great. Rock 'n' roll bands can do that because the whole thing is about monitors – if the lead guitarist has got a stack [of speakers] thirty feet away, you can hear it through your monitor anyway.

Too many gigs are amplified when the size of the venue doesn't call for it.
I think there's an antagonism between sound people and musicians. The 1950s microphone – a vintage ribbon mic used for the bass drum – comes out, and I think "Alright, we're fucked." All you need for a drum is two overheads [mics]. If it's rock, and amplified drums is part of the music, that's another thing. But as

Paul Lovens said, if it's improvised music, you don't need the vintage mic on the bass-drum.

I did a gig where we had a little PA, which we'd agreed we'd use for someone to give a little lecture – and we had a dancer at the end, so they needed the space. And somebody's already put a monitor down! And we're already falling over it. As far as I can see, monitors are only for you to fall over. They're always in a place where you're going to break your ankle – and of course they're black, so if it's dark you don't see them. I hate them. These are things that people put down without even thinking about it.

Most musicians, because of the rock influence, always assume you need a PA.
Yes, it's ridiculous.

We had a gig in Berlin with Lore Lixenberg. She said, "I want to do a duet with my hairdresser." We didn't know what was going to happen. The hairdresser showed up, and Lore said, "We need to amplify the scissors" – so we realised she was going to have her hair cut as part of the performance, and sing through this. She wanted to amplify the scissors. I did have an amp, and a clothes-peg contact mic, so she tried that on the scissors, and held the amplifier. It was very funny. She was amazing. She sang her head off, mainly about "Please don't make it too short!" The hairdresser was totally focused on cutting the hair – she did a very good job!

* * *

Thinking about your recent, unreleased solo piano recording...
It's a stereo microphone stuck inside a piano. What more are you going to do?
You wouldn't produce it yourself.
I wouldn't produce my solo piano record – that's narcissistic! I can't see how it would not be self-indulgent. You can't be objective. I don't think you should publish your own books either for the same reason.

But maybe a solo piano record is narcissistic.

I'd love to work with Pat Thomas – if he wanted a producer, I'd be very happy to produce a Pat Thomas solo record.
What's your reason for making recordings?
I like records very much – I think they're great.
As artefacts? LPs?
Yes. I like CDs as well. I like recordings of music. I still get a real thrill when I'm on a new record, and I like playing records of improvised music. I think they're

more interesting than most other records. There's this cliché, "I like it live but I don't like it on record." People are entitled to feel that, but I don't think it's true. In *The Wire*'s *Invisible Jukebox*, Derek Bailey claimed not to recognise anything he was played – "All sound the bloody same to me." Listening to records, he argued, "introduces the endgame to something that is [not] about endgame.... The point of the record is that you can play it again.... It'll all eventually become mood music, right?"[4]
I think Derek has a point.
But obviously he could tell those tracks apart.
I think it's partly a wind-up.
The pianist Artur Schnabel refused to make recordings because, he said, "I have a terrible fear of making a record of a Beethoven sonata and somewhere, someday, someone is going to listen to it while eating a liverwurst sandwich."
A very sensitive chap.

* * *

A really good improvisation is one you can examine again and again – at least as much as analysing a notated piece. Very often people who write notated music will encode stuff. They'll have an overall pattern that they'll fill in with pitches. All you're doing is decoding something that's been encoded, whereas with improvised music those structures are often unconscious. Sometimes you'll think "I did this sound at the beginning, I'll do it at the end." But you don't know if it's going to be the end if you're playing in a group. You might go back to the beginning stuff, but people will carry on because they want to continue, or they just want to be awkward. Then that's your coding gone.
There's the idea that improvisation should be process, not product.
That's true of all music, isn't it, whether it's Thelonious Monk or Alfred Brendel? That's why Glenn Gould went back and recorded the *Goldberg Variations* again, he had a different way of playing them. His idea about them had changed.
The power of recording has meant that in classical music, playing a wrong note is seen as a disaster.
I think that classical musicians have changed their mind about a lot of things – certainly the ones I know, like Mandhira de Saram and Anton Lukoszevieze. They don't have the idea that a wrong note is a disaster.

A "perfect" recording of classical piano pieces might well have been created from different recordings on different pianos in different studios.

I knew that classical recordings are often collages – but I assumed they were collages of different takes in the same studio!
One of the great skills – it's a particularly daft skill to have – is to make one piano sound like another.

[Italian composer Salvatore] Sciarrino wrote a set of solo violin pieces, *Six Caprices*. Aisha Orazbayeva recorded them in different places in London – a very resonant empty warehouse, her front room, on a traffic island. They cut these together in a very nice way – they're great, and they question the concept of "perfect" recordings. It's exactly the opposite to the usual process, which is about attempting to conceal the edits and the different qualities of the various takes.

What do you make of the resurgence of LPs?
I think it's a fad. People need an artefact – for instance, to give as a present – and the CD has been devalued out of existence. The music industry almost cut its own legs off. Of course it didn't deal with downloading, and Napster – it was really hopeless.

I don't think your average punter is going to buy vinyl. But then the average punter doesn't go to a record shop. The record shops that survive are the really tiny specialist ones like Honest Jons, and Rough Trade off Portobello Road.

Do you prefer LPs to CDs?
Well, first of all, those CD jewel cases are really horrible. They're badly made, and the hinges break constantly.

They must be cheaper to make than cardboard.
But what an absolute waste. It's a bit like milk cartons. For maybe thirty years, milk cartons in Britain didn't work. You were supposed to tear it apart and pull it forward, but they never got the glue right – you'd always have a ragged-looking spout, and the milk would go everywhere. When I went to the States, I'd get a milk carton that made a perfect spout.

And jugs, teapots and toilet seats.
You can have a product that is absolutely badly designed and it endures for decades.

More people buy classical CDs, and the numbers mean it's still more viable for those labels than for jazz. But the economics never were very good, and God knows what they are now.
In Foyle's, the contemporary classical section is pretty impressive.

Simon Reynell [of the label Another Timbre] seems to be going towards paper composition – it seems like that's what's making the impact now.

The view that we – and other musicians – have, that downloading is a rip-off of musicians, is a tiny minority view. Most non-musicians just don't see a problem. Perhaps people think "Why should you be paid for doing something that you like?" It's non-alienated labour, certainly, in the case of free improvisation – people play the music because they love doing so. They identify with what they are producing. Maybe a second violinist in some rather depressing symphony orchestra doesn't identify with the music on that level. It's certainly not as alienating as screwing on door handles in a Ford factory.

But the point is, we should *all* be paid for doing things we like – the whole world should be doing what it likes, and getting paid for it!

Musicians are expected to live off nothing – for instance, they were asked to perform at the London Olympics for nothing.

Of course that's disgraceful, but many people were expected to do stuff at the Olympics for nothing. The music industry, the fashion industry, the film industry – they all have interns. They build their work on people who get paid nothing. That happens because people want to be part of the fashion industry.

Visual artists can make fortunes – that's not why most them are doing it, but it is why some of them are.

Obviously, [Britartists like] Damien Hirst – but they're more like pop stars. There are people in music making a lot of money – Robin Thicke's record that we discussed earlier, with the resemblance to Marvin Gaye, they made huge amounts from it.[5] Stockhausen was getting gigs from the Shah of Iran, I guess he got well paid for that – if you want to do those sort of gigs! So there are people making money out of weird music, but not many of them. And it's not the case that all visual artists are rolling in it.

Do you have any more top tips for improvisers?

TOP TIP No. 7: Don't expect to make a living from improv.

POSTSCRIPT, May 2020.

In the course of our conversations, we've patronised several modest, good-value Asian restaurants in London. Sadly, several closed under COVID and may never reopen. One of our favourites was Loong Kee, in Hoxton.

That's been renamed – it's now Nom Nom. The menu changed quite radically – some people said that it's not as good as it used to be.

We also frequented Makan near Portobello Road, and Asakusa in Mornington Crescent – and a Burmese restaurant in Edgware Road.
That's long gone.
We also went to an amazingly cheap Ethiopian place near King's Cross – Marathon.
And a Turkish place near Café Oto.
Somine.
There was still no ban on large gatherings for those three gigs [for my seventieth birthday at Café Oto].[6] Immediately after that, I did a gig with Evan [Parker], Mark [Sanders] and John [Edwards] that was a fundraiser for Louis Moholo. Mark was absolutely miraculous, and I thought the night was totally inspiring and wonderful.

Then I did a gig that was going to be a fundraiser for Café Oto – they just needed some equipment. That was a duo with Thurston Moore, something I haven't done before – I really like working with him. There were very few people in the audience and the music was clearly affected by [COVID]. I think the music was really different, and then that was it. There are no more groups now – unless you put them together by putting everybody on Zoom.

Notes

1 Steve adds (July 2020): "More recently I've been in the studio a lot."
2 So that saxophone and drums don't drown out piano, for instance.
3 www.youtube.com/watch?v=Fhe6cW3ho_s
4 *The Wire,* issue 178, December 1998, tested by Ben Watson.
5 See Chapter 16.
6 Beresford's interview with Robert Worby of BBC Radio 3, recorded during the weekend, is available here: https://vimeo.com/403757587.

Steve Beresford Discography

Thanks to Daniel Garel for compiling this discography, which is based on the one at www.efi.group.shef.ac.uk/mberes.html

1970/72, *Journey into Space*, York University, (no label), Trevor Wishart.
1970/72, *Journey into Space*, Paradigm Discs, PD18. Trevor Wishart. CD reissue of York University LPs.
1973, *All Day – York Pop Music Project,* York Electronic Studios, YES 1. Various artists.
1973, *Plays the Popular Classics*, Transatlantic, TRA 275, The Portsmouth Sinfonia.
1974, *Hallelujah*, Transatlantic, TRA 285. The Portsmouth Sinfonia.
1974/1975, *Teatime*, Incus 15.
1974/1975, *Teatime*, Emanem 5009. Reissue of Incus 15.
1974/1975, *Not Necessarily "English Music,"* EMF CD 036. Two solo tracks on this compilation CD.
1977, *Company 6*, Incus 29.
1977, *Company 7*, Incus 30.
1977, *Fictions*, Incus 38. Company.
1975, *Three Pullovers*, Quartz Mirliton Cassette 12.
1975/1978, *Three & Four Pullovers*, Emanem 4038.
1977/1979/1980, *The Bath of Surprise*, Piano Records 003/Amoebic CD AMO-VA-03.
1978, *Alterations*, Bead 9.
1978 & 1980, *London Musicians' Collective . . . the First 25 Years*, LMC Rec8.2CD/Res9.1CD. Duos with Roger Turner & Michael Parsons and an Alterations track on this compilation CD (and see below, 2000).
1979, *The English Channel*, Parachute. Eugene Chadbourne.
1979, *20 Classic Rock Classics*, Philips 9109231. The Portsmouth Sinfonia.
1979, *My Body*, Canal 01. General Strike.
1979, *White String's Attached*, Bead 16. Duo with Nigel Coombes.
1979, *White String's Attached*, Emanem 5032. Duo with Nigel Coombes; reissue on CD with additional material.
1979, *Whirled Music*, Quartz 009. With Eastley, Burwell, Toop.
1979–81, *Voila Enough!*, Atavistic/Unheard Music Series ALP239. Alterations.
1980, *The 49 Americans*, Choo Choo Train CHUG 1. The 49 Americans.
1980, *Up Your Sleeve*, !Quartz 006. Alterations.
1980, *Too Young to Be Ideal*, Choo Choo Train CHUG 2. The 49 Americans.
1980, *Double Indemnity*, Y Records 9. Duo with Honsinger.

1980, *Double Indemnity/Imitation of Life*, Atavistic/Unheard Music Series ALP224. CD version of Y Records releases (+/-). With Honsinger, etc.

1981, *Launderette/Private Armies*, Virgin 10158. Vivien Goldman.

1981, *The Peel Sessions*, BBC SFRSCD052. The Slits; SB on 3 tunes playing keyboards etc. Recorded 12 December 1981.

1980, *Typical Girls Live In Cincinnati And San Francisco USA*, Basic Records, BASE2. LP, The Slits.

1980/1981, *In the Beginning*, Freud CD 057. The Slits.

1980/81/83, *Alterations Live*, Intuitive Records, IRCD 001.

1981, *Return of the Giant Slits*, CBS 85269. The Slits.

1981, *Imitation of Life*, Y Records 13. With David Toop, Tristan Honsinger, Toshinori Kondo.

1981, *I Never Knew*, Choo Choo Train CHUG 3. The Avocados.

1981, *We Know Nonsense*, Choo Choo Train CHUG 4. The 49 Americans.

1981, *Luton – Centre of the Universe,* Fringe Benefit Records FBR33 (cassette). With Jon Rose, John Russell, Tony Wren.

1981, *The Promenaders*, Y Records Y31.

1981, *Cry Tuff Dub Encounter Chapter 3*, Daddy Kool DKLP 15/Pressure Sounds CD007. Prince Far-I and the Arabs.

1982, *The Forty-nine Americans*, Choo Choo Train CHUG 1.

1982, *La Paloma*, Chabada OH5. The Melody Four. Reissued on La Paloma compilation Trikont US-0220.

1983, *Couscous*, nato 157. Lol Coxhill.

1983, *Privilege*, Rough Trade 59. Ivor Cutler and Linda Hirst.

1983, *Watch Yourself*, Tommy Boy BR 5003. Akabu.

1983, *Sept tableaux phoniques Erik Satie*, nato 59/nato 53005.2. Steve Beresford on one track.

1984, *My Favourite Animals*, nato 280. Alterations.

1984, *Love Plays Such Funny Games*, Chabada OH6. The Melody Four.

1984, *Le chat se retourne*, nato 257. Tony Coe.

1984, *Touch Travel Package*, Touch T3.

1985, *Gestalt et jive*, Moers Music MM 2038. Alfred Harth.

1985, *Danger in Paradise*, Touch TO2. General Strike.

1985, *Myths 2-System of Flux and Energies*, Sub-Rosa SUB 33002-3. General Strike on one track.

1985, *Eleven Songs for Doris Day*, Chabada OH7 (10")/Chabada 53034 (CD).

1985, *Si Señor!*, Chabada OH11 (10"). The Melody Four.

1985, *We are Frank Chickens*, Kaz LP 2. Frank Chickens.

1985, *The Inimitable*, nato DK 018 53039.2. Lol Coxhill.

1985, *Dancing the Line*, nato 565.

1986, *Kazuko Hohki chante Brigitte Bardot*, nato 985829/nato HS10049.

1986, *Tell Mandela*, Tout Ensemble 12 Lute 5. Mwana Musa.
1986, *Deadly Weapons*, nato 950 (LP and CD)/53021/HS10051. With David Toop, John Zorn, Tonie Marshall.
1986, *TV? Mai oui!*, Chabada DK 018 53008.2. The Melody Four.
1986, *Sleepwalking*, Streetsounds. Family Quest.
1987, *Joyeux Noël*, nato 1382. Compilation featuring various musicians.
1987, *Avril Brisé*, cinenato ZOG1/nato 112035.
1987, *Directly to Pyjamas*, nato 1330 (LP)/777 727 (CD). Duo with Han Bennink.
1987, *Aveklei Uptowns Hawaiians*, Chabada OH 18. Mike Cooper/Cyril Lefebvre.
1987, *More Tales From the City*, Flim Flam Harp LP1. The Band of Holy Joy.
1985, *Get Chickenized*, Flying Stir 1. Frank Chickens.
1988, *Shopping for Melodies Vol. 1*, Chabada OH19 (10"). The Melody Four.
1988, *Shopping for Melodies Vol. 2*, Chabada OH21 (10"). The Melody Four.
1988, *Shopping for Melodies*, Chabada 777 761 (CD). The Melody Four.
1988, *Welcome*, Sidewinder Musa LP88.
1988, *Not Fade Away*, Sidewinder Musa 88 12/1. X-Boys.
1988, *Bandes original du journal de Spirou*, nato 1715/1774. Compilation album.
1988, *L'extraordinaire jardin de Charles Trenet*, Chabada OH23/Nato HS10055.
1988/1989, *Love in Rainy Days*, Chabada 600-310. Kazuko Hohki.
1988–1995, *Cue Sheets*, Tzadik 7501.
1989, *Pentimento*, cinenato ZOG3.
1989, *Hulabaluh*, Hipshot Records HIP 008. Includes tracks by the Uptown Hawaiians.
1990/1999, *Spectral Soprano*, Emanem 4204. One Melody Four track + track with London Improvisers' Orchestra on Lol Coxhill compilation CD.
1991, *I Will Cure You*, Sigh 1-11/Island IMCD 242. Vic Reeves.
1991, *The Bear*, Bimhuis 003. Quartet of Evan Parker, Steve Beresford, Arjen Gorter, Han Bennink.
1991, *October Meeting 1991: Anatomy of a Meeting*, Bimhuis 004. Trio with George Lewis, Michael Vatcher; duo with Guus Janssen.
1992, *At Close Quarters*, These 7 CD. Compilation CD, various artists. (Track 1: John Butcher/ Steve Beresford).
1992, *Vol pour Sidney (aller)*, nato 53001. Two tracks on Sidney Bechet compilation album.
1992, *The Same Elephant*, These 7 CD. Duo with John Butcher on a compilation CD.
1992, *Boss Witch*, SRR CD 002. Shaking Ray Levis.
1993, *AngelicA 93*, CAICAI 004. Solo plus other combinations.
1993, *Conduction 31*, New World Records 80484. Lawrence D. 'Butch' Morris.
1993, *Conduction 31*, New World Records 80485. Lawrence D. 'Butch' Morris.
1993, *Fish of the Week*, Scatter 05:CD.
1994, *Signals for Tea*, Avant AVAN 039.
1994, *Short in the U.K.*, Incus CD 27. With Roger Turner and Shaking Ray Levis.

1995, *AngelicA 1995*, A1 007. Trio with Jon Raskin and Otomo Yoshihide and with Lol Coxhill's Before My Time.
1995, *Les films de ma ville*, nato 112033. The Melody Four plus various artists.
1995, *Burn Baby Burn*, JRVCD 101. The Otherside.
1995, *Museum of Towing & Recovery*, Hot Air EP4YOBS 10" vinyl LP. Duo with Otomo Yoshihide.
1997, *Couleur Café*, Tzadik TZ7116. On Great Jewish Music: Serge Gainsbourg.
1997, *Two to Tangle*, Emanem 4017. Duo with Nigel Coombes.
1997–2000, *Cue Sheets II*, Tzadik 7513.
1998, *Festival Beyond Innocence: 3 1998–1999*, Innocent Records FBI 104. Two solos + track with Altered States on compilation CD.
1999, *Foxes Fox*, Emanem 4035. With Evan Parker/John Edwards/Louis Moholo.
1999, *Proceedings*, Emanem 4201. London Improvisers' Orchestra.
2000, *B + B (in Edam)*, ICP 037. Duo with Han Bennink.
2000, *Agro jazz*, flo records flo013. One track on Panicstepper CD.
2000, *London Musicians' Collective . . . the First 25 Years*, LMC Rec8.2CD/Res9.1CD. Trio with Anna Homler & Richard Sanderson on this compilation CD (and see 1978/80).
2000, *The Hearing Continues . . .*, Emanem 4203. London Improvisers' Orchestra.
2000, *In Praise of the Kitten*, kabuki kore kkcd7. One track on compilation CD.
2000/2003, *I Shall Become a Bat*, QBICO 18. Duos with John Butcher and Richard Sanderson on alternate sides of LP.
2001, *Largely Live in Hartlepool and Manchester*, 30 Hertz CD 15. Jah Wobble & Deep Space.
2001, *3 Pianos*, Emanem 4064. With Pat Thomas/Veryan Weston.
2001, *Freedom of the City 2001: Large Groups*, Emanem 4206. London Improvisers' Orchestra.
2001, *Freedom of the City 2001: Small Groups*, Emanem 4205.
2001, *The All Angels Concerts*, Emanem 4209. Duo with Roger Turner on compilation 2-CD.
2001, *Out to Launch*, Emanem 4086. Lol Coxhill and the Unlaunched Orchestra.
1997–2002, *Steve Beresford*, kabuki kore kkcd11. Solo electronics.
2002, *Freedom of the City 2002*, Emanem 4090. London Improvisers' Orchestra.
2002, *Trap Street*, Emanem 4092. With Alan Tomlinson/Roger Turner.
2002/2003, *Ointment*, Rossbin RS018. Duo with Tania Chen.
2003, *Berlin Toy Bazaar*, Linear Obsessional LOR027. With Anna Homler/Richard Sanderson.
2003, *Bollywood Queen Soundtrack*, MCS Screen 003; includes Najma Akhtar, John Edwards, Aref Durvesh, Eddie Saunders. DVD of film available as SRD 94772.
2003, *Live at the Friends Meeting House*, Planet Mu Records ZIQ082CD. Urban Myth.
?, *(There is No Hidden Meaning)*, kabuki kore kkcd50. One track on compilation CD.

2003/2004, *Responses, Reproduction & Reality: Freedom of the City 2003–4*, Emanem 4110. London Improvisers' Orchestra.

2003/2007, *Improvisations for George Riste*, psi 08.06. London Improvisers' Orchestra.

2004, *Suit*, DVD by Dave Stephens with music by Steve Beresford.

2004, *Conroy Maddox*, Itza CD002. Featuring the voice of surrealist Maddox, with music by Addie Brik, SB, Richard Thomas and others.

2004, *Der Kastanienball: the Fall of Lucrezia Borgia*, Winter & Winter 910 107-2.

2004, *Naan tso*, psi 05.07. With Evan Parker/John Edwards/Louis Moholo.

2005, *Freedom of the City 2005*, Emanem 4216. Trio with Joe Williamson/Roger Turner + London Improvisers' Orchestra.

2005, *Sounds From the Moors*, Music Creator Project MCPCD001.

2006, *Analekta*, Emanem 4138. John Russell.

2007, *Live at the Vortex*, psi 12.01. With Evan Parker/Kenny Wheeler/John Edwards/Louis Moholo.

2007, *Positions & Descriptions*, Clean Feed CF230CD. SFE.

2009, *Check for Monsters*, Emanem 5002. With Okkyung Lee/Peter Evans.

2010, *Lio Leo Leon*, psi 11.04. London Improvisers' Orchestra.

2010, *Snodland*, nato 4190. Duo with Matt Wilson.

2010, *Ink Room*, Creative sources CS 193. With Stephen Flinn/Dave Tucker.

2011, *HMS Concert*, Kukuruku Recordings. London Improvisers' Orchestra.

2011, *Just Not Cricket! Three Days of British Improvised Music in Berlin*, NI-VU-NI-CONNU nvnc-lp001/004. With Tom Arthurs/Tony Bevan/Matthew Bourne/Gail Brand/Lol Coxhill/Rhodri Davies/John Edwards/Shabaka Hutchings/Dominic Lash/Phil Minton/Eddie Prévost/Orphy Robinson/Mark Sanders/Alex Ward/Trevor Watts.

2011, *Overground to the Vortex*, Not Two MW 904. With François Carrier/Michel Lambert/John Edwards.

2012, *Live at Cafe OTO - 'And So Say All of Us'*, Ex 142V. The Ex plus guests.

various, *Le Chronatoscaphe*, nato 574. Commemorative book/3CD package representing twenty-five years of nato and Chabada.

2015, *Will it Float?*, Van Fongool VAFLP010. With John Russell/John Edwards/Ståle Liavik Solberg.

2015, *Blow Out!*, Konsertforeninga Records KF001. With Paal Nilssen-Love/Ståle Liavik Solberg.

2015, *Elaine Mitchener And Steve Beresford Live At White Cube*, VF147 Live 9. With Elaine Mitchener/London Sinfonietta.

2015, *Steve Beresford Live At The White Cube*, VF148 Live 10. With London Sinfonietta.

2015, *OUTgoing*, FMR Records/ColyaKooMusic. With François Carrier/Michel Lambert/John Edwards.

2016, *Eclectic*, Liz Music LMCD0030. With Hyelim Kim/Ute Kanngiesser.

2016, *Landscape: Islands, audet005*, Compilation cassette, various artists – tracks 2 & 3, with Blanca Regina.
2016, *Void Transactions*, Unpredictable series, Alterations. With David Toop/Peter Cusack/Terry Day.
2016, *The Sorter*, Va Fongool VAFCD016. With John Russell/John Edwards/ Ståle Liavik Solberg.
2016, *Utterances*, Linear Obsession (Track 57: Steve Beresford).
2017, *Dirty Songs Play Dirty Songs*, Audika AU-1019-2. With David Toop/ Phil Minton/ Evan Parker/Mark Sanders.
2017, *The Horse Box Vol.1*, IKLECTIK, Compilation album, various artists. (Track 5: trio with John Edwards/Sarah Gail Brand).
2017, *Hesitantly Pleasant*, IRCD07. With Mike Caratti/Rachel Musson.
2018 *Imaginings* by Ian Brighton, FMRCD497-0618.
2018, *20 Years On*, LIO 001. London Improvisers' Orchestra.
2018, *Pleasures of The Horror*, Bisou BIS-OO7 U. With Eugene Chadbourne and Alex Ward.
2019, *What Blue*, Unpredictable SBBR001. With Blanca Regina.
2019, *Shining Leaf*, Unpredictable SBTD001. With Terry Day.
2020, *Old Paradise Airs,* Iluso IR25. With John Butcher.
2020, *Trwst*, Angharad Davies self-released. With Angharad Davies.
2020, *The Phantom Sunrise*, Aural Detritus audet007. With Paul Khimasia Morgan, Richard Sanderson, Blanca Regina.
2020, *Daily Necessities*. Knitted Records DL, forthcoming. With Tania Caroline Chen.

Bibliography and Discography

Bailey, D. (1993), *Improvisation: Its Nature and Practice in Music*, Cambridge MA: DaCapo.
Barre, T. (2015), *Beyond Jazz: Plink, Plonk and Scratch: The Golden Age of Free Music in London 1966–72*, self-published.
Barre, T. (2019), *Convergences, Divergences and Affinities: The Second Wave of Free Improvisation in England, 1973–1979*, London: Compass Publishing.
Bechet, S. (2002), *Treat It Gentle*, Cambridge, MA: Da Capo.
Beresford, Steve (2001), "Toy Piano (1975) and Voice (1974)," *Leonardo Music Journal*, 11, pp. 98–9.
Beresford, Steve (2017), "Small and Medium-sized Things: Their Importance," in Zorn, J. (ed.), *Arcana VIII – Musicians on Music*, New York: Hips Road/Tzadik.
Beresford, Steve (accessed 2019), "Not Necessarily 'English Music' – Steve Beresford: Toy Piano (1975)," https://youtu.be/KLkPVSLShSg.
Brennan, M. (2020), *Kick It: A Social History of the Drum Kit*, Oxford: Oxford University Press.
Cairns, D. (2004), "The Real Godfathers Of Punk," *Sunday Times*, May 30, 2004, http://www.portsmouthsinfonia.com/media/sundaytimes.html.
Chusid, I. (2000), *Songs in the Key of Z: The Curious Universe of Outsider Music*, Chicago: Chicago Review Press.
Coatsworth, C. (2019), *Film: An Audiovisual Medium*, Durham University (undergraduate dissertation).
Cole, George (2006), *The Last Miles: The Music of Miles Davis 1980–1991*, Sheffield: Equinox.
England, P. (2018), "Once Upon A Time In London," *The Wire*, October 2018, pp. 30–7.
Fairhall, A. (2019), "Wooden House," *Little Instruments*, UK: Efpi Records.
Feisst, S. (2009), "John Cage and Improvisation: An Unresolved Relationship," in Solis, G. and Nettl, B. (eds.), *Musical Improvisation: Art, Education and Society*, Urbana and Chicago: University of Chicago Press..
Fishman, H. (2017), "The Shaggs Reunion Concert Was Unsettling, Beautiful, Eerie, and Will Probably Never Happen Again," *New Yorker*, August 30, 2017, www.newyorker.com/culture/culture-desk/the-shaggs-reunion-concert-was-unsettling-beautiful-eerie-and-will-probably-never-happen-again.
Gioia, T. (1988), *The Imperfect Art*, Oxford: Oxford University Press.
Gorbman, C. (1987), *Unheard Melodies: Narrative Film Music*, Bloomington and Indianapolis: Indiana University Press.

Grubbs, D. (2014), *Records Ruin the Landscape: John Cage, the Sixties, and Sound Recording*, Durham, NC: Duke University Press.

Hamilton, Andy (2000), "The Art of Improvisation and the Aesthetics of Imperfection," *British Journal of Aesthetics*, 40: 1, pp. 168–85.

Hamilton, Andy (2007), *Lee Konitz: Conversations on the Improviser's Art*, Ann Arbor: University of Michigan Press.

Hamilton, Andy (2015), "Toy Story," *International Piano*, September/October 2015, available at https://www.rhinegold.co.uk/international_piano/toy-story/.

Hamilton, Andy (2020), "The Aesthetics Of Imperfection Re-Conceived: Improvisations, Compositions And Mistakes," *Journal of Aesthetics and Art Criticism*, 78: 3, pp. 289–302.

Hamilton, A. and Pearson, L. eds. (2020), *The Aesthetics of Imperfection*, London: Bloomsbury.

Jost, Ekkehard (1994), *Free Jazz*, Cambridge, MA: Da Capo.

Kivy, P. (2002), "Note-for-Note: Work, Performance and Early Notation," in his *New Essays on Musical Understanding*, Oxford: Oxford University Press, pp. 3–17.

Kostelanetz, Richard, ed. (2003), *Conversing with Cage*, London: Routledge.

Mwamba, C. (2020), in Hamilton and Pearson eds. (2020).

Nyman, M. (2011), *Experimental Music: Cage and Beyond*, Cambridge: Cambridge University Press.

Pearson, J. (2015), *The Profession of Violence: The Rise and Fall of the Kray Twins*, London: Collins.

Piekut, B. (2011), *Experimentalism Otherwise: The New York Avant-Garde and Its Limits*, Oakland, CA: University of California Press.

Rawes, I. (2016), *Honk, Conk and Squacket: Fabulous and Forgotten Sound-Words from a Vanished Age of Listening*, London: London Sound Survey.

Rose, S. (2017), *The Lived Experience of Improvisation*, Chicago: University of Chicago Press.

Scott, R. (accessed 2018), http://richard-scott.net/interviews/steve-beresford-interview/.

Shoemaker, B. (2017), *Jazz In The 1970s: Diverging Streams*, Lanham, MA: Rowman and Littlefield.

Solis, G. and Nettl, B. eds. (2009), *Musical Improvisation: Art, Education and Society*, Urbana and Chicago: University of Chicago Press.

Stewart, Alexander (2000), "'Funky Drummer': New Orleans, James Brown and the Rhythmic Transformation of American Popular Music," *Popular Music*, 19: 3, pp. 293–318.

Steyn, Mark (2012), "Love Letters," in *National Review*, November 29, 2012, available at https://www.nationalreview.com/corner/love-letters-mark-steyn/

Toop, D. (2016), *Into the Maelstrom: Music, Improvisation and the Dream of Freedom*, London: Bloomsbury.

Toop, D. (2019), *Flutter Echo: Living Within Sound*, London: Ecstatic Peace.

Watson, B. (2013), *Derek Bailey and the Story of Free Improvisation*, London: Verso.
Whitehead, K. (1998), *New Dutch Swing: Jazz and Classical Music and Absurdism*, London: Billboard Books.
Whitmer, T. (accessed 2018), *The Art of Improvisation*, available at https://archive.org/stream/artofimprovisati005713mbp#page/n11/mode/2up
Wilder, A. (1972), *American Popular Song: The Great Innovators, 1900–1950*, Oxford: Oxford University Press.
Zorn, J. ed. (2017), *Arcana VIII - Musicians on Music*, New York: Hips Road/Tzadik.

Index

32-bar pop song 47
49 Americans, The 66, 149
100 Club 159
577 (records) 113
1520 Rooms, The 107
AACM. *See* Association for the Advancement of Creative Musicians
ABBA 237
Abbey Road 170
Abdul-Malik, Ahmed 252
Abrahams, Chris 72
accordion 8, 36, 169
acid house 244
Addams Family, The 236
Adelphi, The 161–2
Adler, Danny 7, 14
Adorno, Theodor 238
Adu-Gilmore, Leila 215–16
Aebersold, Jamey 144
aesthetics 2, 5, 53, 105
   "compositional aesthetic" 29
   of entertainment 219, 229–30
   of film music 165, 174, 232
   of imperfection and perfection 2, 50–1, 105, 114–15, 219, 230
   and John Cage 180, 182
African-American music 10, 160, 205, 231, 246, 249
African musics 101, 155, 217–18, 247
   innovation 145
Afrofuturist musicians 216
Agency, The 62
Ahbez, Eden 238
Ahmed 252
Akhtar, Najma 5, 166
Albania 165
Albert Hall 20–1
Albertine, Viv 71, 239–40, 242
Alexandra Palace 80, 242
Alex von Schlippenbach Trio. *See* Schlippenbach, Alexander Von
Alfred Hitchcock Presents 151
Alice in Wonderland 151
Allen, Marshall 161
Allum, Jennifer 75, 227
Allumés du Jazz, Les 152
alphorn 15, 96
Altena, Maarten 59, 64. *See also* Regteren Altena, Maarten van
Alterations 5, 31, 49, 59, 64–73, 86, 134, 198–9, 201, 209, 253–4
   Alterations Festival 66, 215
AMM 28–9, 32–5, 44, 49, 107–8, 159, 193, 235
Amsterdam 63, 65, 167
   Bimhuis 105
analogue technology 101, 252
anarchy 18, 31, 50, 80, 82
AND (trio) 252
Andrews, Inez 239
Andrews, Julie 24
Ángeles, Camilo 217
anklung 64
Another Timbre 258
Apartment House 185, 213
Arabs, The. *See* Roots Radics
Arad, Ron 184
Archbishop Holgate Grammar School 12
Arditti Quartet 193
Arguelles, Steve 114
Arhoolie 248
Armstrong, Louis 7–8, 112, 115, 247
art
   and craft 42, 83, 85, 117, 142–4, 220, 233
   and entertainment 1–2, 14, 112, 115, 214, 219, 227–32
   high art 88, 112, 142, 238
   light art 215
   movement art 213
   sound art 66, 72, 180, 193, 215, 226
   video art 145, 165, 172, 209, 214

art college   19, 165
arthritis   114
Arts Council   108–9, 197, 202, 215, 230
Asch, Moe   186
Asian Dub Foundation   244
Asian restaurants   3, 50, 193, 226–7, 259–60
Associated Board   9
Association for the Advancement of Creative Musicians   29, 59
Association of Musical Marxists, The   83
Astaire, Fred   24, 111
Aston, Peter   11
Atlantic   10, 229
Audika   66
audiovisual   1, 214
Australia   13, 94, 210
authenticity   2, 24, 166, 237
auto-tune   114–15, 249
avantgarde   17, 34, 39, 53, 63, 72, 100, 102, 149, 156, 172–3, 180, 206, 238, 245
Avant magazine   254
Away   141
Ayler, Albert   20, 27, 86, 231

Babel   113
Bacall, Lauren   95
Bach, Johann Sebastian   10, 12, 181–2, 192–3, 204, 212, 247, 252
Bacharach, Burt   239
Bad Brains   246
BAFTA   222
bagpipes   173
Bailey, Derek   12, 16, 18, 32, 34, 41–56, 85, 110, 116, 119, 139, 154, 257
  as a collaborator   17, 30, 61, 63, 71–2, 80, 83, 98, 114, 126, 128, 141, 156, 158, 160–1, 201, 210, 215, 220, 252–4
  and Company   41, 59–60
  and conventional music   42–3, 220, 228, 239
  and Evan Parker   31, 77–8, 197, 200, 206 (*see also* Incus)
  influence on others   31, 34, 37, 41, 45, 54–5, 189, 199, 223, 240
  and theory of improvisation   41, 119, 200, 203

Baker, Ginger   229
Balanescu, Alexander   80, 166–7, 191, 244
Ballet Rambert   118
banjo   9, 14, 41, 221, 226
Bankhead, Tallulah   148
Banlieues Bleues   150
Barbadian music. *See* calypso
Barbican   8, 180, 244
Bardot, Brigitte   151–2
Barlow, Luke   98
Baron, Joey   147, 153
Barrett Brothers   33
Bartók, Béla   22, 92, 182
Basie, Count   23, 81–2, 155–6
bass   17, 176, 192
  guitar   52–3, 69–70, 72–3, 116, 121, 230
bassoon   175
Bates, Django   155
Batman   158
Battersea Arts Centre   222
BBC. *See* British Broadcasting Corporation
Beach Boys, The   113
Bead   65, 69
Beat Around The Bush, Shepherds Bush   171
Beatles, The   61, 69, 170, 221, 247, 249
bebop   9, 28, 37, 46, 82–4, 155, 183
  hard bop   144
Bechet, Sidney   9, 81
Beckett, Harry   94, 105, 222
Beckett, Samuel   33, 47
Bedford, David   83
Beethoven, Ludwig van   19–21, 74, 192, 257
Begeja, Liria   165
Beiderbecke, Bix   112
Beins, Burkhard   119
Bell, Clive   150
Benford, Douglas   118–19, 227
Benjamin, Walter   97
Bennink, Han   14, 28–9, 42, 44, 48, 50, 61
  as a collaborator   5, 35, 55, 59, 94, 127–8, 201, 220, 222
  and Misha Mengelberg   63–5, 69, 200

Beresford, Steve
  and Anne (sister)   8
  broad musical tastes   1, 68, 113, 162–3, 186, 193, 198, 205
  and commercial music   5, 142–3, 165, 170–1
  and David Toop   206, 210, 221, 236, 247
  and Derek Bailey   5, 27, 29, 35–6, 41, 77–80
  early life   7–10
  and electronics   32, 92, 95, 135, 157, 213, 216, 251–2
  and humour   31, 66–8, 72, 113, 153, 162, 167, 188, 194, 216, 218–20, 241, 245
  and June (mother)   8
  and keyboards   61, 72, 87, 92–3, 107–8, 157–8, 240, 251
  and Les (father)   7, 120, 167
  move to London in 1974   5, 7, 12, 14, 27
  as multi-instrumentalist   14, 80, 87, 100, 113, 186, 202, 240–1
  and Pete (brother)   8, 21, 36
  and piano   62, 67, 87–9, 113, 150, 167, 216
  and politics   167, 190, 206, 224, 231
  and producing   155, 221, 251, 254
  and singing   7–8, 121, 147, 152, 235
  and teaching   141–5
  and toy piano   87–95, 97, 100–2, 168
  and toys   62, 95–6, 99, 113, 150, 186, 194, 241
  and trumpet   209–10, 241
Beretta, Anne Marie   150
Berg, Alban   193
Bergstrøm-Nielsen, Carl   66
Berio, Luciano   35–6
Berlin   67, 119, 180, 192, 211, 223, 256
Berns, Bert   248–9
Berry Street studios   244–5
Berwick Street   158
Bes, Nico   253
Beyls, Peter   253
Biel, Michael von   44
Biggelaar, Johan den   253
bird sounds   31, 81, 99, 241

Birtwistle, Harrison   23–4, 83, 151, 229
Biscoe, Chris   210
Bishop, Jeb   161
Black, Cilla   85, 239
Black Power   27
Black Top   252
Black Uhuru   242
Blackwell, Ed   32
Blair, Tony   217
Blake, David   11
Blake, Steve   177
Blectum, Blevin   173
Bley, Carla   87, 205
Bley, Paul   2, 28, 64, 94, 105, 114
Blondie   247
Blonk, Jaap   105, 120
Bloodvessel, Buster   221
Blue Note (records)   94
Blue Notes, The (band)   156
blues   14, 23, 35, 39, 101, 117, 155, 170
Blues Committee   39
Blunt, Alison   105
Bob Kerr's Whoopee Band   14
Bohman, Adam   105, 117–19, 167, 225–7
Bohman, Jonathan. *See* Bohman Brothers
Bohman Brothers   219, 225–7
Bolan, Marc   229
Bolden, Buddy   205
Bollywood   165–6, 247
Bologna   206
Bongo Joe   248
Bonnington Centre, The   226
Bonzo Dog Doo-Dah Band, The   14, 21
Booker T and the MGs   9, 248
Boone, Daniel   13
Boone, Pat   192
Borge, Victor   24
Borrowers, The   151
Boston   231
Boulez, Pierre   2, 48, 82
Bourgeois, Gérard   152
Bovell, Dennis (aka Blackbeard)   13, 221, 240, 242
Braben, Eddie   225
Bradfield, Polly   197
Brand, Sarah Gail   80, 110
Branson, Richard   204
Brassaï   190

brass bands   211
Braxton, Anthony   59–60, 128, 230
Bread and Cheese   7, 13, 36, 107, 112
Bream, Paul   32, 117
Brecht, Berthold   54, 176
Brendel, Alfred   88, 91, 257
Brennan, Matt   249
Brenner, Andrew   147, 149–50
Brentano String Quartet   215
Breuker, Willem   44, 63, 65
Brick Lane   166
Brighton   30, 74, 86, 149, 202
    Brighton Art College   86
    Brighton Festival   86
Brighton, Ian   37, 54
Brillig Arts Centre, Bath   66
Bristol   77
British Broadcasting Corporation   14, 29, 42, 80, 216, 235
    BBC2   222
    BBC Radio 3 (see Jazz in Britain)
    BBC Third Programme   12
Brookmeyer, Bob   83
Broonzy, Big Bill   247
Brotherhood of Breath   154–6
Brötzmann, Peter   16, 28, 35, 54, 65, 94, 159
    as a collaborator   63, 77, 211
Brown, David (aka candlesnuffer)   72–3
Brown, Earle   179–80
Brown, James   14, 70, 222, 230–1, 253
Bryars, Gavin   5, 17–21, 28, 46–7, 59, 223
Buck, Tony   72, 108, 162
Buckethead   50
Buckingham Palace   190
Buddha   113
Budgie   80, 242
Burma   99
Burn, Chris   90–3, 158–9
Burns, Ken   205
Burton, Richard   108
Burwell, Paul   86, 203
Butcher, John   106, 109, 145, 158–62
    as a collaborator   5, 80, 92, 147, 173–4, 180, 184, 199–200
Butts, Johnny   229
Buzzcocks   222

Byard, Jaki   255
Byrd, Bobby   230

cadenzas   183, 213
Caesar, Shirley   239
Cafe Montmartre   27
Café Oto   66, 71, 105, 177, 198–201, 210, 212, 215, 223, 236–7, 260
Cage, John   11, 12, 20, 32–3, 52, 70, 88–92, 100, 143, 159, 167, 179, 185, 211, 252
    and improvisation   216
    Indeterminacy   5, 18, 92, 140, 180, 186–8, 190–1, 223
    influence   180, 186
    and popular culture   189
    and rules   187
    and scores   182–3, 190–1
    and visual art   177
California   50, 172
calypso   3, 152
Cambridge   235
Camden Jazz Festival   82
Camper Van Beethoven   61
Campi, Gigi   246–7
Canada   61
Cannon, Ace   3, 236
Canterbury   82, 210
Cardew, Cornelius   17, 32–4, 48, 108, 154, 179, 181, 188, 190
Carlin, George   224
Carnegie Hall   23
Carney, Harry   111–12
Carpal Tunnel Syndrome   47
Carpenter, Patrick   166 (aka DJ Food)
Carpenters, The   23
Carr, Katy   142–3
Carrier, Francois   49
Carroll, Lewis   66
Catlett, Big Sid   210
celeste   92–3
cello   21, 32, 56, 67, 74–5, 86, 162, 182, 192, 247
Central Office of Information   169–70
Chabada Records   81–2, 149
Chadbourne, Eugene   46, 59, 61–2, 147, 153, 210, 220
Channel   41, 167, 222

Chantenay Villedieu, near Le Mans 82, 148, 152
Charing Cross Station 100
Charles, Neil 213
Chattanooga, Tennessee 157–8
Cheapo Cheapo Records, Berwick Street 158
Chelsea College of Art and Design 215
Chen, Phyllis 90, 101
Chen, Tania Caroline 5, 18, 92, 97, 138, 180, 186–9, 193, 223
Cher 115
Chernobyl exclusion zone 67
Cherry, Don 182–3, 245
Cherry, Neneh 242, 245
Chic 73, 231, 246, 249
Chicago 29, 225
Chilingirian, Levon 193
China 73, 91, 180, 184
Chisholm, George 211, 227
Cholmondeleys 177
Chopin, Frédéric 90
Chusid, Irwin 23
Cissgee, Rollo 59, 61–2
Clapham Common 99
Clapton, Eric 169
clarinet 9, 17, 21, 63, 81–3, 98, 151, 161, 165, 173, 176
Clarke, Kenny 176. *See also* Kenny Clarke–Francy Boland Big Band
Clarvis, Paul 23
classical music 115, 145, 147
　conservatism 18, 21, 87, 197
　contemporary 83, 92, 100, 102, 108, 111, 193, 202, 213, 237
　and extemporisation 213
clavichord 91
Clements-Croome, Derek 193
Clerkenwell 243
　Clerkenwell Square 85
CMN. *See* Contemporary Music Network
Coe, George 82
Coe, Tony 41, 51–2, 77, 80–3, 85, 121, 148–51, 202
　as a collaborator 5, 133, 212, 222, 246
Cole, BJ 5, 184, 222
Cole, Nat "King" 111, 238

Coleman, Ornette 11, 27, 147, 155, 183, 203–4, 229
Collins, Bootsy 230–1
Cologne 247
Coltrane, John 8–11, 14, 24, 27–8, 37–8, 51, 94, 160, 247. *See also* John Coltrane Quartet
COMA 193
comedy 1, 13, 216, 219–25, 235
　and improvisation 224
　musical comedians 227
Communist Party 206, 242
Company 65, 78, 98, 128, 240
　Company Week 56–7, 59–60, 98, 252
Compendium Bookshop, Camden 221
Concertgebouw 64
conduction 68, 105–6, 161, 186
Confucius 154
Connolly, Billy 220
Contemporary Music Network 105, 108
Conway Hall 189
Coogan, Steve 171
Cook, Peter 235
Cook, Richard 69
Cooke, Sam 239
Coombes, Nigel 14–15, 18–19, 21, 31–2, 60, 74, 191–2, 228–9
　as a collaborator 78, 86, 130, 153, 210
Cooper, Mike 39, 83, 199, 252
Cooper, Tommy 186
Copepod Records 98
cor anglais 161
Corbyn, Jeremy 10
Corbyn, Piers 10
Cornell, Joseph 87, 95, 177
cornet 8, 14
Cotton Club 43
Country & Western 46, 187, 236
COVID 259–60
Coward, Noel 149
Cowell, Henry 88, 90, 92
Coxhill, Lol 30, 33, 47, 81–6, 121, 200, 205, 209
　as a collaborator 5, 39, 59, 77, 80, 105, 128, 133, 148–9, 155, 167, 210, 221, 245–6, 252
　memorial shows 36, 212
Craft, Robert 45

Creation Rebel   245
Crouch End Festival Chorus   212
Crumb, George   90
Cry Tuff   243
Cry Tuff Dub Encounter   243, 245
Cunningham, David   149, 210, 238
Cunningham, Merce   177, 186
Cusack, Peter   64–5, 67–8, 71, 134, 254
Cutler, Ivor   1, 5, 219–21

DAAD. *See* German Academic Exchange Service
Dada   1, 14, 19, 59–60, 78, 87, 91, 192, 213, 215, 219–20
Daddy Kool   245
Dafeldecker, Werner   119
Dahinden, Roland   180
Dalaba, Lesley   197
Dali, Salvador   220
Dalston Junction   236
Damned, The   85, 246
dance bands   8, 21, 42–3, 46, 52, 82, 167
Danish Radio Big Band   83
Dankworth, John   110
Davidson, Martin   3, 29, 31, 34, 56, 74, 88–9, 199, 210
Davies, Angharad   119
Davies, Hugh   56, 118–19, 197, 226
Davies, Ray   212
Davies, Rhodri   3, 7, 69, 119–20, 159
Davies, Tansy   213
Davis, Eddie "Lockjaw"   158
Davis, Howard   193
Davis, Matt   119
Davis, Miles   1, 9, 51, 83, 176, 220, 229
Dawes, George   188
Dawson, Les   224
Day, Doris   121, 147, 149, 167, 235
Day, Terry   31–2, 64–5, 67, 69, 71–2, 86, 105, 134, 141, 200, 215
  and making instruments   145
  and visual art   177, 226
Dead Days Beyond Help   98
de Beauvoir, Simone   44
Debroy Somers Society Orchestra   8
Debussy, Claude   82
Dedication Orchestra   5, 147, 155
Delbecq, Benoît   193–4

Delivery   83
Denmark Street   84
Depeche Mode   244
Desai, Poloumi   177
de Saram, Mandhira   1, 12, 118, 137, 191, 193–4, 209, 227, 257
de Saram, Rohan   193
Desert Island Discs   22, 86, 249
Desmond, Paul   160
Deutsche Grammophon   237
Ding Foundation, The   162
Dion, Celine   247
Dixieland   14, 85
Dixon, Reginald   158
DJ-ing   166, 172–3, 188, 241, 243
Doc Martens   240
Dolphy, Eric   28, 61, 63–4, 235
Donovan   225
doo-wop   69, 236, 243
Dorham, Kenny   94
Dörner, Axel   119
Dorsey, Tommy   7
Douglas, Dave   147, 150
Dr Doolittle   151
Dreben, Burton   203
drums   28, 31, 50, 55, 63, 67, 86, 141, 144, 147, 156, 161, 201, 229, 248
  cymbals   95
  drum machines   69–70, 171
  free drummers and time drummers   210–11
  history of   249
  and male bias   198
  snare   35, 97, 248
dub (reggae)   5, 43, 213, 235, 241, 243–5
  dubstep   244
Dublin   82
Duchamp, Marcel   91, 177, 243
Duck Baker Trio   98
Durham Jazz Festival   206
Durrant, Phil   92, 119
Durvesh, Aref   203
Dury, Ian. *See* Kilburn and the High Roads
Dyani, Johnny   34, 155
Dylan, Bob   246
dynamics   35, 44–5, 52, 55, 69, 91, 116, 154, 160, 181–2

Ealing, West London   141
East Asian philosophy   180
Eastley, Max   37, 39, 66, 84, 86, 118, 165, 177, 244
Eastman, Julius   193
echo   33, 182
Echtzeitmusik   49, 120
ECM   56, 197
Edgware Road   260
Edinburgh Fringe   222
Edwardians   14, 19
Edwards, Bernard   73, 246
Edwards, John   78, 80, 98, 110, 116, 118, 156, 159, 168, 215-16, 227
Edwards, Mrs (piano teacher)   9
Eisler, Hanns   11
electric keyboards   92, 107, 161, 188, 221, 251
   Casio MT68   71
   Casio SK1   93
   Mattel Optigan   171
   M-Audio Keystation   93
Electric Light Orchestra   171
Electro-Acoustic Ensemble   77
electroacoustic music   17, 72, 213
   improvisation   32
electronics   31-2, 37, 69, 92, 94, 157, 161, 188, 192, 213-14, 218, 251-2
Elektra   33
Elgar, Edward   170
Ellington, Duke   7, 51, 82, 94, 115, 229, 253
Ellington Orchestra   111
Emanem   31, 83, 88, 105, 210
Endresen, Sidsel   120
Engineer, The   91
engineering (sound/recording)   89, 167, 244, 254-5
Eno, Brian   5, 17, 21
Ensemble (octet)   92
Environmental Music Festival   150
Epping, Essex   92
Epstein, Brian   69
Epstein, Marie   81
Ernst, Max   177
eSwatini   217-18
euphonium   5, 21, 30, 44, 65, 80, 86, 125, 210, 221, 240-1

Evans, Bill   24, 47, 94, 200
Evans, Gil   87
Evans, Mrs (piano teacher)   9
Evans, Nick   155
Evans, Peter   24, 74, 209
Evans-Stickland, Deborah   238
Expensive (band)   121
experimental
   composition   34
   film   166-7
   music   18-19, 33-4, 159, 163, 165, 180, 185, 187, 189, 193, 213, 219, 238, 244
Experimental Musical Instruments magazine   119
Ezra Read Orchestra   19

Fairhall, Adam   27-8, 87, 100
Fall, The   187
Farley, John   21
Father Ted   232
Fawlty, Basil   230
Featherstonehaughs   177
feedback   30, 85, 115, 145, 158-9, 161, 220
Feldman, Morton   11, 33, 143, 179-80, 185, 188
feminism   197, 241
Feminist Improvisation Group   167, 198
Fennesz, Christian   109
Ferneyhough, Brian   182, 191-2
Ferrar, Sue   105
Feza, Mongezi   155
field recordings   71, 101-2, 168
FIG. *See* Feminist Improvisation Group
figured bass   181
Finnissy, Michael   38
Finsbury Park   36
   Town Hall   184
Fires of London, The   151
Fisher Turner, Simon   17
Fitzgerald, Ella   121
Five Blokes. *See* Four Blokes
flamenco   205
Flowers of Romance   239-40
flugelhorn   240
flutes   63, 65, 88, 151, 221, 243
   bamboo reed   67-8, 145

Peruvian 217
Fluxus 65, 186, 213, 226
Flying Lizards, The 5, 66, 149, 192, 235, 238–9
Flynn, Steven 254
folk 20, 36, 39, 101–2, 108, 147, 237, 247, 253
Folkways 186
Forebrace 98
Forster, Ariane (Arianna) Daniela. *See* Up, Ari
Foster Jenkins, Florence 22–3
Four Blokes 156
Four Pullovers. *See* Three Pullovers
Fox, Charles 12
Fox, Christopher 185
Foxes Fox (group) 80
Foyle's 258
Foyle's Law 232
Frank Chickens 68, 150–1
Franklin, Aretha 10, 160
Free (band). *See* Kossoff, Paul
Freebop 141
Freedom of the City 210
free improvisation 27–8, 32, 34–8, 74, 85, 92, 116. *See also* improvisation
   archival investigation 203
   audiences 203, 214, 227
   beginnings 41
   and classical music training 213
   and combativeness 51
   and danger 30
   enduring groups 199
   first generation 27, 102, 253
   freedom 27, 83, 116, 152, 215, 218
   and free music 36, 44, 152, 157
   funding 202
   gender imbalance 197
   generational differences 37, 67
   and hierarchy 29, 49
   as an idiom 48
   recognition 212
   second generation 1, 27, 31, 152
   and teaching 143–4
   UK scene 162
free jazz 27–9, 32, 34, 41, 46–7, 49, 61, 80, 114, 141, 160, 210, 231, 237

and free improvisation 34, 105–6, 116, 160, 200, 203
and male ethos 198
Freeman, Bud 84
French horn 15, 77, 161
Frisell, Bill 54, 147, 153
Frith, Fred 12, 54, 148, 153, 199
Front, Rebecca 171
Fuhler, Cor 94
Fukuda, Satoko 5, 12, 74, 136, 162, 191, 209
funk 50, 152, 230
Funkadelic. *See* Parliament (band)

G, Kenny 169
Gainsbourg, Serge 151–2
Gal, Sharon 5
Galvin, Elliot 95, 117
gamelan 90, 101, 205, 247
Gamelan Padhang Moncar 215–16
Garden Furniture Ensemble, The 19–20
Gare, Lou 28, 32
Gateway Studio, Kingston-on-Thames 155
Gaumont 8
Gaye, Marvin 248, 259
Gayle, Charles 88–9
General Strike 138, 149, 210
genius 42, 62, 82, 112, 118, 154, 197, 200, 224, 233, 236
Gere, Richard 165
Germany 96, 198
   East 88, 91, 242
   German Academic Exchange Service 67
Gershwin, George 48
Getz, Stan 81
Ghana 215
Gibson, Jon 189
Giles, Mike 71
Gillespie, Dizzy 81, 83
Gillman, Andrew 170
Gioia, Ted 50
Giuffre, Jimmy 28
Glenn Miller Orchestra 111. *See also* Miller, Glenn
Globe Unity Orchestra 77
glockenspiel 90, 118

Godard, Jean-Luc   72, 173
Godzilla   151
Gold, Harry   85
Goldsmith's College   39, 142, 167, 189
Gomelsky, Giorgio   153
gong   55, 75
Gonsalves, Paul   82
Goodman, Benny   7, 182
Gorbman, Claudia   173, 175
Gordon, Dexter   63
Gorecki, Henryk   154
gospel   82, 213, 239
Gould, Glenn   257
Graham, Larry   53
Grant, Hugh   23
Graves, Milford   94
Great American Songbook   236
Green, Al   236
Green, Dave   222
Green, Freddie   54
Greenaway, Peter   166, 169–70
Groening, Matt   220
groove   27–8, 71, 83
Grubbs, David   32, 52, 182, 216
Guillemots   212
guitar   9, 30, 32, 37, 41–2, 98, 145, 154, 175
  12-string   63
  acoustic   36, 52–4, 61, 86, 101
  dobro (brand)   63
  electric   31, 52–3, 61, 161
  extended techniques   53
  harmonics   45, 52
  lap-steel   36
  pedals   52–3, 153–4, 251
  pedal-steel   222
  prepared   115
  semi-acoustic   52–3
  Spanish   53, 228
Gustafsson, Mats   198
Guy, Barry   27, 77, 200

Hacker, Alan   5, 81, 83, 150–1, 165
Hackney   43, 80
Haino, Keiji   159
Hall, Jim   43, 47, 238
Hallett, Sylvia   105, 162, 167, 184
Halvorson, Mary   54

Hamelberg, Geert   253
Hamleys   97
Hamlyn Foundation   109
Hammond, Paul   221
Hampstead Heath   61
Hancock, Tony   108, 232
Hands, Fred   8
Hands, Jim   8
Happy House   245
Hardy, Russell   67
Harle, John   160
harmolodics   204
harmonium   8, 118, 221
harpsichord   91, 107
Harris, Rolf   245
Hatton Gallery, Newcastle   167
Havens, Richie   10
Hawaiian music   39, 118
Hawkins, Alexander   156
Hawkins, Coleman   9, 112, 160
Haynes, Roy   204
Hayward Gallery, London   66
Hayward, Robin   106, 119
Hazard, Merle   46
hcmf. *See* Huddersfield contemporary music festival
Heathrow Airport   150
Hefti, Neal   23, 158
Hendrix, Jimi   10, 61, 246, 248
Henry VIII   107–8
Herbert Spliffington Allstars, The   36
Herman, Woody   21
Herring, Richard   222
Herrmann, Bernard   170, 175–6
Herzfeld, Dave   7, 13, 36
Hession, Paul   161–2
Heywood, Eddie   233
Hill, Benny   233
Hill, Harry   187
Hill, Tim   252
hiphop   66, 68, 71
  experimental   244
Hi Records   236
Hirsch, Shelley   107, 120
Hirst, Damien   259
Hirst, Linda   221
Hit Run   245
Hodges, Johnny   7, 83, 111, 222

Hohki, Kazuko   147, 150–2
Holcombe, James   226
Holiday, Billie   48, 89, 121–2
Holland   44, 63–4, 81, 94, 253
  Holland Festival   64
Holland, Dave   29, 56
Hollywood   165, 175, 204
Honest Jons   35, 155, 241, 258
Honsinger, Tristan   39, 126, 128, 241
Hooker Green   7, 9
Hoorgi House Records   221
Hope, Bob   225
Hopkin, Bart   119
Horak, Steph   142
Horne, Maartje ten   149
Horniman Museum, South London   30
Hot Air   157
Houtkamp, Luc   79
Hove, Fred van   16, 28, 35, 63, 94
Howerd, Frankie   225
Huddersfield contemporary music festival   94, 109, 185
Huddersfield University   185
humour   5, 84, 148–9, 210
  accidental   74, 246
  in films   169
  irony   21, 219, 232
  in music   64, 69, 227, 240
Hundred Years Gallery, Hoxton   118
Hunt, Dave   148, 167, 221, 244, 254–5
Hutchings, Shabaka   5, 117, 156, 162, 193, 209, 217–18
Huynh, Dam Van   213

ICA. *See* Institute of Contemporary Arts
ICES. *See* International Carnival of Experimental Sound
I Ching   180, 190
ICP. *See* Instant Composers Pool
ideology (in music)   47–8, 67, 114, 189
Iggy Pop and the Stooges   68
Iklectik   105, 213, 226
Iluso   113
IML. *See under* Leeds
improvisation   15, 18, 24, 174. *See also* free improvisation
  and imitation   38, 226
  non-idiomatic   41, 47, 119

  as process   257
  values   198
improvisation and composition   2, 73, 107, 158, 193
  compositional structure   28, 109
  faking   105, 107, 112
  improvisation as a compositional method   108–9, 202
  indeterminacy   159, 180, 192
  interpretation of composed works   110, 179–82, 185, 191
  paper composition   108–11, 258
  total improvisation   28
  work-concept   108
Incus   31, 41–2, 44, 55, 77, 83
Indian music   247
Inedible Cheese Sandwich, The   14
Innes, Neil   14
Instant Composers Pool   35, 44, 63–5
Institute of Contemporary Arts   65, 78, 99
International Carnival of Experimental Sound   189
iPhone   118
Irish Catholicism   232
Iskra 1903 (group)   29
Island Records   20, 29, 240–1
Isley, Ron   239
Isley Brothers   248
Italian Instabile Orchestra   15
Italy   206, 227, 258
Items 4 & 10 (ensemble)   98
Ives, Charles   19, 70, 218
I Went This Way   113

Jackson, Al   248
Jackson, David   15
Jackson, Jesse   231
Jackson's Lane Community Centre, North London   228
Jam, The   246
Jamaica   84, 213, 236, 244–5
  Kingston   243
  Spanish Town   243
James Ulmer's Black Rock Coalition   246
Janet Smith (band)   192
Jansch, Bert   39

Japan 41, 56, 73, 99, 119, 149–52, 170, 184, 186, 188, 200, 210
Jarrett, Keith 220
jazz 7–9, 12, 14, 24, 32, 36–7, 41–3, 81, 83, 108–9, 116, 141, 147, 171, 241
  and chord symbols 181
  history 203
  modal jazz 176
  modern jazz 77, 112
  improvisation 116–17, 144
  relation to free improvisation 46, 49, 78, 95, 117, 160
  snobs 154, 237, 246
  standards 7, 42, 46, 48, 79, 82, 94, 199
Jazz Cafe 114
Jazz in Britain 253
Jazzpar Prize 81
Jazz Services 201
Jeffrey, Christine 56, 197
J. Hudson & Co. Whistles Ltd., Birmingham 99
John Coltrane Quartet 79, 156. *See also* Coltrane, John
Johnny Rondo Trio 85
Johns, Jasper 186
Johnson, Boris 112
Johnson, Linton Kwesi 242
Johnson, Robert 246
Jones, Booker T 9. *See also* Booker T and the MGs
Jones, Elvin 36, 114
Jones, Spike 220–1, 227
Joseph Holbrooke (group) 41
Jost, Ekkehard 27
Jurd, Laura 117, 198
Jurek, Thom 242
Just Not Cricket 223

Kadare, Ismail 165
Kagel, Mauricio 90
Kaiser, Henry 61, 188
Kandinsky, Wassily 177, 181
Karajan, Herbert von 106, 237
karaoke 151
Karas, Anton 175
Kaufmann, Achim 79
Kay, Janet 13
Kay, Peter 220
Kaye, Carol 52
kazoo 71, 96
Keane, Shake 46
Keller, Hans 48
Kellers, Willi 211
Kelley, Greg 119
Kennedy, Nigel 237
Kenny Clarke–Francy Boland Big Band 246. *See also* Clarke, Kenny
Kent 81
Kentish Town 237
Kenton, Stan 111
Kent University 81, 214
Kevin Ayers and The Whole World 83
Keystone Cops 213
Khan, Nusrat Fateh Ali 247
Khimasia Morgan, Paul 145
Kieffer, John 202
Kiev 63
Kilburn and the High Roads 67
Kimberley, Nick 221
Kinch, Soweto 206
King Crimson 72
Kings Place 105
King Tubby 242
Kinks, The 115, 144, 152, 212, 235
Kit Records 217
Kivy, Peter 181
Kjaer, Julie 198
klangfarbenmelodie 44–5
Klee, Paul 33, 177
Knight, Tony 84
Knoop, Mark 183, 185
Kobata, Kazue 215
Kode 9 (producer) 244
Koglmann, Franz 63
Kondo, Toshinori 153
Konitz, Lee 1–2, 39, 42, 48, 55, 79, 111, 114, 160, 200–1, 249
Kontakte Trio, The 37
Korwar, Sarathy 217
Kossoff, Paul 70, 121
Kostelanetz, Richard 90
Kowald, Peter 161
Kraabel, Caroline 5, 105
Krall, Diana 239
Kray Twins 43

Kruegers, Gallien 13
Kubrick, Stanley 170
Kukuruku 105

Lacy, Steve 41, 51, 53, 63, 65, 128, 253
Lady Gaga 71
Ladysmith Black Mambazo 155
La Faro, Scott 47
Lake, Steve 96
Lamb, Neil 7, 13–14, 35–6
Lambeth North station 170
Lampard, James 19
laptops 97, 227, 251
Lard, Keith 220
Lash, Dominic 98
Latin music 249
Laubrock, Ingrid 94, 162
Laurel and Hardy 64, 232–3
Laurence, Chris 80
LCC. *See* London College of Communication
LeBlanc, Keith 245
Lee, Arthur 10
Lee, Okkyung 5, 74, 159, 209
Lee, Stewart 1, 5, 24, 112, 211, 219–20, 222, 225
 and Cage's "Indeterminacy" 5, 18, 92, 140, 180, 186–8, 223
Leeds 70, 161, 239
 Improvised Music Leeds 161–2
 Leeds College of Music 211
 Leeds Trades Club 154
 Leeds University 161
Lefebvre, Cyrille 39
Lehn, Thomas 252
Leigh, Mike 116
leitmotif 173, 175
Lennon, John 220, 235
Levi-Strauss, Claude 96
Lewis, George 5, 147, 153, 213
Lewis, Martin 17
licks 35, 111, 244
Ligeti Quartet 183, 193
Lightsey, Kirk 246
Lindsay, Arto 72
LIO. *See* London Improvisers Orchestra
Little Richard 8
Little Theatre Club 15, 29, 33, 56, 78

Lixenberg, Lore 5, 256
Li Yuan-chia 167
LMC. *See* London Musicians' Collective
Loach, Ken 190
Lockwood, Annea 189
London 3, 10, 12, 15, 28, 29, 31–2, 36, 41, 44, 61, 66, 99, 150, 153, 162, 173, 193, 215–17
 Greater London Council 30
 improvised music scene 77, 113, 189, 198, 201, 212
 London Jazz Festival 199
 London University 158
 Olympics 259
 Palladium 225
 West End 29, 42, 222
London College of Communication 66, 143
London Improvisers Orchestra 5, 34, 53, 67–8, 94, 105–6, 113, 132, 192, 216, 226
London Jazz Composers' Orchestra 211
London Musicians' Collective 5, 27, 37–9, 61–2, 91, 150–1, 167, 252
London New Winds 211
London Sinfonietta 159, 213
London Skyscraper 5, 105
Lovens, Paul 200, 256
lower-case music 74, 105, 119
Lowry, L. S. 22
Lubin, Numar 81
Lucier, Alvin 159, 227
Lucked In Sound System 216
Lukoszevieze, Anton 257
Lydon, John 239–40
Lyttleton, Humphrey 82
Lytton, Paul 28, 35, 77, 84, 143, 200, 219, 229

McCartney, Paul 220
McDermott, Jamie 142
McGonagall, William 23
McGregor, Chris 155
Mack, David 46
McLaren, Malcolm 246
McPhee, Joe 161
McQueen, Steve 169
Magagula, Bhemani 217

Maguire, Alex   64
Majorca Orchestra, The   19
makhweyane   217–18
Mala (Digital Mystikz)   244
Malfatti, Radu   49, 119, 154
Malle, Louis   176
Malone, James   36, 202
Manchester   157, 211
   Manchester Art Gallery   167
Mancini, Henry   81
mandolin   67
Mansfield, Jayne   148
Mao Zedong   73, 190
   Maoism   154, 190
Marclay, Christian   5, 162, 165, 172–4, 180–1, 184–5, 211, 213, 217, 237
Marine Ices   189
Marks, Phil   211
Marks & Spencer   56
Marley, Bob   33
Marley, Brian   3, 30–1
Marmalade (records)   34
Marsalis, Wynton   154, 203–5
Marseilles   41
Marsh, Tony   105
Marshall, Hannah   5, 94, 118, 147, 161–3, 216
Marshall, Julian   239
Marshall, Tonie   131, 147–9, 165
Martyn, John   70
Marx, Groucho   248
Marx Brothers   149, 248
Marxist music   190
Mary Poppins   151
Masada   121, 147
Matchless Recordings   32–3, 75
Matrix (ensemble)   81
Matusow, Harvey   189
Maxwell Davies, Peter   83, 151
Mayas, Magda   72, 75, 96
Mayes, Martin   15, 35, 77, 96
Mayfield, Curtis   10, 239
Mayhem Quartet   252
M.C. Doc. Murdoch   241
medieval music   179, 181–2
Meehan, Norman   2
Melbourne   72
Mellers, Wilfrid   10–11, 15

Melly, George   97–8
melodica   80, 99, 138
Melody Four, The   5, 18, 81–2, 86, 121, 133, 199, 252
Memphis   84, 236
Mendelssohn, Felix   19, 192
Mengelberg, Karel   63
Mengelberg, Misha   31, 63–5, 94–5, 200
Mengelberg, Willem   63
Merce Cunningham Dance Company   185. *See also* Cunningham, Merce
Merton, Paul   43
Messiaen, Olivier   2
metal   147, 153, 202, 246
Metcalfe, Neil   88, 105
metre   27, 149, 224, 229, 240–1
microphones   145, 159, 255–6
Miller, Cassandra   185
Miller, Glenn   7. *See also* Glenn Miller Orchestra
Miller, Harry   155
Miller, Hazel   155
Miller, Steve   83
MIMEO. *See* Music in Movement Electronic Orchestra
Mingus, Charles   255
minimalism in music   154, 189, 231, 245
Minsky's   225
Minton, Phil   155, 167
Miro, Joan   177
mistakes   20, 30, 47, 51, 65, 231
Misty in Roots   242
Mitchell, Nicole   80
Mitchell, Roscoe   230
Mitchener, Elaine   5, 80, 209, 213, 218
modernism   31, 46, 144, 191
Moers   96
Moholo-Moholo, Louis   78, 147, 155–7, 218, 260
Moir, James. *See* Reeves, Vic
Mole Jazz   83
Molitor, Claudia   185
Monk, Thelonious   8–9, 94, 227, 257
Montgomery, Wes   53, 63, 162
Monty Python   190
Moore, Dudley   235
Moore, Michael   232

Moore, Thurston   98, 260
Moorman, Charlotte   189
Moor Mother   213
Mopomoso   92, 200, 216. *See also* Russell, John
MOR   27, 158
Morecambe, Eric   224–5
Morecambe and Wise   42–3, 64, 222, 224, 232
Morley, Paul   166–7, 222
Morricone, Ennio   147, 175
Morris, Chris   171
Morris, Joe   98
Morris, Lawrence "Butch"   5, 105–6
Morrison, Clifton "Bigga"   245
Mortimer, Bob   222
Mostly Other People Do The Killing   24
Motor Neurone Disease   47, 223
Motown   7, 9–10, 14, 121, 248
Mozart, Wolfgang Amadeus   64–5, 82, 193, 242
Muir, Jamie   55–6, 71, 197
Muldowney, Dominic   78, 107
Mumbai   166
Munich   239
Murray, Sunny   27
Museum and Hall of Fame of Towing and Recovery   157. *See also* Chattanooga, Tennessee
music for film and TV   1, 5, 27, 41, 83, 141–2, 147, 162, 165–76
  underscore   173–5
Music for Strings, Percussion and Celeste   92
music hall   31, 42, 227. *See also* variety
Musicians' Co-op. *See* London Musicians' Collective
Musicians' Union   7, 190
Music Improvisation Company, The   29, 41, 56, 72, 77, 197
Music in Movement Electronic Orchestra   33
Musics magazine   27, 160, 197
musique concrete   161, 226, 231
Musson, Rachel   80, 105, 113, 198
Mussorgsky, Modest   192
Muswell Hill   212
Mwamba, Corey   179

Naked City   147, 153
Napster   258
Narnia   151
Nash, Ogden   176
Nath, Pran   247
nato   65, 72, 81–2, 147–9, 151–2
NATO. *See* North Atlantic Treaty Organisation
Naxos   19
Necks, The   108
Neidlinger, Buell   94
Neill, A. S. *See* Summerhill
Neumann, Andrea   119
New Age Steppers   245
Newcastle   110, 210
New Complexity   192
New England   13
New London Silence   92, 120
Newman, Chris   192
Newman, Hayley   99
New Musical Express   70
New Orleans   85
Newport Jazz Festival   63
New York   13, 21, 41, 93, 107, 147, 153, 188, 197, 216, 225, 253
New Zealand   78, 215
Nicolls, Sarah   185
Nicols, Maggie   34, 144, 155, 162, 197
Nigerian Juju music   71
Night Light Collective   217
Nilsson-Love, Paal   198
Nimbus   81
Nixon, Richard   231
NME. *See* New Musical Express
Noble, Liam   94, 193
Noble, Steve   64, 98, 166, 215–16, 252
Noh (Japanese drama)   247
noise   32, 34, 68, 72, 83, 226, 231, 240, 245
noisemakers
  Cracklebox   251, 253
  Crackle Synth   253
Nonesuch   12
Nono, Luigi   190
Noordijk, Piet   79
North Atlantic Treaty Organisation   148
Northern Dance Orchestra   85
Northover, Adrian   105

Norwegian Vital insurance company   171
notation   35, 47, 106–10, 142, 182, 184, 201
   graphic   161, 174–5, 179–85
   stave   162, 179, 181–2, 185
Nottingham   201
No Wave   72
Nuttall, Paul   24
Nyman, Michael   17, 21, 159, 166, 169–70, 176

oboe   161
Ogun   155
Ol' Dirty Bastard   48
Olewnick, Brian   109
Ono, Yoko   235
On-U Sound   244
opera   11, 18, 23, 81, 112, 194, 205, 222, 242
Opportunity Rocks   17
Orazbayeva, Aisha   12, 258
Orbitone Records, Harlesden   236
organ   78, 87, 93–4, 98, 158
   Farfisa VIP500   158, 240
   Hammond   7, 9–10, 14
Orkney Islands   158
Ornette Coleman Quartet   229. *See also* Coleman, Ornette
O'Rourke, Jim   221
Orton, Richard   11
Otomo Yoshihide   5, 147, 157–8
outsider music   23
Ovaltine Power   171
Oxley, Tony   17, 27–8, 41, 46, 54–5, 65, 167, 211. *See also* Tony Oxley's Quartet and Celebration Orchestra

Pace, Ian   23, 175, 185, 191
Painkiller   147
Palm Court   85
Palmer, Neil   252
Palmolive (The Slits)   239–40
Paloma (The Slits). *See* Palmolive
Paolini, Patrizia   227
Paris   18, 81, 150, 176, 216
Parker, Charlie   8, 38, 55, 155, 180
Parker, Evan   3, 5, 12, 15, 16, 18, 27–31, 33, 35–7, 41, 55–6, 105, 128, 152, 205, 238
   as a collaborator   63, 66, 77, 141, 155–6, 160–2, 197, 200, 222, 260
   and Derek Bailey (*see under* Bailey, Derek)
   and special status   162, 254
   and visual art   177, 215
Parker, Maceo   230–1
Parker, William   213
Parliament (band)   230
parody   14, 20, 65, 171, 220, 231–2
Part, Arvo   154
Partch, Harry   119
pastiche   14, 21, 31, 72, 149, 200, 214, 247
Pateras–Baxter–Brown   72
Patterson, Lee   118–19
Paul Hamlyn Award for Artists   5, 168, 252
Peel, John   220
People Band   67–8
People's Liberation Music   33
percussion. *See* drums
Peregrine's Pianos   88
performance art   59
Pergola   217
Perry, Lee "Scratch"   242, 244
Peterson, Oscar   111
Petrushevsky, Igor   193
Petts, Helen   93, 166–7
Philadelphia   242–3
Phillips (records)   20
Phillips, Crucial Tony   245
Phoebe's, Hackney   43
piano   30, 32, 34, 39, 47, 49, 67, 74–5, 111, 180, 185, 188
   and classical heritage   160
   Fazioli   88–9
   Fender Rhodes   240
   prepared piano   88, 115, 167–8
   Schoenhut (toy piano)   90–1, 101
   Steinway   88, 90
   Wuyi (baby piano)   92
   Yamaha electric   240
   Zimmerman baby grand   88
Piano Orchestra   151
piccolo   93
Piekut, Ben   182, 216
PiL. *See* Public Image Ltd
Pimlott, Amelia   162

Pinckney, St. Clair 231
Pink Floyd 32, 235
Pinnell, Richard 74
Pisaro, Michael 185
Pizza Express 56
Plaatjies, Dizu 217
Planck, Max 118
playfulness 5, 167–8, 215–16
Plomley, Roy 22
Plytas, Nick 14
poetry 23, 66–8, 120, 219–21, 231
   Black Radical poetry and prose 80
   sound poetry 120, 226
Poland 15
polka 246
Pollitt, Tessa 241 (aka Bassie)
Pollock, Jackson 33
Polwechsel 159
Polynesian music 39. *See also*
   Hawaiian music
pomposity 18, 39, 190, 220
Pop Group, The 231, 240, 242
popular music 14, 17, 27, 37, 59, 66, 86, 114, 117, 142, 187, 200, 235–49
   Japanese pop 151
   narrow gradations between styles 248
   power ballads 247
   white 246, 248
populist music 154
Porter, Cole 24, 94
Portobello Road 50, 98, 157, 167, 241, 258, 260
   Portobello Market 97
Portsmouth 83
   Portsmouth College of Art 17–18
   Portsmouth Sinfonia 5, 10, 14, 17–24, 78, 153, 193
postmodernism 144
Potter, Sally 84
Powell, Bud 89
PowerPoint 251
practising 36, 48, 81, 105, 113–14, 183, 224, 230
Presle, Micheline 148
Presley, Elvis 13, 182, 248
Previn, André 224–5
Prévost, Eddie 27–8, 32–3, 75, 143, 159
Primal Scream 244

Prince 246
Prince Buster 36, 86
Prince Far-I 5, 235, 243–5
Prince Hammer 245
Princeton 216
Promenaders, The 86, 149
Proms 12, 23
   Electric Prom 212
Pryer, Anthony 179
Pryor, Richard 224
Psi 105
Public Image Ltd 240, 244
Pukwana, Dudu 155
Pullen, Don 94
punk 5, 17, 72, 83, 149, 222, 235, 240–2, 244, 246

qawwali 247
Queen (Elizabeth II) 225
Queen Victoria 23

Ra, Sun 11, 17, 60, 149, 242–3
Rachmaninov, Sergei 19, 192
racism 24, 160, 246
Radical Jewish Culture Series 147
radio 12, 29, 37–8, 41, 222–3, 226, 253
RAF. *See* Royal Air Force
Raincoats, The 242
Rainey, Bhob 119
Rainey, Tom 94
Raksin, David 220
Ramanan, Roland 105
Ramones, The 246
R&B 39, 84, 159, 248
Rands, Bernard 11, 35
rap 48, 152
Rasmussen, Mette 198
Rauschenberg, Robert 87, 95, 177
Rawes, Ian 194
Read, Ezra 19
Reading 39
Recedents, The 39, 83, 85
Redding, Otis 7, 14, 248
Red Rose Theatre 88, 92, 105, 216
reductionism. *See* lower-case music
Reed, Lou 245
Reeves, Jim 236
Reeves, Vic 1, 5, 219, 222
Regent Street 97

reggae   5, 13, 27, 65, 241–5
Regina, Blanca   5, 66, 116, 145, 165, 177, 209, 214
Regteren Altena, Maarten van   128.
    See also Altena, Maarten
Renbourn, John   20, 39
repetition   24, 68, 73, 108, 111, 116, 169, 230–1
Resonance 104.4FM   226
Resonant Spaces   158
reverb   13, 33, 56, 210, 246
Reynell, Simon   258
rhythm   23, 45, 155, 161, 166, 173, 189, 244–6
    complexity   93–4, 102, 142
Richard, Cliff   239
Richmond, Sophie   246
riffs   50, 70, 116, 230–1, 244
Riley, Howard   27–8
Rip, Rig & Panic   240, 242
Roach, Max   32
Robair, Gino   143, 159
Roberts, Dawn   149
Roberts, Sonny   236
Robinson, Heath   95
Robinson, Orphy   180, 252
Rochard, Jean   81, 147–50, 152
Rochard, Yves   82
rock   38, 61, 68, 72, 84, 147, 229, 237, 242, 244, 246, 248, 255
    black   246
rock 'n' roll. See rock
Rodgers, Nile   73, 246
Rolling Calf, The   213
Rolling Stones   170, 246
Rollins, Dennis   231
Rollins, Sonny   31, 63, 183, 200, 203
Romantic music   31, 74, 181, 192
Rome   107
Ronettes   170
Ronnie Scott's   29, 36–7, 77, 167, 199
Roogalator   7, 14
Roots Radics   243–4
Rose, Jon   53, 94
Rose, Simon   41
Ross, Annie   22
Rossbin   186

Rothenberg, Ned   107
Rough Trade   221, 240, 258
Roundhouse   48, 184, 189, 212
Rousseau, Douanier   22
Rowe, Keith   27–8, 32–4, 44, 109, 118
Royal Air Force   83, 141, 220, 235
    School of Music   141
Royal College of Art   67
Royal Conservatory at The Hague   63
Royal Festival Hall, London   167
Ruffer, Nancy   183
Russell, John   14, 31, 37, 48, 54, 78, 92, 192, 200, 210, 216
Russia   81
Rust, Brian   9
Rutherford, Paul   27–8, 33, 41, 141, 161, 210

Sachiko M   119
Sager, Gareth   240
St Mary's, Stoke Newington   105
salsa   248
Sam and Dave   7, 14
Samartzis, Philip   72
sampling   93, 115, 166, 215, 251
Sanders, Mark   12, 78, 80–1, 95, 168
    as a collaborator   5, 92, 113, 159, 184, 260
Sankeys   8
Satie, Erik   12, 14, 19, 200
Savile, Jimmy   239
Savile Row   170
saxophone   31, 70, 77–86, 112–13, 121, 198, 205
    and Alan Hacker   151, 165
    alto   147, 161, 231
    classical   160, 201
    jazz   117
    and John Butcher   92, 145, 158–61
    and male bias   198
    plastic   155
    sopranino   63
    soprano   86, 151, 161, 165, 222
    tenor   31, 161, 236, 252
scat   115
Scelsi, Giacinto   190
Schlippenbach, Alexander Von   28, 77, 200

Schlippenbach Quartet. *See* Schlippenbach, Alexander Von
Schnabel, Artur   257
Schoenberg, Arnold   12, 45, 82, 176–7, 192, 238, 253
Schonfield, Victor   32, 108, 228
Schweizer, Irene   197
Schwitters, Kurt   87, 95, 167
Sciarrino, Salvatore   258
score. *See* notation
Scorsese, Martin   170
Scotland   23, 158, 173, 219
  Glasgow   220
Scott, Jimmy   242
Scott, Richard   154
Scratch Orchestra   17, 33. *See also* Cardew, Cornelius
Seamen, Phil   228–9
Second World War   99
semiotics   13
Serame, David   155
serialism. *See* twelve-tone music
seriousness   14, 17–20, 37, 59–60, 62, 68–9, 72, 92, 162, 190, 202, 204, 214, 224, 229, 237, 241, 252
Serious Productions   205
Sex Pistols   246
Shaggs, The   3, 23, 236, 241
Shah of Iran   259
Shaking Ray Levis, The   5, 60, 158
Sharp, Elliott   54, 80, 107
Shaw, Artie   7–8
Shaw, Sandie   239
Shearing, George   157
Sheffield   28, 41, 46
Shepp, Artie   8
Sheppard, Andy   205
Sherlaw Johnson, Robert   11
Sherwood, Adrian   5, 235, 243–6
Shifa   113
Shipp, Matthew   159
Shockabilly   61
Shooting Stars   188, 222
Shoreditch   92, 193
Shostakovich, Dmitri   109
Shrewsbury   8
Shropshire   9, 11. *See also* Wellington, Shropshire
Shropshire Schools' Symphony Orchestra   7, 20–1
Sibyl Madrigal's Boat-Ting   216
silence   49, 73, 106, 110, 119–20, 143, 168, 180, 211
Silvers, Phil   225
Simpsons, The   175, 219–20
Sing Sing Correctional Facility   216
Sir Jack Lyons Concert Hall   77
Ska   3, 83, 85
skiffle   32
Slits, The   5, 13, 43, 80, 158, 173, 221, 235, 239–45
Sly and the Family Stone   10. *See also* Stone, Sly
small instruments   5, 32, 69, 113, 118, 162, 186
SME. *See* Spontaneous Music Ensemble
Smell of Reeves and Mortimer, The   222
Smith, Bruce   80
Smith, Ian   105
Smith, Linda Catlin   185
Smith, Roger   31–2, 48, 54, 74, 158, 228–9
Smith, Wadada Leo   59–60, 105, 128, 188, 193, 214
Smoker, Paul   204
SoftWax   241
Soho Poly Theatre   30
Solomon, Dave   7, 14–15, 31, 36, 67
So Percussion   215
Sorry (duo)   14
soul   7, 9–10, 14, 121, 152, 155, 236, 243
Sound and Music (institution)   108–9, 202
Sounds Positive   211
soundtracks (film)   81, 148, 165, 171, 216
South Africa   155–7, 217–18
  apartheid   156–7
  Cape Town   156
  Johannesburg Jazz Festival   156
  North-West University, Potchefstroom   217
South America   188
South Bank   187
Space Invaders   163
spaghetti Westerns   175
Spain   214

Sparky's Magic Piano   115
Spector, Phil   65
Spike Jones Orchestra   211. *See also* Jones, Spike
Spillane, Micky   14
Spirits Rejoice (band)   156
Splinters   141
spontaneity   2, 32, 50, 68, 105, 108, 110–14, 116, 215–16, 218, 225, 230
Spontaneous Music Ensemble   11–12, 29, 32, 34, 74, 83, 116, 141, 158, 228–9
Spouge   3, 236
Springfield, Dusty   238–9
Springheel Jack   106
Springtime!   20
Squarepusher   161
squeezebox   227
Sri Lanka   193
Stabinsky, Ron   24
Stacey, Cara   217–18
StaggerLee Wonders   80
Stalinism   11
Stalling, Carl   175
Stax   9–10, 155
Steele, Jan   13
STEIM. *See* Studio for Electro-Instrumental Music
Stevens, John   12, 27–9, 36, 45, 47, 50–1, 110, 141, 144, 160, 229
    as a collaborator   55, 70, 158, 211, 225, 228, 235, 247
Stewart, Louis   82
Stewart, Mark   244
Stewart Lee Show, The   80. *See also* Lee, Stewart
Stockhausen, Karlheinz   9, 32, 37, 179, 247, 259
Stoke Newington literary festival   240
Stone, Keith   245
Stone, Sly   53, 231. *See also* Sly and the Family Stone
Strange Umbrellas   193, 209
Strauss, Richard   20, 175–6
Stravinsky, Igor   2, 182
Streep, Meryl   22–3
Strong, Barrett   238
Studio for Electro-Instrumental Music   253

stylophone   188, 245
Summerhill (school)   220
Sun Ra's Strange Strings   17. *See also* Ra, Sun
Sure deodorant   171
surrealism   97, 189, 192, 220, 222
Surrey University   92, 158
Swallow, Steve   28, 205
swing   7, 27, 41, 117, 181, 192, 210, 248
Switzerland   5, 96, 147, 153, 172–3, 185
Sydney   239
    Sydney Opera House   203
synaesthesia   177
Szigeti, Joseph   73

tabla   117, 203
TableMusic   193
Taguchi, Kazumi   150
Tan, Margaret Leng   90–1, 101
tape splicing   161
Tate   177
    Tate Modern   92
Tati, Jacques   84
Tavid, Elvis   61
Taylor, Cecil   9–10, 15, 24, 27–8, 31, 64–5, 89, 94, 116, 156, 203, 210
Taylor, Trevor   37
Tchaikovsky, Pyotr Ilyich   20
Tchicai, John   31, 235
Templeton, Alec   182
Temptations, The   71
Thames   216
Thatcherism   212
theatre   7, 15, 80, 83, 150, 162, 176
    experimental music theatre   213
    improvisational theatre   116
theremin   14, 96, 214, 252
These Records, South London   160
They Might Be Giants   61
Thicke, Robin   248, 259
This Is Not This Heat   98
Thomas, Pat   80, 94, 96, 113, 168, 193, 252–3, 256
Thomas, Philip   185–6
Thomas, Richard   226
Thomas, Rufus   84
Thomas the Tank Engine   150
Thompson, Danny   70

Thompson, Shirley   11
Thompson, Tony   73
Thornhill, Claude   111
Three Pullovers   31, 34, 66, 68–9, 74, 91, 199
thumb piano   145
Tibetan music
   Buddhist   30, 143, 247
   throat-singing   205
Tiger (shop)   97, 99, 188
Tilbury, John   12, 32–4, 185, 252
timbre   34, 175
   and Derek Bailey   44–5, 52
   of electronic devices   53
   and toy pianos   101–2
Tinguely, Jean   95
Tippett, Keith   80, 156
Tippetts, Julie   155
Titanic   100
Titchfield St   141
Todd, Garry   14, 31, 210
Tokyo   119, 150
Tomlinson, Alan   21, 105, 184, 203, 209–11, 227
tone-colour. *See* timbre
Tony Knight's Chessmen. *See* Knight, Tony
Tony Oxley's Quartet and Celebration Orchestra   252
Toop, David   31, 66–9, 71, 100, 109, 116, 143–5, 147–51, 177, 203, 205–6, 210, 216
   as a collaborator   5, 65, 86, 131, 134, 136, 153, 213, 221, 228, 238–9, 243–5, 247
Top of the Pops   66, 222, 235, 239
Tosh, Peter   33
Tottenham   13
Touch   149
toy instruments   30–2, 44, 65, 91, 171
toys as instruments   39, 68–9, 80, 226
Tracey, Stan   109
Transatlantic   20
Travis, Geoff   221
tremolo   160, 173
Trenet, Charles   149
Trevor Watts' Moiré Music   93. *See also* Watts, Trevor

Tristano, Lennie   28, 49, 141, 144
trombone   21, 63, 141, 155, 203, 211, 222, 255
   plastic   155, 193
Trøndelag Centre, Trøndheim   167
Trotskyism   190
Troupe, Quincy   1
Trump, Donald   34
trumpet   5, 7, 9, 12, 17, 21–2, 59, 75, 79, 161, 210, 214, 231, 241
   and Chris Burn   92
   and Dave Douglas   147
   and Duke Ellington   115
   and Han Bennink   63
   Harmon-muted   176
   jazz   198
   and Laura Jurd   198
   and Lesley Dalaba   197
   and Louis Armstrong   112
   and Matt Davis   119
   and Paul Smoker   204
   and Peter Evans   24, 74, 209
   slide   193
   toy   14
   and Wynton Marsalis   204
truth (in music)   1, 194
tuba   106, 119, 242
   plastic   193
Tucker, Dave   105, 211, 254
Tudor, David   180, 182, 186–7, 190–1
Tudor-style keyboard music   108
Tufnell Park   221
Turetzky, Bert   11
Turin   15
Turner, Roger   5, 39, 60, 83, 94, 162, 167, 173, 209–11
twelve-tone music   46, 82, 108, 253
Tyner, McCoy   8
Tzadik   42, 147

uhadi   217
UK Indie Chart   221
ukulele   139
umrhubhe   217
Unity Theatre, London   36
Unpredictable Series, The   209, 215
Up, Ari   239, 241–2, 244–5
Usurp Gallery, West Harrow   177

Vancouver Jazz Festival   155-6
van Houdt, Reinier   185
Varèse, Edgard   93
variety   225, 227. *See also* music hall
  Royal Variety Performance   225
Vatcher, Michael   79
Vaughan, Sarah   121-2
Vaughan Williams, Ralph   166, 170, 192, 212
VCS3 (synthesiser)   65
Velvet Underground, The   14, 246
vibrato   160, 173, 176, 194
Vicious, Sid   240
Vic Reeves Big Night Out   222
Victoria Tea   170
Vienna   119
  Second Viennese School   44, 46
Vietnam   61
Viltard, Guillaume   156
Vine, Jeremy   112
vinyl   101, 157, 172, 258
viola   75
violin   8, 21, 31, 36, 48, 73-4, 79, 82, 86, 160, 166-7, 169, 175, 192-3, 258
  bowing   71, 75, 117, 226
  in classical music   8, 183
  design   181
  Sanctus Seraphin   193
Virgin (records)   245
virtuosity   5, 24, 45, 63, 67, 91, 94, 111, 117-18, 145
  in improvisation   111
Vishnick, Martin   53
visual art   66-7, 142-4, 162, 169, 177, 181, 209
Viva La Black   156
vocalists   84, 107, 120-2, 147-8, 155, 213, 245
Voce, Steve   41
vocoder   115
Volkov, Ilan   12, 192
Vortex, Stoke Newington   78, 83, 89, 156, 209, 216, 240

Wachsman, Phil   105
Wagner, Richard   175
Wailer, Bunny   33
Waisvisz, Michel   251, 253

Wales   144, 182
Wales, Ashley   105-6
Walker, Junior   10
Walker Brothers   226
Wallen, Byron   184
Waller, Fats   111
Wandsworth Trio   19
Wapping Project   203
Ward, Alex   42, 46, 98, 180, 193
Ward, Eugene   46
Warner Brothers   175, 248
Warwick, Dionne   152, 160, 239
Wastell, Mark   30, 119
Watson, Ben   54, 56, 59, 223
Watts, Charlie   48
Watts, Trevor   27-8, 34, 80, 110, 141, 162. *See also* Trevor Watts' Moiré Music
Webern, Anton   11, 31, 34, 44-7, 53, 110
Webster, Ben   160, 252
Webster College, St. Louis   147
Weekertoft   113
Weill, Kurt   19, 176
Wellington, Shropshire   5, 7-8, 10
Wellins, Bobby   94, 109
West, Adam   158
Westbrook, Mike   155
Westminster University   11, 66, 141-3, 165, 217
Weston, Veryan   79, 93-4, 162
Wheeler, Kenny   29, 48, 85, 110, 141, 156, 202
White, John   20
Whitechapel Gallery   173
White City   148
White Cube   217
Whitmer, T. Carl   112
Who, The   235
Wierbos, Wolter   222
Wiesemann, Bernd   90
Wilder, Alec   24
Wile E. Coyote and Road Runner   99, 236
Wilen, Barney   176
Willem Breuker Kollektief   63. *See also* Breuker, Willem
Williams, Allan   69
Williams, John   176

Williams, Michael James. *See* Prince Far-I
Williamson, Joe   94
Wilson, Teddy   111
Wilson, Tom   246
Wimbish, Doug   245
Winant, William   188
Winckel, Christoph   211
Windmill, The   225
Winnie The Pooh   151
Winslet, Kate   100
Wire, The   3, 48, 209, 248, 257
Wishart, Trevor   14, 17
Wolff, Christian   32, 180, 185, 190
Wollesen, Kenny   147
Wolverhampton   9
Wooding, Jeremy   165–6
Woodyard, Sam   51
working men's clubs   7, 12–13, 91, 220, 224
world music   202, 237, 241, 247
Wright, Frank   28
Wright, Geoff   206
Wright, Seymour   117, 206
Wyatt, Robert   221

Xenakis, Iannis   2
xylophone   90
    African   101

YACHT   221
Yanomami shamanism   66
Yarde, Jason   5, 105, 156, 213
Yee, Lydia   173
Yehudi Menuhin School   74
Yellow Magic Orchestra, The   151
Yiddish   73, 117
York   12, 14, 17, 36, 78, 84, 112, 202
    York Arts Centre   33
    Yorkshire   17, 167
    York University   7, 10–15, 35–6, 43, 72, 77, 121, 145, 189
Young, Lester   38, 121
YouTube   102, 158, 167

Zappa, Frank   246
Zeitgeist   82
zither   175
Zoom   260
Zoom sampler   115
Zorn, John   5, 21, 42, 50–1, 61, 66, 72, 87, 89, 95, 99, 121, 131, 148, 150, 153–4
    and Christian Marclay   184
    as a collaborator   253
    and *Cue Sheets*   147, 165, 171–2
    game pieces   147, 153
Zurich   193
Zu Space   153

www.ingramcontent.com/pod-product-compliance
Lightning Source LLC
Chambersburg PA
CBHW072124290426
44111CB00012B/1774